INK AND EXILE

A MULTIDISCIPLINARY EXPLORATION OF DIASPORA

EDITED BY

ABHISHEK BHARDWAJ
DR. MADHUMITA GUPTA
DR. SANOBAR HAIDER
DR. SHWETA MISHRA

INDIA · SINGAPORE · MALAYSIA

ISBN 979-8-89363-357-3

Contents

Contents

Contents

Acknowledgement

We want to express our special thanks and gratitude to all the authors of the research papers who readily agreed to be a part of this intellectual journey and were kind enough to share their vast experience and knowledge through their papers and contributed towards the completion of this project.We also wish to take this opportunity to thank all our friends for their academic motivation and for the time-to-time review and feedback of the work that has been fruitful and has had a positive impact on the final creation. This book is a team effort, and we are thankful to everyone who helped us along the way. We would also want to thank our families for their support and care throughout the making of this book.

Mr. Abhishek Bhardwaj

Assistant Professor,
Department of English,
Maharaja Bijli Pasi Government P.G. College, Lucknow

Mr. Abhishek Bhardwaj is a dedicated scholar and an Assistant Professor in the Departmentof English at M.B.P. Government P.G. College, Lucknow. Hailing from esteemed almamaters such as D.P.S. R.K. Puram (Delhi), Delhi University, and Panjab University, he brings academic expertise and a fervent passion for literary exploration. Currently pursuing a doctorate, his research interest lies in the hyphenated space between the binaries concerning Indian women freedom fighters. This intersectional approach to studying history not only enriches the understanding of the past but also serves as a compelling testament to his commitment to uncovering hidden narratives. In the academic sphere, he has made notable contributions by publishing research papers in esteemed journals. He has been actively involved in organizing international webinars and seminars at his college. In his department, he has also initiated a magazine called *Splashes* that showcases the creative talents of young students. The venture into editing is not his first foray into the editorial realm. Having previously served as an editor both during their collegiate years and in freelancing capacities, he brings a wealth of editorial insight and a keen eye for crafting compelling narratives. As he finds his footing in academia, this collection not only showcases his burgeoning expertise but is also a testament to his dedication to fostering interdisciplinary dialogue.

Editor's Note

Mr. Abhishek Bhardwaj

Exiles cross borders, break barriers of thought and experience.

(Edward Said, "Reflections on Exile")

In crafting the editor's note for this book, I found myself navigating the intricate interplay of editorial voice and scholarly discourse, seeking to strike a delicate balance between personal reflection and academic inquiry. Leafing through the manuscript, I found myself swept right back to my formative years at Ramjas College and Amitav Ghosh and V.S. Naipaul, writers who burrow under your skin and stay there. These authors have left an indelible mark on my understanding and appreciation of diaspora studies. With each stroke of the pen, I navigated the web of diasporic narratives, drawing upon a vast reservoir of theoretical frameworks and empirical evidence to illuminate the nuances of the diasporic experience. Yet, as I grappled with the urge to offer novel insights in this note, I realized that sometimes the most profound truths lie not in groundbreaking discoveries but in the timeless resonance of shared human experiences, underscoring the enduring power of storytelling to transcend boundaries and unite us in our collective quest for understanding and connection.

The epigraph, from Edward Said's "Reflections on Exile", aptly encapsulates the essence of diaspora as a state of being that transcends geographical boundaries and delves into the realms of thought and experience. Moreover, exploring diaspora and its intricate dimensions, while a focal point of contemporary academic interest, is hardly a phenomenon of the modern era alone. Historically, whenever individuals ventured far from their native lands to establish new lives elsewhere, the dynamics of diaspora inevitably emerged. For writers, it was the dilemma of depicting their newfound environments and cultures and the ways of preserving the traditions and principles of their homeland. The economists examined remittances, labor, cultural capital, transnational spaces, and policy implications. Political scientists investigated political participation, lobbying, conflict resolution, and the impact of diaspora movements on domestic and foreign policies in both the countries. These considerations held significance for ancient Romans making homes in Gaul or Malta and Normans in the United Kingdom, just as they did for the British in India, Germany in Africa, Spaniards in South America, and the Indians dispersed worldwide in contemporary times.

The notion of homeland, a concept as elusive as it is central to the diasporic condition, serves as a touchstone for the discussions within this volume. Homeland stands not merely as a geographical entity but as a source of foundational narratives, values, and traditions that inform one's consciousness and *weltanschauung*. However, this connection to the homeland often brings with it feelings of loneliness, alienation, nostalgia, a sense of loss, and rootlessness. For the diaspora, thus, the imagined connection with the homeland fosters a sense of belonging and identity that is both rooted in the past and continuously reshaped by the present diasporic context. Through a creative response to this in-betweenness, the diaspora coalesces homeland and host land cultures to produce unique forms of dress, cuisine, language, culture, and religion. Over time, this new sense of identity becomes a nuanced form of resistance as well as an integral strategy of survival to circumvent the dominant cultural framework to which they mostly remain outsiders. The title's contrasting imagery – the permanence of ink set against the impermanence of exile – reflects the enduring cultural legacy carried by the diaspora despite their physical distance from the homeland.

The collection of academic papers in *Ink and Exile: A Multidisciplinary Exploration of Diaspora* provides a panoramic yet nuanced view of the Indian diaspora through diverse lenses— economic, social, legal, and literary, to name a few. In *A Companion to Diaspora and Transnationalism*, editors Ato Quayson and Girish Daswani give an interesting example of a dispute between the U.S. Patent Office and India over the patenting of "basmati" in the late 1990s. Rice Tec's attempt to patent cross-bred rice and monopolize the basmati name in North America clashed with India's view of "basmati" as a culturally and geographically specific product akin to cognac or champagne in France. This confrontation underscored the cultural economy surrounding agricultural products for Indians, extending beyond patents to the nostalgic connections diaspora communities maintain through products like basmati, linking them to their homelands and preserving complex cultural identities through everyday practices. Therefore, it is crucial to transcend disciplinary boundaries for a holistic examination of the various factors shaping diasporic communities.

In an increasingly globalized world, understanding the experiences of diaspora is no longer a niche pursuit but a cornerstone of navigating our interconnected society. *Ink and Exile* is a humble and timely addition to this discourse as migration patterns intensify and issues of cultural identity, belonging, and integration come to the forefront. While delving into the stories, experiences, and analyses in this compilation, it is vital to remain mindful of the deep currents of homeland that flow beneath the surface of diasporic life. These currents illuminate the intricate interplay of continuity and change that defines the Indian diasporic experience. The editors extend their deepest gratitude to the contributors whose insights have enriched this volume immeasurably. In closing, the editors invite the readers to immerse themselves in the pages of *Ink and Exile*, listen to the echoes of the past and the whispers of the future, and bear witness to the enduring spirit of the Indian diaspora.

Dr. Madhumita Gupta

Assistant Professor,
Department of Commerce,
Maharaja Bijli Pasi Government P.G. College, Lucknow

Dr. Madhumita Gupta (Ph.D.) is a faculty member at the Commerce Department at Maharaja Bijli Pasi Govt. P.G.College, Lucknow. She holds dual P.G. degrees in Commerce and Economics. She holds a doctorate in Commerce, and her research area is Human Resources. She comes from a family of academicians who have left their mark in higher education. She has more than 17 years of experience in teaching P.G. and U.G. students and has to her credit more than 10 research papers published in both international and national journals of repute. She has also contributed chapters to several books. Apart from this, she has presented numerous papers at international and national seminars. She is an academic counsellor for IGNOU.

She holds membership in the All India Commerce Association. Apart from her academic responsibilities, she has worked extensively to promote awareness towards the enrolment of new voters for Central and State elections. Considering her human approach and adaptability to difficult situations, she was chosen to head a Covid Counselling Cell during the peak of the pandemic. Her work during that difficult time has been well appreciated. She is known as a hard taskmaster, and her students are testimony to this fact. She is an avid reader, and her core competence is team building and leadership development.

Editor's Note

Dr. Madhumita Gupta

'Diaspora' word has Greek origins (loosely, it means–scattering of seeds) and refers to the mass movement of Jews away from their homeland. In contemporary times, diaspora refers to people living away from their homeland for various reasons. Indian diaspora is the group of people living outside India (temporarily or permanently) whose origin is in India. The Indian diaspora is a heterogeneous international community representing diverse types, forms, and geographies. Thus, it requires varied and distinct approaches to engage and connect with India. The common thread that binds them is the idea of a mother nation, i.e., India, and its core values. Overseas Indian communities comprising People of Indian origin (PIO) and Non-Resident Indians (NRI) have made their presence felt across the globe and have significantly added noteworthy contributions, not only to India but to the entire world in terms of knowledge, innovation, and development. The Indian diaspora makes up an engaging saga of trials, tribulations, and triumphs of determination and hard work. Many have made their presence felt in host countries, occupying leadership positions there.

With advancements in information technology and cheaper transport services, diasporas, as compared to situations prevailing earlier, are able to maintain connections with people and networks back home more effectively. These diaspora associations help to channel remittances, capital, and investments to benefit not only their home communities but also by developing partnerships with the host country, which is for the mutual benefit of both. These 'Global Indians' can serve as bridges and sources of investment, expertise, knowledge, and technology. By their informed participation, they can shape and help articulate the need for policy coherence in the countries of destination and origin. This requires not only the home country to establish conditions and institutions for a sustainable, symbiotic, and mutually rewarding engagement with the diaspora—central to our programmes and activities; but for the diaspora to project itself as an intrinsically motivated and progressive community. The Government of India has initiated several measures to ensure the welfare of the diaspora. Prominent among them arePravasi Bhartiya Diwas and conferences, online voter participation, overseas citizenship scheme, Indian community welfare fund, and many more.

The articles penned by scholars for the book, *Ink and Exile*, reflect their hard work, knowledge of the subject, and the importance that the diaspora commands within a country, which will go a long way in benefitting their motherland.

Dr. Sanobar Haider

Assistant Professor,
Department of History,
Maharaja Bijli Pasi Government P.G. College, Lucknow

The author is an avid Lucknowite, with a keen interest in teaching the history of India, and a doctorate in the subject. The author has scripted several research papers, which have since been published in national and international journals. The author's research topic for her Ph.D. – "Law and Justice in the United Provinces, 1877-1937" provided her with an insight into the administrative set-up of the erstwhile kingdom of Awadh, immersing her deeply into the exploration of the fabled city of Lucknow. Having excelled in academics at all levels, she has to her credit a number of academic accomplishments. Besides excelling in various competitive examinations, the author also has to her credit the founding of the Avadh Girls Degree College Alumnae Association, which saw the light of the day due to her initiative and dynamism. The author regularly delivers talks on the radio and is otherwise socially active.

She has organised multiple seminars and webinars over the years and has been associated as an editor for several publications. The author also has keen leanings toward researching the history and culture of Awadh and has published several research papers, articles, and books related to the subject.

Editor's Note

Dr. Sanobar Haider

Diaspora refers to groups of people who share a common heritage and even homeland but have migrated to other lands and have been living there for years. Members of the diaspora community contribute towards the development of their home country both directly and indirectly, which is crucial for the economic development of the motherland. Diaspora promotes trade, brings in foreign investment, and contributes tothe sharing of skills and knowledge. The role of the Indian diaspora has been particularly noteworthy in this aspect.

Indian diaspora represents a valuable conduit of goodwill for strengthening India's relations with the world as full partners in growth and development for broader well-being and prosperity. With its civilisational values of peace, plurality and universal fraternity in the true spirit of 'VasudhaivaKutumbakam,' India has traditionally been at the pivot of promoting global peace and progress, and the diaspora has played that role in its true meaning. Indian diaspora is one of those communities existing in the world territory, which plays a very significant and appreciable role in the development of India. Their contribution to the Indian economy in all forms is recognisable and is a matter of pride for all Indians. This community living in other nations keeps on adding to the growth potential of our nation in many aspects.

Through this book, we have tried to highlight the contribution of the diaspora towards the growth and development of the home countries as defined by various academics and educationists. This book is a compendium of the research work of the scholars who have, through their multiple themes, brought to the readers the history, dynamics, and achievements of the different diasporas settled across the world.

This edited book, *Ink and Exile*, is an effort by the editors to underline the contribution of the diaspora, which forms the backbone of the various professional networks between the home country and the host country. Talking about the Indian diaspora in particular, the Indian communities residing abroad have contributed significantly towards enhancing the relations between India and other countries in many domains. By doing this, the Indians living overseas have improved ties between India and other nations in a variety of fields. There is, however, a further need to raise global awareness about the importance and value of diaspora engagement and provide capacity building for diaspora groups and organisations.

Happy Reading…

Dr. Shweta Mishra

Assistant Professor,
Department of English,
Maharaja Bijli Pasi Government P.G. College, Lucknow

Dr. Shweta Mishra is an Assistant Professor in the Departmentof English at M.B.P. Government P.G. College, Lucknow, India. A gold medalist in M.A. English from the University of Lucknow, she has authored several research papers published in various reputed journals. Creative writing is what she passionately loves to do. Her poems have been published in various national and international anthologies. Her notable works include, *What is a Woman: This is Trash. Leave it* (2016) and *Image of Girlhood in the Fiction of African-American Women Writers: Paule Marshall, Anne Moody, Maya Angelou, Toni Morrison, Alice Walker, Ntozake Shange* (2011). Her collection of poems, *The Most Orange,* was published in 2018. Her book *A Smothering Selfless Epitome: Sita* was published in July 2020 through Kindle Direct Publishing. A collaborative venture,

Lucknow Imprints: A Poetic and Historical Account of the Golden City of the East, has been published by Notion Press, Chennai, in 2021. In 2022 and 2024, she co-edited books titled *The Platinum Threshold: Celebrating 75 Years of Indian Independence,* and *Aatmnirbhar Bharat: Resurgent India,* respectively.

Editor's Note

Dr. Shweta Mishra

बाबा के साथ बाज़ार से खरीदे मिट्टी के खिलौने हैं;

एक किताब है कहानियों की;

दादी के हाथों का बुना बटुआ है।

इतना-सा सामान है;

सफर पर हूँ...

पानी का जहाज़ है, संग लहरों का शोर है।

बक्से में बचपन आज भी है, पर आँखों में अश्क रोज़ नहीं आते -

ये अतीत की यादों जैसे हैं, ये आते-जाते रहते हैं...

एक आईना भी है,छोटा-सा; पर खुद से मिलना इतना सरल नहीं अब,

पहचान बहुत आसान नहीं अब...

चेहरा बदलता गया, पहचान पर सवाल रहे;

छोटा-बड़ा, कम-ज्यादा, मैं-तुम-कोई के बीच,

कई अपने दूर, और, कुछ अंजाने साथ रहे।

– श्वेता मिश्रा 'शौर्या'

Defined as the voluntary or forcible movement of people from their homelands to new regions, diaspora can be explained as an experience that is collective as well as individual, and resolutely unique. Initially, the term applied to the Jews who were sent to exile beyond Israel, establishing the historical connotation of the term. Primarily understood as Jewish dispersion, it now applies to the Indian, African, Irish diaspora, as well as many others. The reason for this relocation can be both, forced or by choice. Historically speaking, there have been hundreds of mass migrations or diasporic movements across the globe for political reasons like the Africans who were brought on slave ships to America; many due to expulsion and discrimination like the Jewish Diaspora; or, due to natural calamities like famine, as in the case of Irish diaspora. Philosophically speaking, human beings cannot separate themselves from this diasporic experience because, according to Hindu mythology, the moment we are born, the soul gets separated from the Greater Soul; therefore, the human situation is diasporic. The concept of diaspora is relatable and can be understood by everyone, even if one has not crossed the borders of one's own nation. For instance, Kamala Das, in "My Grandmother's House," nostalgically remembers her grandmother's house, which stores her childhood memories and pines for the love of her grandmother. The nostalgia is so intense that she remembers the windows and craves the "frozen air" and "armful of Darkness."

Various facets, like economic, political, cultural, historical, psychological, educational, and literary, of the diaspora have been discussed in the different chapters incorporated in this book. The emphasis is more on the Indian diaspora. The relevance of the book also rests on the fact that in the age of globalisation, fast-paced networking, the internet, improved communication, and the use of artificial intelligence, diaspora is playing a crucial role in making races, ethnicities, and cultures, blend into one and come under one umbrella. The most unique impact cast by diaspora, be it of any cultural, religious or ethnic context, is that they have had a definitive impact on the formation of a multicultured collective world.

Ink and Exile is a scholarly collection of various ideas on the theme of diaspora, with a special focus on the Indian diaspora. Deliberations on diaspora are significant as they contribute to global progress and mutual understanding. This book is a record of the research papers by educationists and academicians who have enthusiastically researched to come up with prominent parameters on the subject.

Ink and Exile: A Multidisciplinary Exploration of Diaspora is, thus, a mosaic of a multitude of thoughts and views that revolve around, or, are associated with diaspora, their experiences and their impact, in all fields and facets of human society and the world at large. As the editor of the book, it is a matter of great honour and immense pleasure for me to invite the readers on an expedition to the informative journey.

Chapter 1

Evolution of Indian Culture Within Diaspora Communities

Dr. Shalini

Assistant Professor
Department of English
Govt. Girls P. G. College, Hamirpur
Email Address- shalinimona467@gmail.com

Abstract

Diaspora literature is instrumental in safeguarding and passing on the rich tapestry of culture, history, traditions, and languages from one's homeland to subsequent generations. By capturing the essence of these elements in written works, diaspora literature ensures that the collective memory and heritage remain vivid, even in foreign lands. This literary endeavour not only serves as a cultural repository but also fosters a profound connection to one's roots, offering a bridge between the past and the present for those living in a diaspora. In essence, diaspora literature plays a pivotal role in preserving and nurturing the cultural identity of communities dispersed around the globe. The Indian diaspora, widely dispersed worldwide, makes significant contributions not only to their host countries but also to India. They invest in the Indian economy, support philanthropic initiatives, and maintain deep cultural and familial connections. These contributions create a vital and lasting link between the diaspora and India, fostering both economic growth and social development.

Keywords: Indian diaspora, literature, homeland, cultural identity, economy

Introduction

The term "Diaspora" originated from the Greek word for dispersion and was initially used to describe the global dispersion of Jewish people from their homeland, Israel. The Jewish Diaspora emerged as a response to repression and refusal to assimilate, with Jewish communities surviving through migration, adaptation, and the preservation of faith and traditions. Other communities, such as Armenians, Chinese, Africans (due to slavery), and Indians, later adopted a similar model. However, unlike the Jewish Diaspora, Indian communities chose migration as a means of dispersion.

The Indian diaspora's origin is deeply rooted in regional social structures, and distinct regional cultures and languages have given rise to Bengali, Punjabi, and Telugu diasporas. Despite these regional differences, there is a strong sense of belonging to the larger Indian diaspora, united by shared cultural heritage. The globalisation of the Indian diaspora began during the emigration period to plantation colonies, with terms like *"Jahajibhai"* and *"dipuabhai"* symbolising a sense of brotherhood beyond caste, religion, and language, fostering a globalised feeling among the Indian diaspora. In Europe, associations and "circles of friends" played a crucial role in bringing Indians together, fostering a sense of belonging to Indian cultural heritage, and maintaining connections with India.

Advancements in technology, such as telecommunication and cyber technology, facilitated cross-border relations, helping different Indian communities connect and develop a sense of collective transnationalism across borders. This laid the foundation for what is now recognised as the Indian diaspora, a global Indian community with a shared heritage and connections spanning the world.

Literature and Diaspora

Literature and the diaspora are intimately connected, and diaspora literature is a vibrant genre that explores the experiences, identities, and challenges of people living outside their countries of origin. Literature and the diaspora are interconnected through the narratives, stories, and voices of individuals living outside their countries of origin. Diaspora literature serves as a powerful tool for self-expression, cultural preservation, and social commentary, making it a significant and influential genre in the world of literature.

1. Expression of Identity: Diaspora literature often serves as a platform for individuals to express and explore their identity, both as members of their ethnic or cultural diaspora and as individuals navigating complex cultural landscapes. Writers use literature to reflect on their experiences, struggles, and self-discovery.

2. Preservation of Culture: Diaspora literature plays a crucial role in preserving and transmitting the culture, history, traditions, and languages of the homeland to future generations. It helps maintain a connection to one's roots, even when living in a foreign land.

3. Cultural Hybridity: Many diaspora writers explore the concept of cultural hybridity or "third space." They navigate between their cultural heritage and the culture of their host country,

creating new forms of expression and cultural identities in the process.

4. Exile and Displacement: Diaspora literature often delves into the themes of exile, displacement, and the search for a sense of belonging. Writers explore the emotional and psychological impact of being uprooted from one's homeland.

5. Political and Social Commentary: Many diaspora authors use their works to comment on political and social issues related to their home countries, host countries, and the diaspora experience. Their literature can raise awareness and advocate for change.

6. Representation and Visibility: Diaspora literature provides a platform for marginalised voices and underrepresented communities. It helps challenge stereotypes and misconceptions about diaspora populations and contributes to a more inclusive and diverse literary landscape.

7. Transnational Narratives: Diaspora literature often transcends national boundaries, offering a transnational perspective. These narratives highlight the interconnectedness of the world and underscore the global nature of the diaspora experience.

8. Language and Linguistic Diversity: Many diaspora writers grapple with language as a fundamental aspect of their identity. They may write in multiple languages or explore how language evolves and changes in a diaspora context.

9. Literary Genres: Diaspora literature encompasses various genres, including novels, poetry, short stories, autobiographies, and essays. These diverse forms of expression allow writers to convey their experiences in different ways.

10. Prominent Diaspora Authors: There are numerous renowned diaspora authors from various backgrounds who have made significant contributions to world literature. Some examples include Jhumpa Lahiri, Salman Rushdie, Chimamanda Ngozi Adichie, and Junot Díaz.

11. Diverse Diaspora Communities: Diaspora literature is not limited to one specific group; it encompasses a wide range of communities from around the world, such as the Indian diaspora, African diaspora, Jewish diaspora, and many others.

Journey of Indian Diaspora

The journey of the Indian diaspora is a complex and multifaceted story that spans several centuries. The Indian diaspora refers to people of Indian origin who have settled in various parts of the world, often due to historical, economic, or political factors. Here is a broad overview of the journey of the Indian diaspora:

1. Historical Migration

- Indentured Labourers: One of the earliest waves of Indian migration occurred during the 19th and early 20th centuries when many Indians were brought to various British colonies, such as the Caribbean, Fiji, and South Africa, as indentured labourers to work on plantations.

- Early Traders and Settlers: Prior to indentured labour migration, there were Indian traders and merchants who settled in different parts of Southeast Asia, the Middle East, and Africa.

2. Post-Independence Migration

- East African Migration: After India's independence in 1947, significant numbers of Indians migrated to East African countries like Kenya, Tanzania, and Uganda. Many of them were involved in trade and commerce.

3. Migration to Western Countries

- United Kingdom: The 20th century saw a significant migration of Indians to the United Kingdom. Many of these early migrants were primarily from the Punjab region.

- United States and Canada: Indians started migrating to North America in the 20th century, with a substantial wave of professionals, particularly in the fields of medicine, engineering, and technology, settling in the U.S. and Canada.

4. Gulf Migration

- In the latter part of the 20th century and into the 21st century, there was a large-scale migration of Indians to the Gulf countries, particularly the United Arab Emirates, Saudi Arabia, and Qatar. This migration was driven by opportunities in the oil and construction industries.

5. Global Spread

- Indian diaspora communities are now found virtually in every corner of the world. They have established themselves as influential and successful communities in diverse fields, including business, technology, medicine, politics, and culture.

6. Cultural and Social Integration

- Indian diaspora communities often face challenges related to cultural adaptation and integration. However, they have also contributed significantly to the cultural and social fabric of their host countries. They have enriched global cuisine, arts, and traditions and have been instrumental in fostering cultural diversity.

7. Contributions to India

- The Indian diaspora has not only been influential in their host countries but has also contributed to India in various ways. They invest in India's economy, participate in philanthropic initiatives, and maintain strong cultural and familial connections.

8. Challenges and Opportunities

- The journey of the Indian diaspora has been marked by successes and challenges, including issues related to identity, racism, and discrimination, as well as the struggle to preserve cultural heritage while adapting to new environments.

9. Continued Migration

- Migration from India to other countries, whether for educational, professional, or family reasons, continues to be a prominent feature of the Indian diaspora's journey.

In summary, the journey of the Indian diaspora is a testament to the resilience, adaptability, and contributions of people of Indian origin around the world. It is a story of migration, settlement, cultural integration, and success, and it continues to evolve with each generation. The Indian diaspora is a dynamic force that connects India to the rest of the world in myriad ways.

Evolution of Indian Culture Within Diaspora Communities

The evolution of Indian culture within diaspora communities is a dynamic and multifaceted process influenced by a variety of factors, including the host country's culture, the length of time the community has been established, generational changes, and individual experiences. The evolution of Indian culture within diaspora communities is a complex and ongoing process influenced by cultural exchange, generational shifts, and interaction with the host country's culture. It results in a vibrant, dynamic, and evolving cultural landscape that reflects the rich diversity of the Indian diaspora worldwide.

1. Hybridisation of Culture: Over time, Indian culture in the diaspora undergoes a process of hybridisation. It blends with the culture of the host country, resulting in a unique fusion of traditions, customs, and values. This fusion creates new forms of cultural expression, including food, fashion, music, and art.

2. Generational Shift: The evolution of Indian culture within diaspora communities is influenced by generational changes. The first generation often maintains strong ties to traditional Indian culture, while subsequent generations may adapt and blend Indian and host country cultural elements to create their own unique identity.

3. Language and Communication: Language is a crucial aspect of culture, and it often evolves in diaspora communities. The younger generations may predominantly speak the host country's language, which can lead to changes in communication patterns and the incorporation of host country slang and idioms into their speech.

4. Cuisine: Indian cuisine in the diaspora has evolved significantly. It adapts to local tastes and ingredients, resulting in the emergence of fusion foods and restaurants that offer a combination of Indian and host country dishes.

5. Cultural Events and Festivals: Diaspora communities celebrate Indian festivals and cultural events, but these celebrations may incorporate elements of the host country's traditions. This fusion can create unique celebrations that appeal to a diverse audience.

6. Media and Entertainment: The Indian diaspora consumes Indian media and entertainment, such as Bollywood films and music. These cultural products play a role in preserving traditional Indian culture and connecting diaspora communities to their roots.

7. Religion and Spirituality: Religion is a significant aspect of Indian culture, and diaspora communities often maintain their religious practices and traditions. However, adaptations and syncretism can occur as they interact with other religious traditions in the host country.

8. Community Organisations: Diaspora communities often have cultural and community organisations that work to preserve and promote Indian culture. These organisationsorganise cultural events, classes, and gatherings to strengthen cultural ties.

9. Education: Educational institutions within diasporic communities may offer language and cultural classes, helping to transmit Indian culture to the younger generations. These institutions play a vital role in preserving language, arts, and traditions.

10. Global Perspective: As diaspora communities interact with various cultures in their host countries, they develop a global perspective on Indian culture. This broadens their understanding of cultural diversity and enriches their cultural experiences.

11. Maintaining Cultural Traditions: While adapting to their host country's culture, many diaspora communities remain committed to preserving core aspects of Indian culture, including traditional clothing, music, dance, and rituals.

Role of Indian Diaspora in Social Development

The Indian diaspora, which is one of the largest and most widespread diaspora communities in the world, plays a significant role in social development, not only within India but also in their countries of residence and in global contexts. The Indian diaspora is a dynamic and influential community that contributes significantly to social development in multiple ways, not only in India but also in the countries they call home. Their contributions span economic, cultural, educational, and philanthropic domains, making them a vital force in the global social landscape.

1. Remittances: Indian diaspora members often send remittances back to India, which contribute significantly to the country's economy and the well-being of their families. These funds can be used for education, healthcare, housing, and other basic needs, thus improving the social and economic conditions of many households.

2. Philanthropy and Charity: Many members of the Indian diaspora are actively engaged in charitable activities and philanthropy. They support a wide range of social causes, including education, healthcare, poverty alleviation, and disaster relief, both in India and globally.

3. Technology and Innovation: Indian diaspora members have made significant contributions to technology and innovation in their host countries. This, in turn, has created employment opportunities and contributed to advancements in various sectors, leading to social development.

4. Cultural Exchange and Promotion: The Indian diaspora actively promotes Indian culture, art, music, dance, and cuisine in their host countries. This cultural exchange fosters

cross-cultural understanding and appreciation, contributing to social cohesion and diversity.

5. Education: Many individuals in the Indian diaspora are involved in education, whether as students, teachers, researchers, or administrators. They contribute to the development of educational institutions and the dissemination of knowledge, which is crucial for social progress.

6. Advocacy and Networking: Indian diaspora communities often advocate for social and political issues, both in their host countries and with respect to India. They use their collective influence to raise awareness and push for policy changes that can have social impacts.

7. Entrepreneurship and Job Creation: Indian diaspora members are involved in a wide range of businesses, from small enterprises to multinational corporations. Their entrepreneurship leads to job creation, economic growth, and social development in their host countries and India.

8. Healthcare and Medical Initiatives: Indian diaspora healthcare professionals often participate in medical missions, volunteer work, and knowledge-sharing, which can improve healthcare infrastructure and services in India and other regions.

9. Diaspora-Home Country Partnerships: Many members of the Indian diaspora actively engage in partnerships and collaborations with organisations and institutions in India. These initiatives may focus on healthcare, education, technology transfer, and various development projects.

10. Diaspora Investment: The Indian diaspora invests in India's infrastructure, real estate, and businesses, which can stimulate economic growth and create employment opportunities, ultimately contributing to social development.

11. Networking and Knowledge Transfer: The Indian diaspora often serves as a bridge for knowledge transfer, whether it is in science, technology, medicine, or other fields. They facilitate collaborations between experts in different countries, fostering innovation and development.

12. Advocacy for Migrant and Expatriate Rights: Indian diaspora communities also work to ensure the rights and welfare of migrants and expatriates in their host countries. Their efforts contribute to social justice and the well-being of diaspora members.

Role of Diaspora in Promoting Indian Art, Music and Dance

The Indian diaspora plays a significant role in promoting Indian art, music, and dance around the world. Indian culture, with its rich and diverse traditions, has a global appeal, and the Indian diaspora actively contributes to the preservation and dissemination of these cultural forms. The Indian diaspora plays a vital role in preserving, promoting, and popularising Indian art, music, and dance globally. They act as cultural ambassadors, educators, and patrons, bridging the gap between Indian traditions and the rest of the world. Here are some of the ways in which the Indian diaspora promotes Indian art, music, and dance:

1. Cultural Exchange and Fusion: The Indian diaspora often resides in multicultural environments, leading to a natural exchange of cultural ideas. This exchange can result in fusion art forms, where Indian elements blend with other cultures, creating new and innovative expressions. For example, Indian music fusion with Western genres has gained popularity globally.

2. Cultural Festivals and Celebrations: Indian diaspora communities frequently organise cultural festivals which

showcase various forms of Indian art, music, and dance. These events provide a platform for artists to perform and share their talents, helping to preserve traditional art forms and introduce them to a broader audience.

3. Dance and Music Schools: Indian diaspora communities often establish dance and music schools to teach traditional Indian forms. These institutions help pass down the skills and knowledge to the next generation and also serve as centres for cultural promotion and preservation.

4. Art Exhibitions and Galleries: Indian artists within the diaspora often exhibit their work in local art galleries, contributing to the global art scene. These exhibitions not only promote Indian art but also create a bridge between cultures.

5. Online Platforms: With the advent of the internet and social media, the Indian diaspora can easily share their cultural expressions with the world. Many Indian artists, musicians, and dancers use online platforms to reach a global audience, thereby increasing the reach and popularity of Indian art forms.

6. Cultural Associations and Groups: Indian diaspora communities often form cultural associations and groups dedicated to preserving and promoting Indian culture. These organisationsorganise events, workshops, and performances, serving as hubs for cultural exchange.

7. Support for Traditional Artists: The Indian diaspora often supports traditional artists from India by providing them with platforms to perform or exhibit their work abroad. This support can be instrumental in helping artists gain recognition and financial stability.

8. Cultural Diplomacy: The Indian diaspora also serves as unofficial ambassadors of Indian culture. Through their

interactions in their host countries, they promote India's rich cultural heritage and strengthen cultural diplomacy between India and their adopted homelands.

9. Cultural Education: Indian diaspora communities emphasise the importance of cultural education for their children, ensuring the continuity of traditional art forms. They often encourage younger generations to learn classical music, dance, and other artistic practices.

10. Collaboration and Networking: The Indian diaspora connects artists, musicians, and dancers from India with opportunities abroad. This facilitates collaborations and cross-cultural interactions that benefit both the artists and the promotion of Indian culture.

Conclusion

Diaspora literature serves as a bridge that maintains a deep connection to one's roots, even when individuals are living in foreign lands. Capturing the essence of a culture through stories, languages, and traditions ensures the preservation of a rich cultural identity and heritage for posterity. The Indian diaspora, spread across the world, makes substantial contributions to India beyond their achievements in their host countries. They invest in the country's economy, support philanthropic endeavours, and nurture deep cultural and familial ties. These contributions create a vital and enduring link between the diaspora and India, fostering both economic growth and social development.

References

- Bhabha, Homi K. *Location of Culture*. Routledge Publications, 1994.

- Bhabha, Homi K. "The Third Space."*Identity: Community, Culture, Difference*. Edited by Jonathan Rutherford. Lawrence &Wishart, 1990.

- Cohen, Robin. *Global Diaspora: An Introduction*. Routledge Publishing, 2008.

- Karanjkar, P. (2014, March 11). "Religious Education and Current Education System of India." Retrieved from www.speakingtree.in/blog/religious-education-and-current-education-system-of-india Sharma, D. (2020, August 11).

- Mishra, Vijay. *The Literature of the Indian Diaspora: Theorising the Diasporic Imaginary*. Routledge Publication, 2007.

- "National Education Policy (NEP) 2020: Promotion of Indian Languages, Multilingual Education, Arts and Culture." Retrieved from www.collegedekho.com/articles/national-education-policy-nep-2020-promotion-of-indian-languages-multilingual-education-arts-and-culture/

- Nayar, Pramod Kumar. *An Introduction to Cultural Studies*. Viva Books, 2008.

- Rushdie, Salman. *Imaginary Homelands; Essays and Criticism(1981-91)*.Granta Books, 1991.

- Singh, Bijender. *Critical Essays on Indian Diaspora*. Hauz Khas Enclave, 2015.

- Spivak, Gayatri Chakravorty. *The Postcolonial Critic: Interviews, Strategies, Dialogues*. Routledge Publishing, 1990.

Chapter 2

Shadows of Colonialism in Diasporic Writings: A Reading of Nirad C. Chaudhuri's Autobiography *Thy Hand, Great Anarch*

Mr. Ajeet Kumar Gupta

Research Scholar,
Dept. of English, University of Lucknow.
Email Address- ajeetgupta512@gmail.com

&

Prof. S. C. Hajela

Prof. & Head, Department of English,
Shri JNMPG College, Lucknow
Email Address- sudheer.hajela@gmail.com

Abstract

Colonialism stands for political dependence, economic exploitation and social alienation in the day-to-day life of the colonised people. Political analysts and historians in India and abroad have delineated the subtle ways in which colonial powers operated to generate the discourses of India's backwardness, superstitions and regional/ethnic complexities, overall portraying India as a land of darkness. Political thinkers and critics like Foucault and Edward Said pointed out how the construction of such 'discourses' generated powers to rule over the colonised all over the world. Critics like Ngugi wa Thiong'o and Frantz Fanon in the west and Ashish Nandy, Partha Chatterjee, Ranjeet Guha, Rajeshwari Sunder Rajan and Makarand Paranjape in India researched how the self of the colonised is dehumanised, degraded and pushed to an inferiority complex in matters of the capabilities, consciousness and cultural identities of the colonised. The subtle ways of colonialism leave more impact on the psyche of the colonised. While the impact of the physical atrocity lasts for a generation, the impact of colonial rule hangs over the mindset of many successive generations and cripples the imagination to have new systems and fresh viewpoints. The present paper attempts to examine Nirad C. Chaudhuri's *Thy Hand, Great Anarch* (1987) as one of the diasporic texts where, consciously or unconsciously, a colonial mindset can be seen when he depicts India's major political events during the crucial period of India's freedom struggle from 1921 to 1952. The attempt bears significance as Chaudhuri projects his autobiography as political history and vouchs it through his own experience and observations.

Keywords: Colonialism, Nirad C. Chaudhari, *Thy Hand, Great Anarch*, diasporic texts.

Nirad Chandra Chaudhuri was born on 23 November 1897 in Kishoreganj, Bengal Presidency of British India (present-day Bangladesh). He lived his first twelve years in Kishoreganj and the next thirty years in Kolkata (then Calcutta) as a student and an intellectual in the quest for knowledge. He was fluent in English, French, German, Greek, Latin, Bengali, and Sanskrit by the time he earned a first-class degree in history from Scottish Church College. His academic pursuits encompassed a wide range of subjects, including biology, geography, historical military affairs, art, architecture, anthropology, and archaeology. He had an excellent undergraduate record, but dropped out of graduate school. He supported himself with menial work in the Military Accounts Department and spent much of his time studying in Kolkata's Imperial (now National) Library. After appearing in the prestigious English-language publication Modern Review in Kolkata, he temporarily served as its deputy editor. As the editor of Shanibarer Chithi (The Saturday Letter), he gained notoriety in Bengali letters for his conservative opinions. After his 1932 marriage to Amiya Devi, the couple had two sons. He started working as Sarat Chandra Bose's personal secretary in 1939. Sarat Chandra Bose is the older brother of Subhash Chandra Bose and a prominent nationalist in Bengal.

At the age of fifty-four, Chaudhuri released his first book in Delhi in 1951. It was his much-maligned yet acclaimed autobiography. As an exquisitely written account of life in Kolkata and small-town Bengal, as well as a chronicle of the Anglo-Bengali contacts that extended beyond the top classes and elites of society, it was bestowed with the rank of an instant classic. Because Chaudhuri dedicated the book to the British for the benefits of their two centuries of control over India, it was derided and despised in the country. In 1955, a British Council grant enabled Chaudhuri to travel to England for the first time. He recorded the experience in *Passage to England* (1959). His major works are *The Scholar Extraordinary* (1974), *Hinduism* (1979), *Thy Hand, Great Anarch* (1987), *From the Archives of a Centenarian* (1997), *Three Horsemen of the New Apocalypse* (1997), and four books in Bengali.

"The very conception of the work was bound to make it a kind of political and cultural history. But even if I had intended to write only an autobiography I could not have excluded the public and collective themes because they were part and the personal lives of all Indians of that age."

After a few lines, he opines:

But there are more matter of fact reasons for making it some sort of a historical narrative. I have come now to the conclusion that no true history of the disappearance of the British Empire in India will ever be written. For one thing, none of those who are now writing full or partial histories of this epoch have any personal experience to be able to appraise the events correctly, far less to be able to recreate the spirit and atmosphere. All of them were too young, and many not even born when the events were happening. The objection would at first seem to be wholly pointless because most historians write about events they have not seen, and even those which are far removed from in time. But these historians have the means by which they can reconstruct the past, both factually and imaginatively, in adequate source material, to interpret which they can bring to bear on them some analogous experience. Both are absent in these of recent Indian history, in spite of recentness (xvi-xvii).

If these statements of this veteran Indian author, who was born and brought up in colonial India and then migrated to England for personal growth, are critically examined, it is quite evident that the historical perspective he presents is entirely based on his personal understanding and experiences, and not based on historical facts or documents. But, why should an author, who had no political role in the Nationalist Movement, mix up his autobiography with political history with such vigour and convictions, is the point of literary enquiry in this paper. And how history can be manipulated in the garb of a personal point of view, to subtly endorse the discourses of the powerful and the beneficiary, is well-illustrated by the significant political events in the book.

However, before scrutiny of this premise is made, it is worthwhile to understand the forms and strategies of the British rulers in India by which they established and perpetuated colonial hegemony in different spheres of public and cultural life, controlling not only the physical and continued in the form of Neo-colonialism, even after the political independence of the country, often visible not only in the functioning of present Indian legal and administrative institutions but in the domain of literary studies and cultural practices. Writing about colonialism and its forms of knowledge during the British rule in India, Bernard S. Cohn talks about their 'investigative modalities' which they used "to classify, categorise and bound the vast social world that was India so that it could be controlled" (Cohn 4-5).

Among other modalities, such as the Observational/Travel Modality, the Survey Modality, and the Surveillance Modality, he emphasises the Historiographic Modality and draws out its three strands from the beginning to the last phase of their colonial rule in India. In the first strand, they conceived of governing India by codifying and reinstituting the ruling practices that had been developed by the previous states and rulers. In the second strand, they were involved in the ideological construction of the nature of the Indian civilisation, the major historical writings of Alexender Dow, Robert Orme, Charles Grant etc., according to Cohn, such historical writings "can be seen to have begun the formation of a legitimising discourse about Britain'scivilising mission in India." (p6).

The third historiographic strand involved the study of representations, whether in England or in India, of specific events. Cohn writes, "Thus stories of Black Hole of Calcutta, the defeat of Tipu Sultan, or the siege of Lucknow involved the creation of emblematic heroes and villains, as individuals and types, who took shape in illustrations, various popular performances and poetry" (p6). There is no doubt such constructions of history helped the colonisers to stress the inferiority of the colonised Indians and thus to strengthen the holds of imperialism in India. It would not be an overstatement that subsequent histories were bound to be influenced by these histories of the colonial period, but the writers in the post-colonial period also could be free from such versions and biases, just as the slaves hate their masters but unconsciously ape the ideology and manners of the masters, so is the relationship of the colonised and the coloniser. The shadows of colonialism have dogged the mental processes of many of our literary masters. A case in point is Nirad C. Chaudhuri's autobiography- *Thy Hand, Great Anarch* (1987), which is a sequel to his *Autobiography of an Unknown Indian* (1951)

The very first statement of Chaudhuri in the introduction of *Thy Hand, Great Anarch,* he says,

This book continues the story of my life and thoughts from the point of time it was left in *The Autobiography of an Unknown Indian,* published in 1951. That was first book, and it gave an account of my childhood and student days which came to an end in 1921, when I was twenty- three years old. How I began to write an autobiography in the middle of 1947, when I was short by six months of being fifty, I shall relate in the last part of this book, which deals with that stage of my life. Here I shall only say that even then it was my intention to bring down the story to 1947, the year of British withdrawal from India, so that I might conclude it with a decisive historical event and be enabled to give a complete account of the decline and fall of Indian Empire of Britain. But the narrative of early life had become so long that there could be no question of including what did and what happened in India after in the same book (xiii).

The above shows the contrast in his intentions – he wants to write a sequel to his autobiography, and simultaneously, he wants "to give the complete account of the decline and fall of Indian Empire of Britain." He indirectly makes an effort to dilute the intensity of the National Movement for Independence of India when he says, "it was my intention to bring down the story to 1947, the year of British withdrawal from India," as if they left India willingly without any resistance faced from Indians.

Chaudhuri admires the rule of the colonial power of Britain in India and considers imperialism as a civilising mission. He says,

So far as British rule had a psychological aspect and a civilising mission in India, its greatest achievement was seen in Bengal. That was the renovation of the culture and mental life of a people who had become almost fossilised culturally, British rule, by bringing European cultural influences to bear on Indian life, created what was virtually a new culture. Its cradle and centre of diffusion was Bengal. Its quality, too was very fine, in spite of its limitations and weaknesses. (xx)

Chaudhuri did not participate in any of the movements going on in his time, not even morally or ideologically. He completely disagreed with the way Indians marched against the British Raj. For him, these ways of Indian resistance against the British administration were totally meaningless, though he did not provide any better alternative to go against the colonial structure.He ridicules the Non-Cooperation Movement launched by Mahatma Gandhi, he says,

> For Gandhian specialities, however, I felt only disdain, and did not mince my words. I said that if we must spin in order to be self-reliant in respect of clothing, we should also plough in order to eat; or, if we were sure to get political independence in six months or a year by not going to schools and colleges, giving up our professions, and resigning from Government services *en masse*, we would get it even sooner by committing mass suicide (p11).

British administrators were staunch believers in the idea that once India got its independence, Indians would not be able to run their administration, and the country would collapse. Chaudhuri had the same opinions of colonial masters about his fellow countrymen. He disagrees with the demand for complete independence from British colonialismwhen he writes, "The leadership of Mahatma Gandhi completed the negation. Before him no political leader had seen the aim of ending British rule apart from the entire fabric of Indian life, which they considered the main duty before them" (p31). He was ready to leave India before its independence, which is evident when hesays, "More anticipation of decadence was to follow. Even before independence came to India, I had begun to think of migrating to England to escape from the Indian decadence, and this too my wife was insistent. But that was not practically possible" (xxv).

Being an Indian, Chaudhuri did not want independence from the British Raj,admired their administration, and considered the regime the best in Indian political history. He writes, "There was, first, my historical view of British rule in India, which I regarded as the best political regime which had ever been seen in India, in spite of its shortcomings and positive evils" (p27). He further continues his appreciation for the British administration and finds them better than the Indians, "....it was the British administration who were more closely in contact with the Indian masses and had the most thorough knowledge of their good as well as bad points, and, besides the greatest practical sympathy for them....The common people of India did have a genuine respect for British rule and British administrators, and also confidence in their fairness when dealing between Indian and Indian" (p30).

Chaudhuri criticises the ideas and initiatives to dismantle British rule on the Indian territory and achieve complete independence for all Indians. He refused any achievements of Gandhism, which was solely based on pacifist ideals and values. He says, "Their stock phrase' passive resistance' is a contradiction in terms, because all resistance is active. I have come to the conclusion that the doctrine of non-violence, i.e., preaching the abjuration of violence, stands for nothing else than merely not killing its corollary – not to be killed themselves. That sort of doctrine can only be described as the moral refuge of cowards who want to take credit for resisting evil without taking the consequent risks. But Mahatma Gandhi'snon-violence never excluded social and psychological violence whose objective was moral coercion" (p42).

Here, his ideas coincide with the ideas of Frantz Fanon, a postcolonial critic who asserts at the very beginning of his book *The Wretched of the Earth* (1961), "National liberation, national renaissance, the restoration of nationhood to the people, commonwealth: whatever may be the headings or the new formulas introduced, decolonisation is always a violent phenomenon" (p35). Fanon further opines, "Decolonization is the meeting of two forces, opposed to each other by their very nature, which in fact owe their originality to that sort of substantification which results from and is nourished from situation in the colonies" (p36).

He critically investigates the personal history and background of Mahatma Gandhi to prove him a person with a lack of knowledge about Indian history, culture and politics and his immature policies to unite Indians to fight against the British regime in the country, for that, he declares his background as the significant reason for his short-sightedness:

He was born and brought up in a backward state of India, one of one hundred and ninety- three princely states in Kathiawar, a fractional area of India. His father intended him to follow in his footsteps and become the Diwan or Chief Minister of the State, and sought to give him an education to fit him for the post. It was with this object that he was sent to first to Bombay, and then to England at the age of eighteen, already married man of six years and a father. Therefore he was expected to qualify himself to become a barrister, and he did (p44).

He criticised the life and philosophy of not only Gandhi but Pandit Jawaharlal Nehru and Subhash Chandra Bose too, "No other leader showed this negation more than the three who really had a hold on the mind of Indian people, namely, Gandhi, Nehru, and Subhas Bose. Over the whole period with which I am dealing none of them put forward a single idea about was to follow British rule" (p31).

The way of presentation of India by Chaudhuri is very much inspired by the idea of Orientalism, which has been a narrative used by Europeans to show their superiority over the Orientals (the eastern countries). Edward Said opines in his *Orientalism* (1978) that"European culture gained in strength and identity by setting itself off against the Orient as a sort of surrogate and even underground self" (p3).

Conclusion

Chaudhuri intended to narrate an account of his personal life with a highly subjective version of the historical events of the period from 1921 to 1952, which he calls the working period of his life. He says he has consciously tried to "write the book on the same lines and in the same spirit as its predecessor." He is quite successful in this -- there is absolutely no difference in style or tone between the two volumes. The self-satisfied stance of wisdomand the complete lack of modesty can be found in the second book- *Thy Hand, Great Anarch*. He makes gratuitous jabs at numerous independence movement icons, none of whom are around to dispute him. While Gandhiji seemed kind, "his demands for money were made in the unabashed manner of all Hindu holy men," he said. He views Subhash Chandra Bose, whom all Bengalis revere as Netaji, "the leader," as being irrational, ineffective, and suspicious, and he holds Nehru accountable for the Cripps Mission's failure. All these are nothing but the shadows of colonialism, which are not visible on the surface but playtheir role at a subconscious level in the writing of an Indian author.

References

- Chaudhuri, Nirad C. *Thy Hand, Great Anarch.* Jaico Books, 1987.

- Cohn, Bernard S. *Colonialism and Its Forms of Knowledge: The British in India.* PrincetonUniversity Press, 2021.

- Fanon, Frantz. *The Wretched of the Earth.* Grove Press, 1961.

- Said, Edward. *Orientalism.* Vintage Books, 1978.

Chapter 3

The Indian Policy of Skilled Migration: Brain Drain Versus Brain Return and Benefits of Diaspora

Dr. Mishu Singh

Assistant Professor,
Department of Chemistry
Pt. DeenDayalUpadhayay Govt. Girls P.G. College, Lucknow
Email Address- mishusingh17@gmail.com

Abstract

This article attempts to analyse the phenomenon of skilled migration in detail, based on the idea that international migration is the most obvious example of globalisation. Because they are highly innovative and specialised, skilled migrants constitute a global population that, despite their small number, has exponentially more influence than lower-skilled migrants. For the past few years, there has been a steady increase in the number of skilled Indian migrants. Their degree of dispersal is so great that, worldwide, they rank second only to the Chinese in terms of diaspora size. In certain aspects, this makes the second justification for concentrating on India even more pertinent: during the last several years, India has emerged as a major hub for highly skilled migration, marking a first for the subcontinent. Is our Indian government more in favour of a brain return, or is it more interested in leveraging the political clout and economic significance of its own diaspora?

Keywords: Migrations, Indian diaspora, brain drain, migration policies, brain return

Introduction

People who have migrated from areas that are currently a part of the Republic of India are collectively referred to as the Indian diaspora. It also suggests something about their offspring. Over 20 million people are thought to be part of the diaspora, which is composed of "NRIs" (Indian citizens who do not live in India) and "PIOs" (Persons of Indian Origin who have obtained citizenship in another nation). The largest diaspora in the world is centred in India. All of the main continents in the world are home to more than 25 million Indian expatriates. Diasporas serve as international representatives of their home countries and are emblems of national pride. The diaspora is now widely acknowledged for its capacity to advance Indian soft power, advocate for the country's interests, and boost the country's economy.

Skilled Brain Drain and International Relations

Given their high rate of innovation and specialisation, skilled migrants' movements are especially important to globalisation and cross-national interaction. With flows coming from north to north, north to south, and south to south, the labour market for qualified workers is becoming increasinglyglobalised. The aforementioned factors include the widespread use of ICTs, the advancement of transportation infrastructure, changes in the population, and the state of the economy (Counihan and Miller 2006). Historically, states have been responsible for ensuring that skilled human capital is mobile; however, in the current global economy, regions, cities, universities, and multinational corporations are vying for the talent of skilled workers. It is imperative for institutions to implement management policies that guarantee their appeal both locally and globally, contingent upon the calibre of skilled human capital they hope to draw (Lucas 2008).

A complex web of circumstances, human variables, and factors influence migration and the international mobility of skilled workers more than the movement of goods, capital, or resources. Policies that are specific to each sector and aimed at each skilled group should be implemented at both the micro and intermediate levels. Numerous developing nations have relaxed their immigration laws in an effort to attract skilled labour and improve their competitiveness in the global talent market. However, the majority of the world's highly skilled labour still comes from developing nations, which is why these nations are losing their most highly skilled workers (Mani S. 2009). The growth and development of a country may be negatively impacted by an excessive exodus of highly qualified professionals. Growth and development in today'sglobalised economy rely on the ongoing relationships and advantages that states maintain with their highly skilled citizens abroad.

In this scenario, India takes the lead due to the increasing number of qualified migrants, especially those with qualifications. With 114.4 million departures in 2010, India is one of the major countries that supplies skilled labour to global markets. India has a vast pool of highly skilled human capital available to businesses worldwide in practically every industry, particularly I.T. and healthcare. Additionally, India is a significantsource of highly qualified human capital, i.e., pupils (Mahroum 1999). The question of whether India is suffering from a brain drain was first debated in the 1960s and 1970s when highly qualified workers left the country. By the twenty-first century, academics were talking about "brain gain," which was partly caused by some extremely skilled Indians returning to their home country and the diaspora's significant economic and political influence on the world stage (Khadria 2006).

It is helpful to take a step back and briefly describe how the demographics of Indian immigrants have changed, as well as to examine the political and economic roles played by the diaspora, before attempting to respond to these queries.

The Pervasive Soft Power of the Indian Diaspora

The Indian diaspora's soft power is primarily derived from Indian political values, culture, and technological prowess. However, there are also difficulties because of India's large territory, second-largest population, and third-largest army. Notwithstanding these obstacles, India benefits from the qualified portion of the Indian diaspora as a competitive advantage in the global marketplace (Khadria 2001). Through remittances, investment flows, or the experience and knowledge of skilled migrants who have returned home, countries can profit from their qualified human capital abroad(Buga and Meyer 2012). These factors offset the adverse effects of brain drain, particularly in nations with small populations or unstable political systems. In these situations, skilled migrants' investments, knowledge sharing, and remittances can positively impact the economies of the recipient nations.

A recent analysis shows a significant negative correlation between the likelihood that a migrant will send remittances and the income levels in their country of origin. The likelihood that a nation's eligible foreign migrants will send remittances is positively correlated with the country's gross national income per capita. In this way, a country's population size has less of an impact on remittances than low-income levels do. The size of the diaspora, low per capita income, and high rates of brain drain are the reasons behind India's dominance in remittances worldwide (Seghal 2004). Research indicates a positive correlation between the amount of foreign direct investment (FDI) that theU.S. invests in a given country and the number of qualified migrants that nation has living in theU.S. It is understandable how this could affectU.S.investors' decisions given that approximately 40% of the Indian diaspora is based in theU.S. However, following the liberalisation of the 1990s, the amount of money that Indian brands have invested abroad in their home country has not been as high as anticipated (Khadria 2007).

Comparatively speaking, Chinese diaspora FDI (10.1% of GCF) has been invested in the Indian economy by the Indian diaspora, which has made relatively small investments (3 per cent of GCF). Certain analysts have observed potential manipulation stemming from a soft power tactic employed by the Chinese diaspora in Southeast Asia. With highly skilled Indian migrants spearheading the development of the burgeoning Indian I.T. industry, the rise of India's competitive I.T. sector is remarkable (Khanna P. 2005).

Transformation of Migratory Flows and the Role of Indian Government

Indian migration has been largely influenced by the Indian government, which has delegated the role of attracting and facilitating the return of expatriates to the market. This is a result of the massive labour force in the nation—518 million people—many of whom are unemployed and impoverished (World Bank 2011). No policies have been put in place by the Indian government to draw in foreign talent or make it easier for eligible Indian emigrants to return home. Instead, in order to handle the substantial amounts of money remitted each year, it has implemented ad hoc measures. As a result, the government is now more concerned with obtaining investments from the Indian diaspora than it is withdrawing in new expats. The Indian government has recently pushed two initiatives: the Ministry of Overseas Indian Affairs in 2004 and the Annual Diaspora Conference in 2003, which attempts to build a community among expatriates, political figures, and economic players. The aforementioned initiatives pertain to special identity documents that grant equal rights to Indian expatriates and domestic Indians, except for the ability to vote and hold public office.

Conclusion

Conclusively, one could argue that the limited yet steady reversal of migration flows towards India in recent years, characterised by the return of many Indian emigrants and the arrival of qualified personnel from overseas, has been primarily driven by economic factors. Other than the ones already discussed, one noteworthy aspect of these economic factors is what can be referred to as the Copernican revolution of the 1990s without fear of exaggeration. Significant progress was made in making India more appealing to foreign investors at the start of that decade when the government initiated a broad liberalisation process of the Indian market. However, managing and allocating the substantial financial resources that citizens remit to their home countries more effectively has been its main goal rather than pushing citizens to return. India must prioritise strengthening its human capital above all other issues if it hopes to maintain its upward trajectory in the global economy.

References

- Buga N, Meyer JB. "Indian human resources mobility: brain drain versus brain gain." CARIM-IndiaRR 2012/04, Robert Schuman Centre for Advanced Studies, European University Institute, SanDomenico di Fiesole, Florence. www.india-eu-migration.eu/media/CARIM-India-2012%20-%2004.pdf. 2012.

- Counihan CR, Miller MJ. "Competing for global talent in an age of turbulence."2006.

- Kuptsch C, Pang E, editors.*Competing for Global Talent*, ILO, Geneva, pp. 259–75. 2006.

- Khadria, B. "India: Country Study—Skilled Labour Migration (the "Brain Drain") from India: Impact and Policies." Jawaharlal Nehru University, 2001.

- Khadria, B. "India: Skilled Migration to Developed Countries, Labour Migration to the Gulf." Jawaharlal Nehru University, 2006.

- Khadria, B. "Conceptualising the Typologies of Indian Diaspora in International Economic Relations: 'Tinker, Tailor, Soldier, Spy', or a 'Great Off-White Hope' of the New Century?"*ISAS* Working Paper No 19, January, Institute of South Asian Studies, 2007.

- Khanna, P. "Bollystan: India's Diasporic Diplomacy."Khilnani S (eds) *India as a New Global Leader*. Foreign Policy Centre, pp. 16–26. www.isn.ethz.ch/isn/Digital-Library/

Publications/Detail/?ots591=0c54e3b3-1e9c-be1e-2c24-a6a8c7060233&lng=en&id=23654, 2005.

- Lucas, R. "International LaborMigration in a GlobalisingEconomy: Trade, Equity, and Development Program," No.92, July, *Carnegie Endowment for International Peace*, 2008.

- Mahroum, S. "Highly Skilled Globetrotters: Mapping the International Migration of Human Capital."*R&D Manag* (30)1:23–31, 1999.

- Mani, S. "High Skilled Migration from India: An Analysis of its Economic Implications." Working Paper 416, Centre for Development Studies, 2009.

- Seghal, M. "Foreign Pros Seeking Jobs in India." Rediff India Abroad, February 11.www.rediff.com/money/2004/feb/11bpo1.htm, 2004.

- World Bank. *Migration and Remittances Factbook 2011*. 2nd edition. World Bank, 2011.

Chapter 4

Identifying Opportunities for Knowledge Transfer and Capacity Building: A Study of the Indian Diaspora

Dr. Madhumita Gupta

Assistant Professor, Department of Commerce,
Maharaja Bijli Pasi Government P.G. College,
Ashiana, Lucknow, U.P.
Email Address- madhugdc@gmail.com

Abstract

Indian diaspora broadly refers to millions of people of Indian origin who have migrated to various countries across the globe in search of jobs, employment, business or some other purpose. Estimates from the Ministry of Overseas Indian Affairs suggest that the Indian diaspora has a sizeable presence of over 30 million, which comprises non-resident Indians called NRIs, citizens placed and located overseas termed OCIs, and persons who are of Indian origin termed PIOs. Of these, over 5.5 million are in the Gulf, 2.2 million in the U.S., 1.7 million in the U.K., and over a million in Canada. Leaving aside the colonial period of indentured labour, the Indian diaspora has evolved over three phases: the quest for employment and education- as a source of Indian remittances, and now, increasingly, as active players in shaping the policies in their host countries.

The economic reforms of India transformed with the changing worldview about India and as we seek the world. The NRIs have lent strength and stability to the management of our economy. As per the World Bank Report, remittances from the Indian overseas community are the highest globally

During periods of foreign exchange crisis, policy managers have invariably turned to the NRI community to enhance capital flows and secure the marketing of India Development Bonds and other Special NRC schemes. These remittances have shored up our reserves and supported the incomes of intended beneficiaries. Subsequently, we have sought these flows as investment vehicles. State governments have competed to attract NRI investments to meet capital shortages, finance projects, and generate employment. The profile of the Indian diaspora varies from the blue-collar workers in the Gulf to professionals in Silicon Valley. Seeking symmetry between changing demand patterns and the supply side needs creativity.

The Indian diaspora has come of age. Many Indian-Americans are high-ranking public officials like Governor Nikki Haley, Congresswoman Tulsi Gabbard, and Bobby Jindal, who is seeking to run for the U.S. presidential election.In the recently concluded parliamentary elections in the U.K., ten Indian-origin MPs won seats in the British Parliament. Scores of Indians like Sundar Pichai, Indira Nooyi, Ajay Banga and Satya Nadella hold top positions in some of the biggest multinational companies.

Keywords: Diaspora, NRI, Foreign Exchange, Migrants, Economic Reforms

Introduction

The Indian diaspora can be broadly classified into two categories. Old diaspora refers to those people of Indian origin who moved away from India to other parts of the globe during colonial rule, which was dominated by contracts. This included labourers taken to British colonies like Mauritius, South Africa, the West Indies, Fiji, and many other countries to work in construction and plantation. The new diaspora is a mix of professionals in the Indian community,including doctors, academicians, and engineers, who have moved away to developed countries, mostly Europe, Australia, and North America, for better career prospects and a better future.

The combined potential of both the diasporas can help in nation-building as it is a reservoir of skill, expertise, technology, and finances, which is mutually beneficial for both the countries, the country of their living and the country of their origin. These mutual benefits create business opportunities; promote foreign direct investments, and transfer knowledge and skills. Several countries worldwide seek diaspora engagement, but only a few have succeeded in actively engaging their diaspora for mutual benefits and interests. This is evidenced in terms of strengthened bilateral relations between the host and home nation, apart from providing aid in the development activities of native states.

The perception in India about the diaspora has changed in successive years from 'brain drain' to 'brain gain' because of the spur by the ever-growing contributions made by the diaspora in various sectors at global platforms, including I.T., medicine, art, culture, international politics and many more. The Indian economy has gained immensely from this dynamic and enterprising diaspora. India received a significant flow of remittances in the world, which is nearly $ 108 billion in 2022. This accounts for approximately 03 per cent of India's GDP. In addition to this, Indians residing abroad hold deposits in Indian banks worth several billion dollars. The Indian economy is undergoing a fundamental transformation comprising all sectors. The distinguishing transformation is happening in India's services export, which has demonstrated growth amidst the pandemic wave gripping the globe in past years. India is home to about 40 per cent of the world's Global Capacity Centres, and they are estimated to comprise 25 per cent of overall I.T. services exports. However, their acknowledgement as an asset is a new aspect of the 21st century, and several policy shifts were madeto integrate the diaspora into the nation's development through knowledge and technology transfer in particular.

Understanding the Indian Diaspora

Earlier, the diaspora was seen as a concept of forced exile, but now it is seen as a more generic concept and is used to describe a transnational population where the cultural origins of that group are said to have arisen in a land other than that in which they now reside and whose social, economic and political networks cut across borders and are even global. Today, there is no inconsistency between being responsible citizens of the host country and continuing to maintain social and cultural links with one's homeland. The bare fact that needs to be considered while describing the diaspora is that although the diasporas are a result of migration, all the migrants cannot be termed diasporas. The crucial element that makes the concept meaningful and legitimate is their self-mobilisation around their awareness of themselves as a diaspora. The continuing existence of migrant communities with their 'self-awareness', 'self imagination' and 'connectedness', to the country of origin not only leads to the formation of diaspora but also helps in the organisation of diasporas.

The Indian diaspora is a generic term to describe the people who migrated from territories that are currently within the borders of the Republic of India. It also refers to their descendants. The diaspora is currently estimated to number over twenty million, composed of "NRIs" (Indian citizens not residing in India) and "PIOs" (Persons of Indian Origin who have acquired the citizenship of some other country). The diaspora covers practically every part of the world. As per the report of the High-level Committee on Indian diaspora 2001, the largest percentage of the populace is concentrated in the Southeast Asia region (32%). The next biggest concentration is in the Gulf region, with 19%; however, it is almost half of Southeast Asia. The USA is home to 10 per cent of Indians. Latin America and the Caribbean, and the U.K. both have 7 per cent of Indian people, closely followed by Mauritius & Reunion and South Africa, both with 6 percent of Indians. Other regions where Indians live are– Canada with 5 percent, Asia Pacific with 4 percent, other European countries with 3 percent and the least number of Indians in East Africa with just 1 per cent. There are three categories of overseas Indians.

- NRIs: Indian citizens staying abroad for an indefinite period for whatever purpose

- PIOs: Overseas Indians who have become citizens of the countries of their settlement.

- SPIO: Stateless Persons of Indian Origin who have no documents to substantiate their Indian Origin (Majority in Myanmar and Sri Lanka).

Contemporary flows from India are of two kinds: The first is the emigration of highly skilled professionals, workers and students with tertiary and higher educational qualifications migrating to developed countries, particularly the USA, UK, Canada, Australia, and New Zealand. This flow started after Indian independence and gathered momentum with the emigration of I.T. professionals in the 1990s. The second is the flow of unskilled and semiskilled workers going mostly to the Gulf countries and Malaysia, following the oil boom in the Gulf countries, mainly from Kerala and other south Indian states (MOIA, 2012). Of late, however, northern states in India like Uttar Pradesh and Bihar have also emerged as the leading states of origin for such migration.

Diaspora and Development

Due to globalisation, the influence and impact of diasporas have increasingly become important, especially in the areas of policy and, in some cases, politics. It is important to see the relationship between the diaspora and the nation's development, and there are two different views about the relationship between diaspora and countries of origin. The first view is the "balanced growth" approach. The theory of economic liberal principle specifies that by working towards providing employment for all, extending economic support by way of remittances and working towards skill development of the migrant population in the country of origin, the inter-country income disparities minimise and eventually make migration unnecessary. Diaspora and development are interlinked and bear a relationship that works on a two-way phenomenon. Diaspora and development interact with each other at two different platforms as follows:

- First, the effect of diaspora in development, in terms of family remittance transfers; demand of services, such as telecommunications, consumer goods, or travel; capital investment and charitable donations to philanthropic organisations.

- Second, development affects migration in the sense that closer economic integration,symbolised by freer trade and investment, can speed up change in developing countries, affecting the scale of international migration itself.

Development Outcomes of Diaspora Engagement

The impact of diaspora on their countries of origin has several dimensions, especially in terms of investment, trade, remittances, trade, philanthropy, networks and so on, but the focus of the present paper is mainly on the impact of diaspora in transferring knowledge and technology in their countries of origin. Since these impacts are not mutually exclusive, it may be pertinent to cover all these aspects:

Remittances: The principal focus of the economic benefits to the countries of origin through their diaspora is in the form of remittances- private transfers from the migrant population to their families. As per the latest World Bank Report (2015), remittances to developing countries amounted to $431.6 billion in 2015, an increase of 0.4 per cent over $430 billion in 2014. India retained its top spot in 2015, attracting about $69 billion in remittances, down from $70 billion in 2014. For many developing countries, remittances are an essential source of family (and national) income and are the largest source of external financing. The total value, including unofficial remittance flows – money and goods sent through family, friends, and informal or semi-formal channels is thought to be much higher. It is also important to mention that remittances do not automatically contribute to national development. According to the International Organization for Migration (IOM), remittances tend to follow through three spending phases-

A. family maintenance and housing improvement,

B. conspicuous consumption (spending resulting from tension, inflation, or in a crisis situation or, at times, ostentatious expenditure as well)

C. productive activities (improvement of land, education or health)

A large percentage of remittances do not extend to the third 6 phase. According to the World Bank, remittances can

   i.   reduce recipient household poverty, with spillover to other households

   ii. increase investment in education and health as well as other productive activities

   iii reduce child labour

   iv   increase entrepreneurship

1. Trade and Investments: There is evidence that indicates a strong correlation between the presence of diaspora residing in a country and trade ties to the country of origin. Another significant role that diasporas play is in the economic development of their countries of origin through investment. Diasporas play a dual role when it comes to investment: either directly investing in their countries or persuading non-diasporas to invest in their countries of origin. The diasporas have unique ownership advantages, which range from their expertise in the area, networks which they have developed over

time, as well as their ability to forecast new developments in their countries of origin. They can also combine this knowledge with the skills, knowledge and networks they have cultivated abroad, yielding significant synergistic advantages. However, available information suggests that investment by its 7 diaspora in the Indian economy is still meagre. The total amount of investments by Indian expatriates (NRIs) over the period 1991-2001 is put at $2.6 billion out of the total $100 billion FDI in India.

2. Philanthropy: Yet another way in which diaspora contributes is through philanthropic engagement in many areas. Philanthropy has a pivotal role in advancing global equity, acting beyond the broader concerns of government and the narrower interests of business. These investments not only contribute to monetary resources but also new skills, fresh thinking, and innovative approaches to global problems. Some diaspora organisations and individuals seek no personal return on investment, but rather pursue charitable enterprises. Such enterprises range from very small-scale, one-off efforts of community groups to more organised and durable efforts, from the donations of single individuals to powerful networks of like-minded donors. There is an absence of any systematic data relating to the contributions made by the diaspora in the areas of philanthropy. In India, there is no mechanism to collect data on diaspora philanthropy, nor is such type of data kept or interpreted by the government authority or any other research organisation.

3. Technology, Knowledge, and Skills Transfers: In many countries, the diaspora acts as a trust, connecting critical components of the public and private sectors to expertise not available within the country and compensating to some degree for the departure of highly skilled emigrants. Some skills and

knowledge-transfer initiatives rely on the temporary (and occasionally permanent) return of skilled diaspora members to the country of origin to teach and train–although these initiatives are hard to scale up because of their high cost and the difficulty of detaching professionals from their regular jobs abroad for meaningful periods of time. Some of the domains in which the Indian diaspora has contributed to endogenous economic development are inter alia - I.T., diamonds, health and education, medicine, and engineering.

Some of the domains in which the Indian diaspora have contributed to endogenous economic development are inter alia - I.T., diamonds, health and education, medicine and engineering. This has generally picked up momentum after the economic liberalisation in India in the nineties. Recently, the government has taken steps to facilitate diaspora investment by instituting a "one-stop-shop" for simplified procedural requirements.

Policy Perspectives and Strategy for Diaspora Engagement in India

The effects of a diaspora are strongly mediated by policies and conditions in the country of origin. Several countries of origin have attempted to formulate policies of diaspora engagement in order to use their overseas communities as a resource for development. Such policies range from securing better welfare conditions for their migrants abroad to promoting investment and contributions to development. To begin with, it is important to ask whether India has a diaspora policy? Is it stated or written somewhere? Is it clear, transparent, and evident in India's dealing with the diaspora? If one looks at it formally, there is no 'whitepaper' on 'Indian diaspora Policy.' This does not mean that India does not have a specific policy on diaspora engagement.

It is the view of this paper that India does have a robust diaspora engagement policy that is evolving with the active involvement of the diaspora itself. This consultative process is mentioned in addresses by the Prime Minister and the Minister for Indian Overseas Affairs at the (Pravasi Bhartiya Divas) PBD, which is one of the best forums for diaspora engagement. It is also significant to mention that the transformation of the ideological climate in India towards diaspora engagement has begun, especially after the 1990s with the success of the I.T. industry.

The Ministry of Overseas Indian Affairs (MOIA) is a unique experiment in diaspora engagement. India, in fact, is only the 11th country in the world to have set up a separate 'Diaspora Ministry'. The MOIA was established in 2004 to "promote, nurture and sustain a mutually beneficial and symbiotic relationship between India and overseas Indians" (MOIA, 2009). The MOIA is the nodal Ministry for all matters relating to Overseas Indians comprising Persons of Indian Origin (PIO), Non-Resident Indians (NRIs) and Overseas Citizens of India (OCI) and also handles all aspects of emigration and return of emigrants. The mission is to establish a robust and vibrant institutional framework to facilitate and support mutually beneficial networks with and among Overseas Indians to maximise the development impact for India and enable Overseas Indians to invest in and benefit from the opportunities in India.

Some of the important points on the Indian policy of diaspora engagement are listed below: Regarding citizenship laws, India does not permit dual citizenship, however, its OCI Card scheme provides for lifetime visa-free travel and full residency and employment rights for Persons of Indian origin who are citizens of other countries. Given India's concerns and pressure from its diaspora, India evolved its own model, which it called the 'Overseas Citizenship of India

(OCI)', which is actually a Card (the OCI card) and is a follow-up of the earlier grant of a 'Person of Indian Origin' or PIO Card. This was a hybrid between dual and single citizenship. India deprived OCIs of political rights while it conferred economic privileges; even those were also restricted in some ways. OCI, therefore, is "not to be misconstrued as a 'dual citizenship'. OCI does not confer political rights".

Similarly, voting rights have not been accorded to Persons of Indian Origin who are citizens of other countries, however, Non-Resident Indians (NRIs - Indian Passport holders settled overseas) right to vote was recently restored by amending rules for registration of voters located overseas. The Indian diaspora holding PIO or OCI cards have the right to purchase property in India (except farms and plantations). Tax incentivesand reduced customs duty regimes for the transfer of residence of overseas Indians returning to India are available, including the retention of NRI status up to three years after return. Provisions for transfer of funds for philanthropy and tax exemption for the same are available. Portable Benefits Through the provision of SSAs (Social Security Agreements), the pensionary benefits of Indian workers and professionals working overseas are both portable and can be totalised in countries where SSAs have been executed.

There are many general laws to promote investments from the Indian diaspora, and several provisions have been put in place, ranging from special incentives for bank depositsto investments in the share marketto certain special provisions for OCIs and NRIs for foreign direct investment. Also, to encourage employment of overseas Indians, amendments to rules for doctors, scientists, academics and accountants have been or are in the process of being amended. The government of India has launched some schemes over the years for the welfare of overseas Indians. To list some of them include, the Indian Community Welfare Fund, PIO/OCI Card PIO card, Pravasi Bhartiya Bima Yojna, Pravasi Bhartiya Divas and Pravasi Bhartiya Kendra, Mahatma Gandhi Pravasi SurakshaYojna, OIFC – Economic engagement, Global INK for Knowledge transfer, IDF – Philanthropy, ICM – migration policy research, SSAs/HRMP, Voting Rights, Gender Initiative – Assistance for women against fraud NRI marriages, Youth – Know India programme/Youth Clubs/Scholarships.

Conclusion

Although infrastructure and policy have been barriers to knowledge and technology transfer in India, one of the main barriers is the IPR, which has hindered the diffusion of technology in the country. However, it is noteworthy that the recent government is taking all the progressive steps toengage the diasporas for the development of the nation. A recent example of this can be related to the amendments in India's IPR policy. The policy is entirely compliant with the WTO's agreement on TRIPS. It also aims to sustain entrepreneurship and boost Prime Minister Narendra Modi's pet scheme 'Make in India.' The Prime Minister on 14th Pravasi Bhartiya Divas exhorted the diaspora to participate in flagship government programmes such as Digital India, Make in India, Start-up India, Swachch Bharat (Clean India) and Namami Gange (Clean Ganga) for the country's all-round development. The Prime Minister of India also launched the VAJRA (Visiting Advanced Joint Research) Faculty scheme by the Department of Science and Technology, enabling NRIs and the overseas scientific community to participate and contribute to research and development in India.

For effective and systematic cooperation with the diaspora, some strategies need to be worked upon, such as mapping the diaspora and preparing "diaspora profiles", formulating diaspora-friendly policies, establishing institutional mechanisms for coordinating the work of different departments within embassies to increase efficiency in building constructive relationships with diasporas and their networks and engaging with multiple stakeholders namely chambers of commerce, investments promotion agencies, trade associations, universities, banks. Thus, for overall national development, it is important for a country like India to tap the capacities of overseas nationals for the development of their motherland as well as countries where they are settled, and it can be done by liberalizing the norms for Non-Resident Indians and Persons of Indian Origin. On a global level, we need to explore the catalytic role of diaspora in reaching the Sustainable Development Goals (SDGs) and the 2030 Agenda for Sustainable Development. Diaspora expertise and contributions must be better leveraged to deliver on the 2030 Agenda, particularly for SDGs that aim to end hunger and poverty, ensuring healthy lives and lifelong learning that are at one end of the spectrum to the larger development goals of sustainable energy, housing, industrialisation, conserving marine resources and ecosystems, combating climate change, promoting peaceful and inclusive societies. Goal 17, which reads 'Strengthen the means of implementation and revitalise the global partnership for sustainable development', in particular, opens several windows, such as technology, trade, finance and capacity building for diaspora contribution.

References

- economictimes.indiatimes.com//news/economy/finance/ indian-economy-benefited-from-diaspora-rbis-michaelpatra/ articleshow/ 100140191.cms? utm_ source= content of interest & utm_medium=text&utm_campaign=cppst

- 'Engaging Diaspora: The Indian Growth Story.' Eleventh Pravasi Bhartiya Divas www.ficci.com/publications, p. 32, 2013.

- High-Level Committee on the Indian Diaspora (2001). The Indian Diaspora, Ministry of External Affairs, Government of India, December 19, 2001, indiandiaspora.nic.in/contents. htm. and gjepc.org/updates/8988/india-and-china-shape-global-diamond-trade-years-come

- IOM, Department of Migration Management, Migration heath Division, Diaspora engagement projects in the health sectors of Africa. Paper Presented at the International Migration Dialogue Diaspora ministerial Conference, 2013.

- Ministry of Overseas Indian Affairs, Annual report (2012-13). Accessed from: www.mea.gov.in/images/pdf/annual-report-2012-13.pdf

- Sahoo, Ajay Kumar and Brij Maharaj. *Sociology of Diaspora: A Reader*. Rawat Publication, 2007.

- World Bank (2015). Migration and Development Brief. Accessed from: www.worldbank.org/migration

Visualising Diasporic Heritage: The Role of Graphic Novels in Preserving and Communicating Cultural Memory

Ms. Archika Vishwakarma

Research Scholar
Department of English and Modern European Languages,
University of Lucknow, Lucknow.
Email Address- archikavishwakarma95@gmail.com

Abstract

The concept of cultural memory in the context of diaspora refers to the transmission and preservation of any community or a group's collective memory, cultural heritage, and identity as they shift and settle in different locations around the world. Mostly, diaspora communities face many problems in maintaining their cultural identity to survive in different locations. While preserving their traditions, cultural memory helps them adapt to new environments. There are many art forms that play a prominent role in expressing and sustaining cultural memory among diaspora communities in which graphic novels are one of the latest forms of literary art that also play a significant role in preserving and expressing cultural memory among diaspora communities. This research paper deals with the concept of cultural memory within a diaspora that is essential for preserving a sense of identity.

The research paper will discuss the 'Diaspora and Graphic Novels' and examine how the diaspora is preserved and communicated through visual storytelling. The research study will introduce graphic novels as a highly unique visual medium for telling stories and explain why these novels are effective in conveying cultural memory with the analysis of selected graphic novels. This paper will also discuss the reflection and evaluation of the impact of these graphic novels in preserving Cultural memory for diasporic communities. It will also help the readers conduct further research studies on the intersection of diaspora, cultural memory, and graphic novels.

Keywords: Diaspora, Cultural memory, Graphic novels, Visual storytelling, Diasporic heritage, Displacement, Identity

Introduction

Diaspora studies examine the spread of populations and cultures to various geographical areas and locations. People from diaspora communities of ten have close social and cultural connections with their homelands or their place of origin while simultaneously also embracing a multitude of cultural identities. In the context of diaspora, cultural memory refers to the collective recollection and preservation of a group's cultural legacy, traditions, heritage, customs and history. This tradition usually continues to be passed down through generations, even after individuals from that culture are dispersed to different parts of the world. It plays a significant role in maintaining a sense of identity and belonging for diaspora communities, as it allows them to remember and cherish their cultural heritage, even when they are separated from their places of origin. Cultural memory encompasses various elements such as language, customs, traditions, rituals, stories and artistic creations, which bind individuals in the diaspora to their cultural background and history. Anh Huaargues inher essay "Diaspora and Cultural Memory" that when she uses the term "diaspora", her reference is to the dispersion of a group of people from a central location to multiple peripheral places, along with the incorporation of collective memory and trauma within such a dispersal. According to her, this interconnection is achievable through the advancement in modern technologies, enhanced global communication, and heightened mobility within our contemporary late capitalist society. Consequently, this leads to the emergence and vivid expression of cultural or collective memories, myths and perceptions of the homeland.

Graphic Novels as a Medium of Visual Storytelling

A graphic novel is one of the highly unique mediums of visual storytelling nowadays. Writing a story in a visual format allows an artist or a writer to communicate through artwork and focus on the power of dialogue instead of describing details. Graphic novels are effective in communicating cultural memory through a blend of visuals and storytelling, which lies in their ability to merge the power of imagery and narrative. The incorporation of visual elements and texts allows for a multi-dimensional understanding of cultural memory, making it more impactful and memorable. Ggolnar Nabizadeh, in his book *Representation and Memory in Graphic Novels,* has discussed the concepts of memory and visual archive and explores the representation of memory in graphic novels and comics from the contemporary era.

Graphic novels play a significant role in diaspora communities as well as serve as a powerful medium for preserving and communicating cultural memory. It can serve as a means to transmit and preserve the cultural heritage and identity of a diaspora community. The production of graphic novels by diaspora authors and artists can be an empowering act. It allows individuals to reclaim their stories, challenge stereotypes, and establish their presence within the cultural domain. Graphic novels also serve as a bridge between diaspora communities and the broader society by facilitating cross-cultural conversion. They offer valuable perspectives on the diaspora journey and encourage discussions on subjects like diversity and inclusivity.

Graphic Novels Analysis

There are several graphic novels that preserve and communicate cultural memory in the context of diaspora. *"Pashmina"* is a touching graphic novel written by Nidhi Chanani and published in 2017 for young adults that explores the journey of an Indian American teenager as she seeks to re-establish her connection with her mother's homeland through a magical and mystical pashmina shawl. It explores the diasporic experience of dislocation and relocation within a multicultural context, as portrayed through the character Nimisha as a lens to explore intricate themes of identity, belonging and the quest for one's cultural roots. Through this novel, Nidhi Chanani explores the hardship and subsequent self-discovery that comes from navigating two different cultures and worlds that represent a relevant example to exemplify the preservation and communication of cultural memory in the context of diaspora study.

Bishak Som is a graphic novelist whose family moved from India to the United States, and that plays a significant role in shaping her graphic novels. Her experience of upbringing in an immigrant household heavily influences her graphic novels. Her books often revolved around South Asian characters on a quest to discover their identity and integration into a foreign culture that can be relatable with diaspora elements and communities. In one of the magazines, Som herself states that the high intention of her work is to initiate the creation of queer/femme utopias, allowing joyous femmes to fully inhabit, dance, frolic and thrive in a queer landscape. *Apsara Engine* is one of her wonderful graphic novels, having a collection of graphic stories that explores gender identity, immigration and cultural displacement within the context of the South Asian diaspora. Rachel Pollack, an American author, has given their opinion on this book that *Apsara Engine* is an outstanding book that achieves something remarkable: it seamlessly combines relatable and meaningful narratives with imagery that transports readers to strange, unfamiliar and otherworldly places. Such stories push the limits of what we consider 'realism' and, moreover, serve as a reminder that reality is not always as it seems.

Another writer is Samhita Arni, an Indian author and graphic novelist best known for her adaptation of Indian epic poetry that preserves Indian cultures and myths. *"Sita's Ramayana"* is the greatest graphic novel developed in collaboration with Moyna Chitrakar. *Sita's Ramayana* is a retelling of the epic *Ramayana* from a woman's perspective, narrated by Sita. The strong focus on the role of women in the midst of the heroic war and the political conflicts between men and the kingdom serves a unique viewpoint. As *Ramayana* is a timeless Indian epic, this book *Sita's Ramayana* is the best example of preserving cultural memory because this book preserves Indian culture through the use of modern technologies that make it more memorable for present society as well as further generations. It is also a valuable piece of historical literature that preserves Indian myths and cultural history by retelling the greatest epic of India, the *Ramayana.*

Visual Storytelling Methods and Techniques

These graphic novels use visual storytelling techniques for telling stories through the use of visual media, such as photography, art, illustration, info graphics and other elements. It involves storytelling from an individual's perspective by using juxtaposed images to create a narrative and offering glimpses into a topic that elicits strong emotion and encourages action. The main purpose of this method of storytelling is to capture the attention of the audience swiftly, as the human brain can rapidly process visual information. This visual storytelling technique can help in preserving and communicating collective memory.

Reflection and Impact of Graphic Novels

There is also a prominent question on the reflection and impact of graphic novels for readers. Graphic novels have played a significant role in preserving cultural or collective memory for diaspora communities in several ways. It has special and unique characters, settings and narratives that reflect the experiences and cultures of diaspora communities as well as provides the best platform for these communities to tell their authentic stories and challenges of life and showcase their history, tradition and identity. It also serves as a visual record that future generations can access, ensuring that crucial events and experiences remain vividly documented and not lost to oblivion. Graphic novels are often used as educational tools for learners to raise awareness about diaspora communities and cultural heritage in a better way that can help promote cross-cultural understanding. To sum up, graphic novels have a powerful impact on preserving the cultural memory of diaspora communities by representing their experiences, chronicling history, creating emotional bonds, spreading awareness among learners, fostering community, and enhancing cross-cultural understanding. These novels stand as a valuable medium for storytelling and the preservation of the cultural richness of diaspora communities.

Conclusion

We can conclude that diaspora communities face lots of challenges and troubles in surviving in a new environment. Their past experiences are also preserved in their memory and represented through different art forms by these communities. This article talks about such an art form called graphic novels, which is a highly unique medium of conveying the stories, experiences, and memories of diaspora communities and other artists. When we describe the term cultural memory within the diaspora, we can see that it evolves over time as new experiences and challenges arise, and it plays a vital role in shaping the identity and resilience of diaspora groups as the novelist Nidhi Chanani describes in a unique way by using the visual arts in her book *Pashmina* and Bishak Som, also the greatest novelist who portrays their real-life experiences in her books. It contributes to the preservation of their unique cultural heritage in the face of displacement and acculturation.

As we can see through the book *Sita's Ramayana,* which can help to preserve our Indian cultural memory, thus we can say that graphic novels represent a medium that can be instrumental in helping to document and communicate this cultural memory to new generations and wider audiences. Critics often praise graphic novels for their effectiveness in conveying cultural memory through visual and narrative techniques. They argue that the bond of art and storytelling allows for a richer and more immersive exploration of history and culture.

References

- Arni, Samhita. *Sita's Ramayana.* Tara Books, 2011.

- Chanani, Nidhi. *Pashmina.* Macmillan, 3 Oct. 2017.

- Hua, Anh. *Diaspora and Culture.* University of Toronto Press, Dec. 2005.

- Nabizadeh, Golnar. *Representation and Memory in Graphic Novels.* Routledge, 2019.

- Som, Bishakh. *Apsara Engine.* Brow Books, 14 April, 2020.

Chapter 6

Unveiling the Historical Odyssey: A Review of the Global Journey and Impact of the Indian Diaspora

Mr. Lavkush Kumar

Assistant Professor
Department Of English
Government Girls P.G. College Hamirpur U.P.
Email Address- lavkushkumar45583@gmail.com

Abstract

The Indian diaspora is one of the largest and most diverse in the world, with a history dating back more than two millennia. This review article provides a comprehensive overview of the global journey and impact of the Indian diaspora, from ancient migration to contemporary international relations. It covers the historical background, post-independence migration, and significant contributions of the Indian diaspora to various fields such as science, technology, medicine, and culture in their host countries. It also examines the challenges faced by the Indian diaspora in terms of identity and integration and explores its increasing political participation. The article concludes by highlighting the importance of the Indian diaspora in shaping the global landscape, making it a topic of great scholarly interest and importance.

Keywords: Indian diaspora, historical journey, global impact, migration, contributions, challenges.

Introduction

The Indian diaspora, a vast and diverse community of people who have migrated from India to different parts of the world, has a rich and complex history spanning from ancient times to the present day. This diaspora has significantly influenced the cultures, economies, and politics of their host countries while maintaining their Indian identity and contributing to the global exchange of culture and knowledge.

From the early migrations that spread Indian languages, religions, arts, and sciences to regions like Southeast Asia, Central Asia, and East Asia to the difficult period of indentured labour migration during the British colonial era, Indian migrants faced numerous difficulties and challenges. Injustices have been tolerated. However, they have also made lasting contributions to their host countries, both economically and culturally.

In the post-independence era, Indian migration took on new dimensions, driven by economic opportunities, educational prospects, and political factors. Indians migrated to Western countries like the USA, Canada, the U.K. and Australia, where they excelled in fields like science, technology, medicine, business and education. This wave of migration has further strengthened the cultural diversity and global influence of the Indian diaspora.

The impact of the Indian diaspora goes beyond individual success stories. He has made significant contributions in various fields, from shaping the Silicon Valley technology industry to enriching the healthcare system in the U.K. Indian culture, including festivals, food, dance, music, and yoga, has been adopted and celebrated around the world. Bollywood films have captivated global audiences, and Indian literature and philosophy have inspired thought and creativity.

However, the Indian diaspora has also faced challenges, including issues of identity, integration, discrimination, and cultural heritage protection. Finding a balance between integrating into host societies and preserving one's Indian roots can be a complex and ongoing struggle.

Despite these challenges, the Indian diaspora remains politically engaged with their host countries and India. They have elected and appointed leaders of Indian origin who have had significant influence on policies and decisions. He actively supports initiatives aimed at improving relations and cooperation between India and the diaspora, as well as supporting India's development and growth. The Indian diaspora plays an important role in shaping the foreign policy and global influence of both India and its host countries, contributing to global peace, security, and cooperation.

In this article, we will examine the historical background, cultural exchanges, challenges, and political engagement of Indians, highlighting the multifaceted and dynamic nature of this global community.

Historical Background

According to Tharoor (2019), Indian culture, religion and trade have a long history of global influence, dating back to ancient times. One of the most important periods for the Indian diaspora was the

British colonial era, when millions of Indians were transported as indentured workers to various parts of the British Empire, such as the Caribbean, Africa, and Southeast Asia. These early immigrants faced many hardships and injustices, but they also played important roles in the economic, social, and cultural development of their host countries (Bhattacharya and Chatterjee, 2018).

Indian migrations in prehistoric times reached many parts of Asia, such as Central Asia, Southeast Asia, and East Asia. Through these migrations, Indian languages, religions, arts, and sciences spread to these areas. For example, countries such as China, Japan, Korea, Tibet, Sri Lanka, Myanmar, Thailand, Cambodia, Vietnam, and Indonesia adopted Buddhism, Hinduism, and Jainism. Indian scripts, literature, architecture, sculpture, painting, and music also shaped the cultures of these countries. Indian merchants, traders, and sailors were connected to different parts of Africa, Europe, and the Middle East by trade and sea routes, allowing the flow of goods, ideas, and people. (Thapar, 2002; Kulke and Rothermund, 2004; Chaudhary and Israel, 2010)

The colonial powers, especially the British, hired millions of Indians as indentured labourers to work in their colonies around the world. Most of these workers were from the lower castes and classes of India, who suffered from poverty, oppression and discrimination in their homeland. They were deported to various regions of the British Empire, such as the Caribbean, Africa and Southeast Asia, where they faced harsh working and living conditions, exploitation and abuse. However, they also maintained their culture, religion and identity and established vibrant and resilient communities in their host countries. They also played a role in the economic, social and political development of their host countries, as well as in anti-colonial and nationalist movements (Bhattacharya and Lucassen, 2005).

The post-independence migration of Indians began in the 1940s when India became independent from British rule. This migration was motivated by various reasons, such as economic, educational and political opportunities, as well as conflict, violence and persecution (Khadaria, 2019). Many Indians migrated to Western countries such as the US, Canada, Britain and Australia, where they sought better prospects in terms of education, employment and standard of living. These migrants were skilled workers, professionals, students, and entrepreneurs who became successful in various fields, such as science, technology, medicine, business and education (Sahu and Patnaik, 2014). While maintaining their cultural and religious ties with India, they also adapted well to their host societies. They also established influential and active diaspora organisations, networks, and associations that supported their interests and welfare as well as their engagement with India and their host countries (Rai and Sahu, 2010).

The Indian diaspora has a long and rich history of global migration, integration and contribution, spanning from ancient times to diverse regions and countries. The Indian diaspora is not a homogeneous group but a complex and dynamic group reflecting multiple waves of migration, diverse ethnic, religious and linguistic identities, and different socio-economic and political conditions. The Indian diaspora has had a significant impact on the world, making it a subject of immense relevance and academic interest. (Shukla, 2008; Jain, 2010; Mishra, 2016)

Post-Independence Migration

According to Roy (2016), India's independence in 1947 triggered a new wave of Indian migration driven by economic, educational and political factors. Many Indians sought better opportunities in Western countries like America, Canada, Britain and Australia. The Indian diaspora became more diverse, including professionals, students and skilled workers. Roy (2016) argues that this wave of migration not only contributed to the economic growth of the host countries but also promoted greater cultural exchange.

According to Kumar (2018), the migration of Indians after independence was mostly voluntary, unlike colonial migration, which was often forced or coerced. The main factors motivating this migration were the lack of adequate opportunities, resources and infrastructure in India, as well as the aspiration for higher education, professional advancement and personal freedom. Many Indians were attracted to Western countries by the prospects of a better quality of life, higher incomes, and greater social mobility. Some Indians also migrated due to political unrest, communal violence, or persecution in their homeland, such as the Partition of India in 1947, the Emergency in 1975, the Sikh riots in 1984, and the Gujarat riots in 2002.

Many host countries welcomed Indians after independence with policies and programs favouring skilled workers, professionals, students and entrepreneurs. For example, the United States enacted the Immigration and Nationality Act of 1965, which removed national origin quotas and created a preference system based on skills, family ties, and diversity. This act allowed many Indians, especially those with scientific, technical, and medical backgrounds, to enter the United States (Bhattacharya and Chakraborty, 2019). Canada also adopted a points system in 1967, evaluating immigrants based on their education, language, work experience, and adaptability. The system was suitable for Indians, who were mostly well-educated, English-speaking, and adaptable (Gupta and Gupta, 2018). The United Kingdom and Australia had similar policies, which attracted many Indians to their lands (Singh and Singh, 2020).

The Indian diaspora is a large, diverse and dynamic group of people who have migrated from India after its independence. They have made significant contributions to the host countries and the world in various fields, such as science, technology, medicine, business, education and culture. Some notable members of the Indian diaspora include Sundar Pichai, Satya Nadella, Indra Nooyi, Raghuram Rajan, Salman Rushdie, and A.R. Rehman. They have also enriched the cultural diversity and exchange of their host countries through their languages, religions, cuisines, arts, music and festivals. The Indian diaspora has also helped strengthen ties between India and itshost countries and promote global peace, security and cooperation. (Sharma and Singh, 2019)

Impact on Host Countries

According to various sources, Indian immigrants have made significant contributions in various fields in their host countries. Some of the areas where they have demonstrated their excellence are science, technology, medicine, business and culture (Chandrashekhar, 2017; Kumar, 2019; Singh, 2020). For example, they have been instrumental in the technological innovation of Silicon Valley (Saxonian, 2006), the U.K. healthcare system (Bhugra and Gupta, 2011), and the cultural diversity of the Caribbean (Roopnarine, 2018).

Indian immigrants have made significant contributions to science and technology, especially in the U.S., where they have shaped the I.T. industry. A report by the National Science Foundation (2013) shows that Indians made up 14% of Silicon Valley workers in 2010 and 15.5% of immigrant-founded startups in the U.S. from 2006 to 2012. Some prominent Indian-origin tech leaders include Google CEO Sundar Pichai, Microsoft CEO Satya Nadella, Sun Microsystems co-founder Vinod Khosla and Adobe CEO Shantanu Narayan. Indian immigrants have also excelled in engineering, mathematics, physics, chemistry, and astronomy, with notable examples being Nobel laureate in Physics Subramanian Chandrasekhar (1983), Nobel laureate in medicine Har Gobind Khorana (1968), and Kalpana Chawla, the first Indian American woman in space (1997).

Indians have played an important role in advancing medicine and health in many countries, both as researchers and physicians. For example, Indians constitute 10% of the medical staff in the U.K. and have helped shape and deliver the National Health Service (British Association of Physicians of Indian Origin, 2017). Some notable examples are MagdyYacoub, a pioneer in heart transplantation (Yacob, 2014), Parveen Kumar, co-author of the widely used textbook Kumar & Clark Clinical Medicine (Kumar & Clark, 2016), and Rajesh Chandra, prominent Royal College of Surgeons (Chandra, 2019). Indians have also contributed to medicine and health in other countries such as the US, Canada, Australia and South Africa, where they have worked as doctors, nurses, pharmacists and public health experts (Bhugra et al., 2010).

Indian immigrants have positively impacted the culture and education of the countries where they live by sharing their languages, religions, cuisines, arts, music and festivals. They have also introduced global audiences to Indian cultures, such as Bollywood films, yoga, meditation, Ayurveda, and vegetarianism, and created new cultural forms such as fusion music, literature and cuisine. They have also excelled in education as students and teachers in various fields such as humanities, social sciences, business, and law. Some prominent scholars and teachers of Indian origin are Nobel laureate in economics Amartya Sen (Sen, 1999), founder of postcolonial studies Gayatri Chakraborty Spivak (Spivak, 1988), and Harvard College Dean Rakesh Khurana (Khurana& Spender, 2012).

As employees and entrepreneurs, Indian immigrants have played a vital role in the economic growth and development of their host countries in various sectors such as finance, manufacturing, retail and hospitality. The Indian diaspora has shown remarkable potential for entrepreneurship, innovation and risk-taking, setting up successful enterprises and creating jobs and wealth. Some prominent business leaders of Indian origin include former PepsiCo CEO Indra Nooyi, Arcelor Mittal Chairperson Lakshmi Mittal, Vedanta Resources founder Anil Agarwal and former Tata Group Chairperson Ratan Tata (Gupta and Ojha, 2018; Khanna and Verma, 2019; Nanda and Khanna, 2010; Ramamurthy and Singh, 2009).

Indian diasporas have significant political and diplomatic influence in their host countries and beyond. They have participated in various levels of politics, advocating their interests and enhancing the diversity of the political landscape. Some prominent examples of Indian-origin politicians are Kamala Harris(U.S. Vice President), Priti Patel (U.K. Home Secretary), Jagmeet Singh (Canadian NDP leader), and Leo Varadkar(former Irish Prime Minister). The Indian diaspora has also promoted ties between India and their host countries as well as other countries through various platforms such as Pravasi Bhartiya Divas, the Global Organization of People of Indian Origin and the Indian Overseas Council (Chanda and Srinivasan, 2006; Kumar and Singh, 2018; Mishra, 2016).

Indian immigrants have made significant contributions to their host countries in various fields, such as science, technology, medicine, business and culture. They have demonstrated excellence in various fields, enhancing the intellectual and economic capabilities of their new homes. Their influence can be seen in Silicon Valley's tech industry, Britain's healthcare system, and the cultural diversity of the Caribbean, among others. The Indian diaspora has also promoted greater cultural exchange and diversity through their languages, religions, cuisines, arts, music and festivals. The Indian diaspora has also been instrumental in strengthening bilateral and multilateral relations between India and their host countries as well as advancing global peace, security and cooperation (Gupta and Oommen, 2018; Jain and Singhvi, 2019; Kumar and Singh, 2020).

Cultural Exchange

The global Indian community has been instrumental in spreading India's culture and heritage. The world has adopted Indian food, art, music and yoga, among other aspects. Bollywood films have enthralled global audiences, enhancing India's soft power. Indian literature and philosophy have also reached audiences around the world, stimulating ideas and innovation across borders (Kumar, 2019).

The Indian diaspora and their host societies celebrate Indian festivals with enthusiasm and joy. Some of the major festivals are Diwali, the festival of lights, Holi, the festival of colours, Navratri, the festival of dance, and Eid, the festival of breaking the fast. These festivals reflect the diversity and richness of Indian culture as well as the principles of harmony, tolerance and peace. They also facilitate cultural exchange and dialogue as people from different backgrounds and religions participate in the festivities. For example, Diwali is celebrated by Hindus, Sikhs, Jains and Buddhists, as well as non-Indians in various countries such as the United States, United Kingdom, Canada, Australia and South Africa (Singh and Singh, 2018).

Many aspects of Indian culture have earned global recognition and appreciation. One of them is Indian cuisine, which offers a variety of dishes that are diverse, delicious, spicy and healthy. Indian cuisine reflects India's rich and diverse history, geography, climate and culture, as well as the influence of various religions, invaders and host countries. Indian cuisine has also created new and fusion dishes that suit the local tastes and preferences of different regions. Some of the famous Indian dishes are curry, biryani, tandoori, naan, samosa, dosa and dal (Acharya, 1994; Jaffrey, 2003; Sen, 2004).

Another aspect of Indian culture that is widely admired and enjoyed is Indian dance and music. These are dynamic and expressive forms of art that convey stories, emotions and messages. Indian dance and music are influenced by various classical, folk and modern styles, as well as various regional and religious traditions. Indian dance and music also include elements from other cultures, such as Western, Arabic and African. Some of the popular Indian dance and music styles are Bharatnatyam, Kathak, Bhangra, Bollywood, Carnatic, Hindustani, and Qawwali (Ghosh and Chakraborty, 2008; Nair and Khokar, 1984; Sharma and Kothari, 1999).

Indian yoga is another aspect of Indian culture that has become a global phenomenon. Yoga is an ancient system of exercises that aims to achieve harmony and balance between body, mind and spirit. Yoga has various benefits, such as improving health, fitness, flexibility and relaxation. Yoga has also been recognisedfor promoting peace, tolerance and intercultural dialogue, as it transcends the boundaries of religion, nationality and ethnicity. Yoga has been adopted by millions of people around the world and is celebrated by the United Nations as International Yoga Day on 21 June every year (Feuerstein and Wilbur, 1998; Iyengar and Evans, 2005; Singleton and Byrne, 2008).

According to Sharma (2020), Bollywood is the name of the Hindi-language film industry of India, which is based in Mumbai and produces more than one thousand films annually. Bollywood films are famous for their vibrant costumes, catchy songs, exciting storylines and romantic themes. Bollywood films have a large and loyal fan base across the world, especially in Asia, Africa and the Middle East. Bollywood films also contribute to India's soft power, as they highlight India's image, values and aspirations to a global audience. Bollywood films have also influenced other film industries such as Hollywood, Nollywood and Lollywood.

Indian culture has global appeal through its literature and philosophy, stimulating thinking and creativity across the world. India's literary and philosophical traditions are diverse and complex, reflecting its linguistic, religious and cultural diversity. They have also absorbed influences from other cultures, such as Greek, Persian, and English, and in turn, influenced other traditions, such as Buddhism, Islam, and Western culture. Some examples of Indian literature and philosophy are Vedas, Upanishads, Ramayana, Mahabharata, Bhagavad Gita, Panchatantra, Kama Sutra, and works by Rabindranath Tagore, R.K. Narayan, Salman Rushdie, and Arundhati Roy (Dasgupta and Mohanta, 2013).

According to Singh (2020), the Indian diaspora has been instrumental in spreading Indian culture and traditions across the world. He said that various elements of Indian culture, such as festivals, cuisine, dance, music, and yoga, have attracted attention and appreciation from across the world. He also argues that Bollywood films have enthralled global audiences, thereby boosting India's soft power. Furthermore, he believes that Indian literature and philosophy have inspired thought and creativity beyond India's borders. He concluded that Indian immigrants have contributed to cultural diversity and exchange in their host countries and around the world.

Challenges and Identity

According to Singh (2020), the Indian diaspora has achieved remarkable success in various domains, but it has also faced some challenges. These challenges include identity, integration, discrimination, and cultural heritage. Finding a balance between assimilating to their new societies and preserving their Indian roots is a complex challenge that many members of the diaspora must deal with.

Identity is a complex and changeable idea; it means how one sees oneself. The Indian diaspora has a diverse and hybrid identity shaped by various factors such as ethnicity, religion, language, culture, nationality and generation. Indian immigrants often struggle with dual or multiple identities, as they must balance between their ancestral and host cultures as well as their individual and group selves. Indian immigrants also have difficulty in identity formation and expression, as they must deal with expectations and stereotypes of both themselves and the dominant communities (Bhugra and Baker, 2005). Integration is a way to become part of a larger society while maintaining one's individuality. Indian immigrants have shown a high level of integration, as they have assimilated and integrated various parts of their host society, such as economy, politics, education, and culture. However, Indian immigrants also face various limitations and challenges to integration, such as discrimination, racism, xenophobia, and violence. Indian immigrants often face prejudice and aggression based on their ethnicity, religion, culture or nationality, which can affect their sense of belonging and safety. Indian immigrants also face the difficulty of social and cultural adaptation, as they must fit in with the norms and values of their host society while maintaining themselves (Vertovec and Cohen, 1999).

Discrimination is the unjust or unequal treatment of an individual or group based on their qualities or characteristics (United Nations, 2020). Indian immigrants have faced discrimination in various forms and levels, both in the past and present, in their host countries. Some examples of discrimination that Indian immigrants have faced include anti-Indian violence in Uganda in 1972 (Mamdani, 1999), Dot busters attacks in the U.S. in the 1980s (Prasad, 2000), and Cronulla clashes in Australia in 2005 (Poynting & Noble, 2006), and the Brexit referendum in the U.K. in 2016 (Virdy & McGeever, 2018). Discrimination can have adverse effects on the health, self-worth and opportunities of Indian immigrants, as well as their relationships with dominant and other minority groups (Bhugra and Baker, 2005).

Conservation of cultural heritage is the act of preserving and passing on to future generations the cultural values, traditions, and practices of one's ancestors (UNESCO, 2019). The Indian diaspora has demonstrated a strong commitment to preserving their cultural heritage, as they have maintained and celebrated their languages, religions, cuisines, arts, music, and festivals (Vertovec, 2000). Indian immigrants have also established various institutions and organisations, such as temples, schools, associations and media, which support and promote their cultural heritage (Jayaram, 2004). However, Indian immigrants also face the challenge of cultural continuity and change, as they face the effects of globalisation, modernisation, and acculturation, which may affect their cultural identity and practices (Mukherjee and Banerjee-Guha, 2012).

Political Engagement

The Indian diaspora has demonstrated high levels of political participation and influence in many countries, especially in the West. They have elected and appointed many leaders and officials of Indian origin who have had significant influence on the policies and decisions of their host countries. Some examples are Kamala Harris (U.S. Vice President), Priti Patel(U.K. Home Secretary), Jagmeet Singh (Canadian opposition leader), and Leo Varadkar(former Irish Prime Minister) (Chakraborty and Dasgupta, 2018; Jain and Singh, 2020; Kumar, 2021; O'Shea, 2019).The Indian diaspora also has various political groups and networks that advocate for their rights and interests, as well as support their candidates and issues (Kapoor, 2010; Thakur and Thakur, 2017).

The Indian diaspora has been more active in engaging with India's politics, society and economy. The Indian diaspora has shown its interest, concern, support and solidarity towards India and its people. The diaspora has also become involved in various efforts and activities aimed at enhancing relations and cooperation between India and the diaspora, as well as supporting India's development and growth. Some of these efforts and activities are Pravasi Bhartiya Divas, Overseas Citizenship of India, Know India Program, and Bharat Vikas Foundation of Overseas Indians (Ministry of External Affairs, 2021).

The Indian diaspora has played an important role in shaping the foreign policy and global role of India and its host countries. They have used various platforms and channels to connect and collaborate within India and their host countries as well as other countries and regions. He has also represented the interests and values of India and his host countries in various international forums and organisations such as the United Nations, Commonwealth and G20. He has also supported global issues and causes like climate change, human rights, democracy, and terrorism that matter to India and the world.

The Indian diaspora has been active in the political affairs of both their host countries and India. They have participated in local and national politics, advocating for their interests and adding to a more inclusive and diverse political landscape. They have also enhanced bilateral and multilateral relations between India and their host countries, as well as promoted global peace, security and cooperation.

Conclusion

The Indian diaspora is a global community of immigrants who have enriched the world with their culture, skills and achievements. They have been migrating to different areas since ancient times, spreading Indian values, beliefs and trade. They have also had a significant impact on their host countries and India's global standing. The Indian diaspora has excelled in various fields, such as science, technology, medicine, business, culture, and politics. They have also preserved and promoted Indian cultural heritage while interacting with their host cultures. However, the Indian diaspora has also faced challenges such as identity, integration, discrimination, and cultural preservation. They have struggled to balance their Indian roots with the expectations of their host society. They have also faced discrimination based on their ethnicity, religion, culture, or nationality, which has affected their sense of belonging and well-being.

Despite these challenges, the Indian diaspora has shown remarkable resilience and adaptability. They are engaged in politics and diplomacy, influencing foreign policies and strengthening international relations in both their host countries and India. Their contributions have made them an important force in the global arena. The Indian diaspora is a dynamic and diverse global community that deserves recognition for its contributions and efforts to overcome the challenges it faces. These immigrants have shaped the cultural, political and economic landscapes of their host countries and contributed to the global advancement of knowledge, innovation and human development.

References

- Bhattacharya, S., and Chakraborty, D. *Indian Diaspora in the United States: Brain Drain or Profit?* Lexington Books, 2019.

- Bhattacharya, S., and Chatterjee, I. editors. *Indian Diaspora: Historical and Contemporary Context*. Routledge, 2018.

- Bhattacharya, S., and Lucassen, J, editors. *Colonial Migration of Indians*. Brill, 2005.

- Bhugra, D., and Gupta, S. *Migration and mental health*. Cambridge UP, 2011.

- Bhugra, D., Gupta, S., Schuler-Oak, M., Graff-Calise, I., Deakin, N.A., Qureshi, A.,... and Ventriglia, A. EPA provides guidance on mental health care for immigrants. European Psychiatry, 25(2), 110-120. doi.org/10.1016/j.eurpsy.2009.09.003. 2010.

- British Association of Physicians of Indian Origin. Contribution of doctors of Indian heritage to the NHS. Retrieved from www.bapio.co.uk/wp-content/uploads/2017/07/BAPIO-Report.pdf. 2017.

- Chakraborty, S., and Dasgupta, D. *The Other One Percent: Indians in America*. Oxford UP, 2018.

- Chanda, R., and Srinivasan, G. *India's Experience with Skilled Migration*. C. Kuntesh and E.F. In Pang (Ed.), Competition for Global Talent. International Institute for Labor Studies. 2006, pp. 215-58.

- Chandra, R. Presidential Address: The Royal College of Surgeons – Past, Present and Future. Bulletin of the Royal College of Surgeons of England, 101(8), 321-325. doi.org/10.1308/rcsbull.2019.321. 2019

- Chandrashekhar, S. *The Other One Percent: Indians in America*. Oxford UP, 2017.

- Chaudhary, K.N., and Israel, J.I. *The Trading World of Asia and the English East India Company: 1660–1760*. Cambridge University Press, 2010.

- Dasgupta, S., and Mohanta, D.K, editors. *Indian Literature and Culture: A Mosaic of Voices*. Creative Books, 2013.

- Foreign Ministry. (2021). Diaspora Engagement. Retrieved from www.mea.gov.in/diaspore-engagement.htm

- Gupta, A., and Gupta, R. *Indian Immigrants to Canada: Cultural Dynamics of Adaptation and Integration*. Springer, 2018.

- Gupta, A., and Oommen, T.K, editors. *Indian Diaspora: Historical and Contemporary Context: Essays in Honor of Professor Chandrashekhar Bhatt.* Springer, 2018.

- Jain, R. "Global Indian Diaspora: An Overview." *The Routledge Handbook of the Indian Diaspora*, edited by R. Jain, Routledge, 2010, pp. 1-19.

- Jain, R., and Singh, A. *Indian Diaspora in Canada: Emerging Identities and Challenges.* Springer, 2020.

- Jain, R., and Singhvi, L.M. editors. *Indian Diaspora: Dynamics of Migration.* Sage Publications India, 2019.

- Kapoor, D. *Diaspora, Development and Democracy: Domestic Impact of International Migration from India.* Princeton UP, 2010.

- Khamriya, B. "Indian Diaspora: Historical and Contemporary Context." M. Amber, C.R. In Amber and I. Sogard (eds.), *Encyclopaedia of Diaspora: Immigrant and Refugee Cultures Around the World*, 2nd edition,Springer, 2019, pp. 1-11.

- Khurana, R., and Spender, J.-C. Herbert A. "Simon on the Problems of Business Schools: More Than A Problem In Organisational Design."*Journal of Management Studies*, 49(3), 2012, pp. 619--39.

- Kulke, H., and Rothermund, D. *History of India.* Routledge, 2004.

- Kumar, A. "The Post-Independence Indian Diaspora: An Overview". *Journal of International Migration and Integration*, 19(4), 2018, pp. 879-92.

- Kumar, A., and Kumar, S. *The Rise of Kamala Harris: A Biography.* HarperCollins India, 2021.

- Kumar, A., and Singh, B. "Indian Diaspora: Historical and Contemporary Context". *Essays in History*, 51(1), 2018, pp. 1-13.

- Kumar, P., and Clark, M., editors.*Kumar and Clark's Clinical Medicine* (9th ed.). Elsevier. 2016.

- Kumar, S., and Singh, B., editors. *Routledge Handbook of Indian Immigrants*. Routledge, 2020.

- Kumar, V. *Indian Diaspora: Socio-cultural and Religious World*. Brill, 2019.

- Mishra, V. *Literature of the Indian Diaspora: Between Theory and Archive*. Routledge, 2016.

- Mishra, V. *Literature of the Indian Diaspora: Diasporic Imaginary Theory*. Routledge, 2016.

- National Science Foundation. Science and Engineering Indicators 2014. Retrieved from www.nsf.gov/statistics/seind14/index.cfm/chapter-4/c4h.htm. 2013.

- O'Shea, B. *Leo Varadkar: A Very Modern Taoiseach*. Merion P, 2019.

- Rai, A., and Sahu, A.K."Indian Diaspora: Transnational Networks and Ethnic Identity". A.K. Sahu and B. In Maharaj (Ed.), *Sociology of Diaspora: A Reader*, Vol. 2, Rawat Publications, 2010, pp. 1005-35.

- Roop Narayan, L. *The Indian Caribbean: Migration and Identity in the Indian Diaspora*. UP of Mississippi, 2018.

- Roy, A. "The New Indian Diaspora: Migration and Identity Formation after Independence". *Journal of South Asian Studies*, 39(3), 2016. pp. 593-609.

- Sahu, A.K., and Patnaik, B.K. *Global Migration and Development: Socioeconomic, Cultural and Policy Perspectives.* Springer, 2014.

- Saxonian, A. *The New Argonauts: Regional Advantage in the Global Economy.* Harvard UP, 2006.

- Sen, A. *Development as Freedom.* Oxford UP, 1999.

- Sharma, A., and Singh, S. *Indian Diaspora: Historical and Contemporary Context.* A. Sharma and S. In Singh (Ed.), The Routledge Handbook of the Indian Diaspora, Routledge, 2019, pp. 1-14.

- Sharma, R. "Bollywood: Cultural Ambassador of India". *Journal of Indian Cinema,* 8(2), 45-60, 2020.

- Sharma S.P., and Kothari K.K. *Folk dances of India.* Abhinav Prakashan. 1999.

- Shukla, S. *India Abroad: Diaspora Cultures of Post-War America and England.* Princeton UP, 2008.

- Singh, G. *Indian Doctors in Kenya, 1895–1940: A Forgotten History.* Cambridge UP, 2020.

- Singh, J., and Singh, K. *Migration of Indians to the United Kingdom and Australia: Trends, Challenges and Opportunities.* Routledge, 2020.

- Singh, R. "Role of NRIs in Promoting Indian Culture and Soft Power". *Journal of Indian Studies,* 6(2), 1-15.2020.

- Singleton M. and Byrne J.A. *Yoga in the Modern World: Contemporary Approach.* Routledge, 2008.

- Spivak, G.C. "Can the subaltern speak?" C. Nelson and L. In Grossberg (Ed.)Uof Illinois P, 1988, pp. 271-313.

- Thakur, R., and Thakur, M. (eds.). *The Indian Diaspora: Hindus and Sikhs in Australia.* Australian National UP, 2017.

- Thapar, R. *Early India: From Origin to 1300 AD*. Penguin Books, 2002.

- Tharoor, S. *Prime Minister of Contradictions: Narendra Modi and His India*. Aleph Book Company, 2019.

- Yacob, M. History of heart transplant. British Medical Bulletin, 111(1), 5-15. doi.org/10.1093/bmb/ldu018. 2014.

Chapter 7

Identity and Otherness: Hanif Kureishi's *The Buddha of Suburbia* as the Voice of Diasporic Community

Dr. Mohd. Faiez

Assistant Professor
Department of English
Rajendra Prasad Degree College,
MJP Rohilkhand University,
Bareilly, Uttar Pradesh.
Email Address- mohdfaiez8@gmail.com

Abstract

For ages, the economy has been driving people to different locations and places of the world to fulfil their needs and desires. This movement of people seems simple in terms of their physical displacement, but it is very much complex from the point of emotional displacement. Those people who moved as first-generation immigrants faced what their generation did not face. It is not very easy to leave the place and settle down at another place that is different in many ways, like language, culture, food, etc. These factors can be considered as the key indicators which mark a line of demarcation between the natives and immigrants. And this led to the alienation and marginalisation of the people in different lands. These people are called diaspora who left their lands for greener pastures. Their issues need special attention as they face situations which are not even thought. Literature plays an important role for all who are unable to express their emotions and raise the voices of pain and trauma of displacement. John McLeod argues in his book regarding the difficult lives of immigrants in the following words:

> *The Location of Culture* addresses those who live 'border lives' on the margins of different nations, in-between contrary homelands. For Bhabha, living at the border, at the edge, requires a new 'art of the present'. This depends upon embracing the contrary logic of the things like history, identity, and community. (McLeod 217)

Different writers have raised issues related to the problematic notions of identity, race, ethnicity, culture, alienation, marginalisation, class, nostalgia, otherness, in-betweenness, and many more. Hanif Kureishi is one such writer whose works are based on the same issues. Kureishi's highly acclaimed novel *The Buddha of Suburbia* is being taken to highlight the issues of diaspora.

Keywords: Hanif Kureishi, *The Buddha of Suburbia*, displacement, diaspora, ethnicity, alienation.

Kureishi's *The Buddha of Suburbia* can be considered as their voice. The main challenge for Asians in foreign countries is to get respect for who they are. Hanif Kureishi himself, born and bred in England, is still considered an Asian writer and not an English one. He has tried to reflect the experiences of his own in his works. I have tried to address this issue with special reference to his work *The Buddha of Suburbia*.

Among various issues, the issue of social consciousness is taken up in a much more comprehensive manner by *The Buddha of Suburbia*, Kureishi's most famous novel. The central character of this novel, Karim Amir, is similar to Hanif Kureishi in many ways. He also has an English mother and a Pakistani father. He says that he is considered a funny kind of Englishman. He also says that he is almost an Englishman. The declaration of this racial anxiety at the very beginning of the novel is significant. The question arises: what are the forces that do not let Karim feel like an Englishman? The novel tries to find some factors behind this anxiety. The novel starts with these words of Karim Amir:

> My name is Karim Amir, and I am an Englishman born and bred, almost. I am often considered to be a funny kind of Englishman, a new breed as it were, having emerged from two old histories. But I don't care - Englishman I am (though not proud of it), from the South London suburbs and going somewhere. Perhaps it is the odd mixture of continents and blood, of here and there, of belonging and not, that makes me restless and easily bored. Or perhaps it was being brought up in the suburbs that did it. (*The Buddha of Suburbia* 3)

The question arises: why does Kureishi begin his first novel with his character announcing his identity and asserting his Englishness? Why does the narrative begin with a detailed note about Karim Amir's identity? Most of the writers with sub-continental connections invariably use their nation's history and their family history in their novels. It can be said that his self-consciousness about identity is also Kureishi's self-consciousness about identity. Karim Amir is considered a funny kind of Englishman because of the colour of his skin. He has an Indian father and a British mother, in other words, he has mixed blood in his veins.

The effort at trying to wash away the mark of mixed identity may land one in trouble. It has something to do with colonial history, which changed the psyche of generations of people in countries once colonised. This identity crisis is one of the various main issues that are faced by the immigrants or diasporas in foreign lands who left their homes in search of greener pastures. Regarding the issue of identity for Indians or Asians, Dr. Tapan Kumar Rath and Dr. Arun Behera put their view in the following words:

> One gains a sense of identity through family, society and culture. For the culturally displaced, this is a difficult endeavor. Numerous such Indians try to identify themselves with the land but with a sense of coyness. Though they keep coming to their home land because it is their parents' or grand parents' place, they are unable to embrace the culture, tradition and beliefs of the land and their ancestral families. They stand between the adopted society and their own, adopted culture and their own, which in turn creates a crisis for them. (Rath and Behera)

These issues of identity are also raised through Haroon, Karim's father, one of the most important characters. He appears very clumsy in matters of dress when he is in his own house. What is most interesting about him is that he is described as a yoga guru. He even talks about different yogic positions at home, for example, about one yogic posture being beneficial in preventing loss of hair and reducing any tendency to greyness. India has had its share of godmen and gurus. The popular version of India's spiritual side is a subjectthat is exotic in nature and has a kind of mystic value. The fact that Haroon commands attention because of his yogic postures is considered exotic. At the very beginning of the novel Haroon goes to Eva's house to give a mystic lesson, which a man present there describes as "a demonstration of the mystic arts" (12). Many cultural and national stereotypes are evoked by white people present in that meeting. A gentleman remarks if the person giving mystic lessons has parked his camel outside. Another person remarks that if he has come on a magic carpet, yet another person wonders why Eva brought the brown Indian to this gathering. It may be recalled that camel and magic carpets belong to the worlds of *The Arabian Nights*. It also has characters who have gorgeous clothes and have enormous appetites.

Obviously, the elements of fantasy and magic predominatein the world of *The Arabian Nights*. It has no relation to the actual life of the people as it was lived in Arabia. For popular Western imagination, the world described in *The Arabian Nights* was the real world of the Asian people. Another thing to note about this conversation is that all Asians, whether they come from Arabia or India, are discussed in the same breath. Camel and magic carpets are more representative of the Arab world rather than the world of this brown Indian. The way natives address the immigrants and have prejudiced and stereotypical images that these immigrants are different from them is very painful for them.

Karim considers himself to be almost an Englishman. The fact that Karim has never visited the subcontinent is important here. Equally important is the fact that he does not understand any language other than English. Also important is the fact that his entire education and upbringing take place in Britain. But all these are not sufficient reasons for him to be considered an Englishman. The question arises as to what a person should do to be considered an Englishman. Karim Amir has all the prerequisites of an Englishman. However, he is not considered an Englishman because he is not white. His colour of skin is not white. All through the narrative, he struggles to know his identity. The forces that impose an identity on Karim, an identity not of his choosing, are too powerful for Karim to overcome. His relationship with Helen is not acceptable to Helen's racist father. He treats Karim very savagely, calling him names and even unleashing his ferocious dog on him. His words are full of hatred and venom against blacks, which are expressed as "However many niggers there are, we don't like it. We're with Enoch. If you put one of your black 'and near my daughter I'll smash it with a'ammer! With a'ammer!'" (40)

In his career as an actor, Karim can achieve success only as an ethnic character. He cannot dream of playing an Englishman. When he is selected for a play, it is not because of his acting skills, his talent, or his qualifications but for his Asian connection. The director asks him many probing questions. He utters a few words in Punjabi and Urdu. The director, Shadwell, did not like the fact that Karim knew no Indian language. He is equally dismayed to learn that he never had the dust of India in his nostrils. He believes that Karim must visit India. His words appear ironical when he says:

What a breed of people two hundred years of imperialism has given birth to. If the pioneers from the East India Company could see you. What puzzlement there'dbe. Everyone looks at you, I'm sure, and thinks: an Indian boy, how exotic, how interesting, what stories of aunties and elephants we'll hear now from him. And you're from Orpington.' (*The Buddha of Suburbia* 141)

Karim is finally chosen to play the role of Mowgli in Kipling's *The Jungle Book* in Shadwell's play. It is really ironic that a writer who is taken to task for his imperialist and racist concerns continues to be used for perpetuating the discourse on race and imperialism. This time, his discourse on race is played out in a Britain that boasts of the success of the model of multiculturalism. Shadwell is excited about the fact that he has found Karim to play the role of Mowgli. Because of his Indian connection, Karim can look authentic in that role. Shadwell words appear to support Kipling's imperialist discourse:

'You're just right for him,'…. 'In fact, you are Mowgli. You're dark-skinned, you're small and wiry, and you'll be sweet but wholesome in the costume. Not too pornographic, I hope. Certain critics will go for you. Oh yes. Ha, ha, ha, ha, ha! (pp 142-143)

The ironic thing is that Karim can speak English with an English accent only. He has all the Englishman's patterns of behaviour. He has the habits of an Englishman. However, he must forget everything he has learned from his childhood. He has to speak his language in a bizarre and strange accent so that he can sound authentic to an audience who can accept Mowgli only as a bizarre creature. And to make matters worse, it is not only the accent but rather animal voices that he has to produce that diminish him in his own eyes. In between his bizarre dialogues, he has to hiss like a snake. To Karim's request that he be spared this agony, he gets no support from anyone, not even from Terry, who is considered an active Trotskyite. Mowgli's dress embarrasses Karim, but he has to wear that dress so that he can look the part. Karim feels insulted and reduced by doing that play. He feels that he and Shadwell "together we're making the world uglier" (146). Regarding prejudiced views, Graciela Moreira Slepoy says, "The prejudices and preconception many of the characters are subject to are rooted in issues connected with power, ideology and historical representation."

Issues of race are also treated in the play, which is offered to Karim by Pyke, a very well-known director. In this play, Pyke also wanted Karim to play someone from his own background, in other words, someone black and not white. Karim has not known any black person in his life, but desperate to do the role, he thought about using Anwar's character for this play. In a moment that sees a colonial becoming a coloniser Karim finds the dilapidated condition of Anwar's shop suiting his artistic purpose. Anwar's poverty and decline could be used for his play. Karim's play includes details of Anwar's search for his Indian roots, the assertion of his Muslim identity, and his headstrong nature. It also includes his insistence on an arranged marriage of his daughter and his hunger strike when the daughter refuses to marry the boy of his choice. Tracey, a black girl who is part of Karim's group, is the only person who can see problems with Karim's representation of Anwar. She rightly believes that Karim portrays non-white people as irrational, ridiculous, and hysterical. She finds this representation not only stereotypical but offensive. To quote Tracey:

> Your picture is what white people already think of us. That we're funny, with strange habits and weird customs. To the white man we're already people without humanity, and then you go and have Anwar madly waving his stick at the white boys. I can't believe that anything like this could happen. Why do you hate yourself and all black people so much, Karim? (*The Buddha of Suburbia*180)

Through Haroon, the novel touches on a very important theme of nostalgia and in-betweenness in postcolonial writing when he says, "We old Indians come to like this England less and less and we return to an imagined India (74)." He makes a conscious effort to remain an important part of his society. However, his friend Anwar, though he appears better settled than Haroon, returns to his Indian roots when he thinks about the marriage of his daughter

Jamila. Jamila, like Haroon, was brought up in England. She has an English education and English manners. She is part of an England which is multicultural. She wants to claim her full rights as an Englishwoman. For her to enter into an arranged marriage with a man she does not know is unthinkable. Her father discovers his Indian and Muslim roots when he insists on the arranged marriage of Jamila. The matter is so important to him that he goes on a hunger strike to force his daughter into this arranged marriage with a boy from Bombay.

Anwar's behaviour is considered shocking by Karim because Anwar is acting as a Muslim in this instance. He had never acted and behaved like a Muslim in his life. In his dealings with Jamila, Anwar had always shown a kind of indifference and Jeeta had shown a kind of indulgent love. That was one reason why Jamila led a very free life. Karim also finds it puzzling that suddenly, Anwar was discovering his Indian roots. It is interesting to know that both Anwar and Haroon considered India a bad place compared to their adopted country. The following paragraph reveals their ambivalent attitude towards the country of their origin:

> Now, as they aged and seemed settled here, Anwar and Dad appeared to be returning internally to India, or at least to be resisting the English here. It was puzzling: neither of them expressed any desire actually to see their origins again. 'India's a rotten place,' Anwar grumbled. 'Why would I want to go there again? It's filthy and hot and it's a big pain-in-the-arse to get anything done. If I went anywhere it would be to Florida and Las Vegas for gambling.' And my father was too involved with things here to consider returning. (*The Buddha of Suburbia* 64)

Not only Anwar, who has spent his early years in India, but also Jamila, who is British by birth and upbringing, faces a crisis of identity. It is at such moments that she starts identifying with "our people in this racist country" (108). Unlike Karim, she thinks about a life beyond herself.

It can be said that *The Buddha of Suburbia* treats issues of race, class, and gender in an exhaustive manner. Kureishi's discussion of these issues is not only perceptive but is novel in many ways. The issues of identity, in-betweenness, hybridity, and otherness, which are so important in postcolonial writings, are treated by Kureishi very insightfully. The treatment of the construction of identity by different discourses makes Kureishi a voice of his period.

References

- Kureishi, Hanif. *The Buddha of Suburbia.* Faber and Faber, 1990. p 3

- ---. *The Buddha of Suburbia.* Faber and Faber, 1990. p 14

- ---. *The Buddha of Suburbia.* Faber and Faber, 1990. p 180

- ---. *The Buddha of Suburbia.* Faber and Faber, 1990. p 74

- ---. *The Buddha of Suburbia.* Faber and Faber, 1990. p 64

- McLeod, John. *Beginning Postcolonialism.* Manchester University Press, 2007.

- Rath, Tapan Kumar and Arun Behera. "Question of Identity and Alienation: A Reading on Jhumpa Lahiri's 'Interpreter of Maladies'", *International Journal of Advanced Research (IJAR)*, *5(8), pp 335-336.*

- Slepoy, Graciela Moreira. "The Legitimising of His/Her-stories in Hanif Kureishi's The Buddha of Suburbia", *Postimperial and post colonial literature in English*. This web essay is based upon a paper the author wrote for Professor Neil Bissoondath's "Postcolonial Literature II" [ANG-64699A], Laval University. 26 Apr 2007 <www.scholars.nus.edu.sg/post/uk/kureishi/gms5.html>

Chapter 8

Succession Planning and Management in Transnational Companies

Mr. Abhishek Kumar Pandey

Assistant Professor, Department of Management & Commerce,
School of Management Sciences, Lucknow, Uttar Pradesh
Email Address- abhishekpandey@smslucknow.ac.in
https://orcid.org/0000-0002-8251-7278

&

Dr. Pramod Kumar Upadhyay

Assistant Professor, Department of Commerce,
Maharaja Bijli Pasi Govt. P.G. College, Lucknow, Uttar Pradesh
Email Address- pramodkrupadhyay76@rediffmail.com

Abstract

Succession planning can be seen as a leadership resilience strategy if organizations want to ensure that they need strong bench strength and business continuity. Past literature offers insight into the fact that companies often ignore such an important topic, which causes huge losses to business operations or survival status. Having a profound leadership pool can provide a number of benefits to existing corporate firms as well as to start-up companies. In this conceptual work, it has been attempted to explore and analyze various key dimensions related to succession planning prevalent in transnational contexts. Findings can be useful for further extension in terms of empirical investigation in the area of leadership research and developing strategies which ensure the availability of future leadership within the organization. Findings have greater significance for new-age companies or ventures that often suffer from leadership issues. Policymakers and practice doers might get useful articulation in the domain of leadership succession and its linkages to transnational organizations.

Keywords: Succession planning, transnational companies, resilience strategy, business continuity, conceptual paper

Introduction

Succession planning in Transnational Companies (TNCs) involves the systematic identification and development of talent to ensure a smooth transition of leadership across borders. Managing succession in a transnational context comes with unique challenges, such as cultural diversity, legal and regulatory variations, and the need for effective communication across different locations.

Definition and Characteristics of TNCs

Scholars often define TNCs as large enterprises that operate in multiple countriesand engage in international business activities. They typically have a centralized management structure and subsidiaries in various locations. Among the largest economic entities in the world are transnational corporations. Rough estimates place the value of the world's productive assetsat around US$5 trillion, or at least 25%, under the ownership or control of the 300 largest transnational corporations (TNCs) (Greer & Singh, 2000).

Here are key considerations for succession planning in transnational companies:

Global Talent Identification

Identify high-potential employees across various regions who have the skills, knowledge, and cultural adaptability to assume leadership roles. Implement a consistent talent review process to evaluate performance and potential on a global scale.

Cultural Competence

Recognize the importance of cultural competence in leadership roles and consider cultural fit when selecting successors. Provide cross-cultural training and development programs to prepare potential leaders for the challenges of leading in diverse environments.

Knowledge Transfer

Facilitate the transfer of critical knowledge and skills across borders by creating opportunities for international assignments, job rotations, and cross-functional projects. Encourage mentorship and knowledge-sharing initiatives among employees from different regions.

Legal and Regulatory Compliance

Understand and comply with local labour laws and regulations related to leadership succession. TNCs should ensure that potential successors are familiar with the legal and regulatory requirements in the regions where they might assume leadership roles.

Communication and Collaboration

Establish effective communication channels to facilitate collaboration among teams in different regions. Use technology to bridge communication gaps and foster a sense of unity among employees across borders.

Succession Planning Policies

Develop and document clear succession planning policies and procedures that consider the unique challenges of a transnational environment. Align succession planning with the overall strategic goals of the company, taking into account regional differences.

Leadership Development Programs

Implement leadership development programs that address the specific needs of potential successors in a transnational setting. Offer training in global leadership skills, including cross-cultural communication, negotiation, and conflict resolution.

Local Succession Teams

Establish local succession planning teams in each region to address specific regional challenges and opportunities. Involve local leadership in identifying and developing successors to ensure a deep understanding of regional nuances.

Data-Driven Decision-Making

Use data and analytics to assess the effectiveness of succession planning initiatives and adjust strategies accordingly. Monitor key performance indicators related to leadership development and succession.

Flexibility and Adaptability

Recognize that the business environment is dynamic, and succession plans may need to be adjusted based on changing circumstances. Foster a culture of adaptability and resilience to navigate unexpected challenges. In this way, Succession planning in transnational companies requires an investigation from a strategic and holistic point of view that considers the organisation's global nature while addressing each region's specific needs in terms of leadership development and successor appointment. It involves nurturing a pipeline of diverse talent and creating a supportive environment for leadership development on a global scale.

Literature Review

Globalization and TNCs

The literature explores how TNCs drive and respond to globalization trends. It delves into their role in shaping the global economy, contributing to economic growth, and influencing international trade patterns. The majority of cross-border organisational practice transfers involve implementation difficulties; nonetheless, the transfer coalition plays a mediating role, acting as a "bridge" between the headquarters and subsidiaries in the transfer of organisational practice. This role has been largely overlooked in the field's important literature (Klimkeit&Reihlen, 2016). Globalisation has an impact on businesses that compete for clients that have high standards for pricing, quality, and performance. The HRM function is under pressure to adapt to evolving organisational needs and provide better value as a result of globalisation (Friedman, 2007). It shows the need for a review of succession strategies prominent in TNCs.

Emerging Trends on Succession and Leadership Management in Transnational Companies

In defining HRM policy, Gunnigle and Morley (2013) compare central HRM control at the corporate level with subsidiary autonomy. They contend that this should be viewed as a continuum, spanning from an organisation where all HRM practices are defined by the headquarters and are only implemented by the subsidiaries to one where each subsidiary defines and carries out its own HRM practices (Nestande, 2013). A balance for all parties may be provided via shorter-term abroad postings. While the company can fulfil a business need like development for succession planning, the employee obtains experience without having to move their family (L, 2021).CEO succession was largely determined by firm performance, which has been the dependent variable in numerous studies.

The effect of the successor's origin—insider versus outsider—on the performance of the post-successor firm has been thoroughly researched prior to 2005 (Giambatista et al., 2005). According to Clayton et al. (2005), CEO succession has a detrimental effect on performance and raises stock price volatility for a company. According to Karaevli's (2007) research, environmental benevolence, past business performance, and changes in the top management team members all mitigate the effect of the CEO's origin on the performance of the company (Farah et al., 2020). The five paradoxes that managers and leaders in the twenty-first century must take into account in order to successfully manage for the success of their organisations are the following: the paradox of response (time focus: short and long-term), the paradox of action (doing and being), the paradox of communication (direct and indirect), and the paradox of knowing (self and other) (Fisher & Geller, 2008).

Objectives of the Study

1. To explore the various practices related to succession planning and management in transnational companies

2. To draw prominentimperatives for succession planning in new-age start-ups based on transnational experiences

Research Method

A conceptual design based on a literature review and exploratory research has been adopted. Peer-reviewed articles and published reports were considered while subtracting key themes and findings from the study. Research articles from the year 2020 to 2023 have been primarily considered. Open-source databases like Google Scholar and Dimension AI have been utilized to get secondary data and published articles.

Findings and Discussion

After exploring the various research papers and articles on succession planning in the context of TNCs, the present study highlights its findings in two broad contexts. These are:

Succession planning strategies in TNCs

Reviews suggest that insider versus outsider orientation is a key consideration when choosing a good candidate for key management positions in transnational companies. There is an emphasis on talent pool development in transnational companies. The majority of succession planning procedures centre on enumerating possible successors for specific roles.(Hub,n.d.). Organisations should build agile succession processes that are more adaptable to shifting leadership roles and talents, as well as flexibility for future leadership demands. Additionally, it is critical to provide much-needed diversity to the majority of organisations' leadership bench. Additionally, organisations must think about ways to reduce selection bias throughout their leadership pipelines (*Succession Planning | Hr Insights | Gartner. Com*, n.d.).

Both Conger and Nadler (2004) and Charan and Colvin (1999) contend that the execution of the succession plan—rather than the plan itself—is the issue. We may have underestimated the significance of organisational culture and the roles of members, the incumbent, top management, and the board, which could lead to execution issues (Cannella Jr &Lubatkin, 1993; Denis, Langley, & Pineault, 2000; Kets de Vries, 1988; Schein, 1992 as cited in Fancher, 2009).

Imperatives for succession planning based on international experiences in modern start-ups

Startups can plan in advance based on international practices of succession. Policies can be framed based on organizational strategy, the cultural context of the business origin, and host countries where businesses have functionality, industry-level attributes, and strategic facets of human resource management. Job rotation of candidates based on shifting candidates in a foreign assignment, short duration project, and exposure to deal with abroad customers on a gradual basis might make readiness in such nascent firms. Start-ups can adopt models of succession from top family firms in Japan, which are known for their longevity (*Building on Tradition — 1,400 Years of a Family Business by Irene Herrera (Works That Work Magazine)*, n.d.). Startups should start developing talent from internal candidates by adopting best practices from TNCs and MNCs. Cross-cultural assignments might offer great exposure to leadership development.

Conclusion

In a nutshell, the present study explores succession planning as a prominent area for multinational, transnational and global companies. Such companies need to design their talent management strategies which connect the leadership requirements at key management positions. Startups can learn from global practices adopted by TNCs, which will provide diverse benefits and ease in managing the talent pool for key profiles and ensuring successor availability. Both family and non–family businesses can adopt proactive succession strategies to achieve their strategic business objectives. Business continuity has linkages with effective succession management in international companies operating in several countries. Succession is related to business longevity, too. Modern day companies need to handle this challenge by developing talent for future roles.

References

- Building on tradition—1,400 years of a family business by Irene Herrera(Works that Work magazine). (n.d.). Retrieved January 11, 2024, from worksthatwork.com/3/kongo-gumi

- Farah, B., Elias, R., De Clercy, C., & Rowe, G. (2020, February 1). Leadership succession in different types of organizations: What business and political successions may learn from each other. *The Leadership Quarterly.* doi.org/10.1016/j.leaqua.2019.03.004

- Fancher, L. "The Link between Culture and Succession Planning." Hansen, C.D., Lee, YT. (eds) *The Cultural Context of Human Resource Development.* Palgrave Macmillan, 2009. doi.org/10.1057/9780230236660_14

- Fisher-Yoshida, B. and Geller, K. «Developing transnational leaders: Five paradoxes for success," *Industrial and Commercial Training*, Vol. 40 No. 1, 2008. pp. 42-50. doi. org/10.1108/00197850810841648

- Friedman, B. (2007, July 17). Globalization Implications for Human Resource Management Roles. papers.ssrn.com/sol3/papers.cfm?abstract_id=2509526

- Greer, J., & Singh, K. (2000). A brief history of transnational corporations. archive.globalpolicy.org/component/content/article/221-transnational-corporations/47068-a-brief-history-of-transnational-corporations.html

- Hub, T. H. C. (n.d.). Global trends influencing succession planning. Human Capital Hub. Retrieved January 11, 2024, from thehumancapitalhub.com/articles/global-trends-influencing-succession-planning

- Klimkeit, D., &Reihlen, M. "Organizational practice transfer within a transnational professional service firm: the role of leadership and control." *The International Journal of Human Resource Management*, 27(8), 2016. 850-875.

- L. (2021, March 11). Global Mobility for Succession Planning – DavidsonMorris. Davidson Morris. www.davidsonmorris.com/global-mobility-for-succession-planning/

- Nestande. (2013). Determinants of Succession Planning in MNCs Operating in Denmark. research-api.cbs.dk. Retrieved January 11, 2024, from research-api.cbs.dk/ws/portalfiles/portal/58430789/jacob_storm_nestande.pdf

- Succession planning | hr insights | gartner. Com. (n.d.). Gartner. Retrieved January 11, 2024, from www.gartner.com/en/human-resources/insights/succession-planning

Chapter 9

Alienation & Challenges Faced by Indian Diaspora With Reference to Select Works of Chitra Banerjee Divakaruni

Dr. Nigar Alam

Assistant Professor
Department of Humanities & Professional Communication
Babu Banarasi Das Northern India Institute of Technology
(AKTU College Code:056)
Guest Lecture – BITS Pilani
Email Address- nigar.alam@yahoo.com

Abstract

The word 'diaspora' was primarily used in association with the dispelling of Jews when they were forced into exile and the consequent nostalgia for their motherland and the cultural alienation experienced by them in the new location. However, today, it means any reasonably large group of people of a particular country or region living outside his country and sharing commontraits that give them an ethnic identity and resultant bonding. In the last few centuries, there has been a rise in migration from India. They may speak different languages, follow different religions, and have different occupations or professions, but they share similarities in their beliefs as they are conscious of their Indian origin, cultural heritage, and strong feelings for India. Diaspora is an experience of dislocation, re-location, and nostalgia. Diaspora acts like a protective shield; its greater visibility makes us invisible. The diasporic vision can, at times, be culture blind, remote, prejudiced or static. Writers like Chitra Banerjee Divakaruni, Shashi Deshpande, Jhumpa Lahiri, Rohinton Mistry, M. G. Vassanji, Kiran Desai, William Safran, Uma Parameswaran and Bharati Mukherjee lend their writing to facile generalizations about various Indian culture, customs, traditions, arranged marriages often occur in their narratives. The changing of home, worry about homelessness, and the impossibility of going back are some of the themes that occur again and again in diasporic literature. This kind of literature deals mainly with the inner conflict in the context of cultural displacement.

Keywords: Ethnic identity, nostalgia, inner conflict, cultural displacement

Mostly, the migrants suffer from the trauma of being far off from their homes; the reminiscences of their motherland, the problem of adjustment in the new place and the anguish of leaving behind everything familiar torment them. They are not able to break the relationship with the ancestral land, which leads to cultural uprootedness. They fail to detach themselves from their original roots and adjust to the land of a new culture. The immigrants try to assimilate, adapt and intermingle with the society of their adopted country. They believe in the continuation of cultural practices and social traditions. Due to this, they find themselves on the margin, belonging neither to their motherland nor their adopted country. Sometimes, they develop dual identities. These diasporas live in what Homi K Bhabha calls that is very disturbing to them, and there is a yearning for 'home' which remains a "mythic place of desire in diasporic imagination." (*The Location of Culture* p.77)

Usually, the first-generation diaspora insists on clinging on to and keeping their religion, language, music, art, dress, food, etc., intact. This obviously highlights their Indianness, which separates them from others and emphasizes their differences. This is perhaps a conscious declaration of belonging to another place. They even make all efforts to pass on their traditions and culture to future generations. However, the second-generation diaspora refuses to carry on these labels to mark their identity rather, they learn to become part of the culture they are living in.

"Diasporic writing draws our attention to an important aspect of our era in which responsibilities of citizens go across national boundaries. The earlier modernist notions of centre and margin, home and exile and familiar and strange are falling apart. The borders defined in terms of geography, culture and ethnicity are being replaced by configurations of power, community, space and time." (*Diasporic Writing and Politics,* p. 33) "Therefore the words exile, diaspora, migration, dislocation, deracination and displacement are the leading metaphors used to express not only disorientation but also ideological and existential fragmentation." (*Diasporic Writing and Politics,* p. 40)

Many Indian diaspora writers have portrayed in their literary works certain community, region, and culture-specific conflicts in the new lands of relocation. However, their major concern about diaspora issues has been dislocation, fragmentation, nostalgia for home, marginalization, racial hatred, cultural and gender hatred, conflicts, identity crisis, generation differences, a transformation of subjectivities, emergence of new patterns of life with cross-cultural interaction and disintegration of the family of the Indian diaspora that leads to dilemma, anguish, and trauma. The inspiration is always drawn from the homeland, and the writer is caught between the past and the present, which often forms a significant factor in expatriate writing. Sometimes, the writer sees his home country as a place of violence, poverty, pollution, and corruption, and sometimes, it is romanticised and eulogized. These and many other issues have been given prominence by Indian immigrant writers through their literary works.

A number of diasporic writers like Salman Rushdie, Amitav Ghosh, Raja Rao, V.S Naipaul and Kovid Gupta, who are of Indian descent, have been dealing with the issue of diasporic identity in their works. However, diasporic women writers have a different take on this issue from male writers. Anita Desai's *Bye-Bye Blackbird* (1971) deals with diasporic migration and is a psychological analysis of the immigrants who suffer mixed feelings of love and hate towards the country they are residing in. The novel explores the lives of three characters– an immigrant refusing to fit in and looking at those who do with scorn, an immigrant trying to belong and loving everything about the new place and a native who marries an immigrant. It is a study of human relationships, cultural encounters, alienation, and loss of identity that the immigrants have to confront in the country of their adoption. Kiran Desai, a young writer, generally narrates about Indian immigrants who find it hard to settle in an alien country, especially America. In her *The Inheritance of Loss* (2006), India's caste/class system is recognisable as every aspect of the characters' lives revolves around their caste or race. The novel portrays themes of alienation, globalisation, multiculturalism, isolation and migration. Desai also shows conflict between past and present and issues related to loss of identity.

Jhumpa Lahiri too delves into various diasporic aspects in her fiction, especially the short story collection *Interpreter of Maladies* (1999) and *Unaccustomed Earth* (2008) and her first novel, *The Namesake* (2003). They acquire a hybrid identity as their ethnic identity is formed by their childhood memories, whereas their youthful identity is influenced by their American experience. The older female characters like Ashima in *The Namesake* or Mrs. Parul in 'Once in a Lifetime' (*Unaccustomed Earth*) face the initial trauma of displacement but then adapt themselves to the American ways. The younger women characters like Shobha in 'Temporary Matters' (*Interpreter of Maladies*) and Moushmi in *The Namesake* Sandhya in 'Only Goddess' (*Unaccustomed Earth*) are independent, strong, and educated women with their own definite identities. They are ready to adopt and accept their existence in the foreign land as they have not gone through the experience of migration directly as their forefathers.

Bharati Mukherjee, another stalwart and a great writer, analysed the experience and dilemmas of being an immigrant and the culture shock and alienation that ensued. She pointed, "Even in Manhattan we'd smile at another Indian if they walked by us," she further added, "You felt an affinity to other Indians that you might not have felt in India." (*Passage from India* by Sandip Roy, California Magazine July-August 2006) She openly proclaimed herself as an American writer and not an Indian American, bringing forth the emotional and mental status of the Indian immigrants in their search for self-identity in her novels and short stories. She rejected the tradition-bound society of the East as she approved of the more empowering and individualistic society of the West.

In a recent interview, she stated her intention to write about the immigrants' fascinating tales. Tara, the protagonist in *The Tiger's*

Daughter (1971), is disappointed when she visits India after seven years. It is difficult for her to adjust to her friends and relatives in India, and she finds the traditions and way of thinking of her own family amusing. She feels alienated in her own country. In her essay 'Day's and Night's in Calcutta' (1977, with Clark Blaise too, she attempts to find her identity in her own land. Some of her other works, such as *Wife* (1975), *Darkness* (1985), and *An Invisible Woman* (1981), expose the immigrants' experience of racism. However, her later works like *Jasmine* (1989), and *The Middlemen & Other Stories* (1988) explore immigrants' experiences rather than nostalgia.

Chitra Banerjee Divakaruni, purportedly a feminist writer of the 21st century of Indian origin based in America, is a gifted and one of the finest storytellers. This fact can be gauged by the numerous novels she wrote with an irresistibly interesting and factual storyline. Her job as a Professor of Creative Writing at the University of Houston vouches for her ability as an acclaimed writer. Although she has been residing in America since 1976, she generously imbibes various Indian cultures, traditions, and beliefs in her stories, perhaps due to her own close involvement with Indian culture when she lived in India till she was 20 years old. She also portrays life in America and the difficulties faced by immigrants due to differences in culture and beliefs between the East and the West. Living in a foreign country makes one yearn for one's own homeland, and also, there arises a different set of problems. This immigrant experience was crucial for her in becoming a writer, she observed. "I did not think I had a story to tell," she wrote on her blog.

Moving to a very different culture and learning to live on my own made me see the world much more clearly…. I thought about

India more than I had ever before. I realized what I appreciated about it; the warmth, the closeness of extended family, the way spirituality pervades the culture. But I also recognized problems [with regard to] how women are often treated. (Interview for Guernica)

Divakaruni debuted on the literary scene with her collection of short stories, *Arranged Marriage* (1995), which won the American Book Award in 1995. Her first collection of short stories, *Arranged Marriage* (1995) developed from her poem 'Arranged Marriage' in *Black Candle,* focuses on the two contradictory cultures of India and America. Both the poem and stories portray the emotions of women whose lives are affected by the Indian tradition of arranged marriages. The stories also explore issues like divorce, abortion, racism and economic inequality. The stories also draw our attention towards the adverse conditions of women living in India, and life in America, too, is not an easy one. These Indian-born women are in conflict between old traditional beliefs and newfound independence and desires. There is a need to understand the emotions of immigrant women as they are torn between Indian cultural expectations and American life.

Divakaruni focuses on both cultures equally, criticising and praising certain aspects of each. She says Mukherjee was a significant influence on her when she started writing about the Indian immigrant experience in her short story collection*Arranged Marriage.* "I remember reading, re-reading & underlining passages in her novel *Jasmine.* I felt she had captured some important aspects of diasporic desires and downfalls" (Hindustan Times). Mukherjee's short story 'The Management of Grief' (1988) is Divakaruni's favourite among the writer's works.

Although I would soon go a different route, using magical realism to explore immigrant problems in the Indian American community in novels such as *Mistress of Spices*, and unlike her, I would always consider myself an Indian American writer, I am grateful to her for giving me the confidence that stories about Indians in America were worth telling, says Divakaruni. (Hindustan Times)

In *Arranged Marriage*, Divakaruni looks into the psychological discord occurring in the minds of her characters as they proceed to adjust to the western way of life and culture. They are in a situation where they cannot erase their past memories nor find themselves fit in the new situation. They try to assimilate two different cultures and traditions for a new life in a foreign country. Her immigrant female characters are more rooted in tradition, so it is difficult for them to break the barrier set by patriarchy and traditional society. She undergoes psychological discord when she experiences something that had been restricted for her earlier; sex before marriage is not approved in Indian society, but when they experience this situation in America, they find it a bit awkward.

The protagonist in the story 'Love' (*Arranged Marriage*) is in a similar dilemma, and her heart is torn apart between two cultures – one represented by her boyfriend and the other by her mother. It is a beautiful story that portrays the dilemma of a girl who lives with her boyfriend, and at the same time, she does not want to offend her mother, who believes in the sanctity of marriage. She wants to confess about her relationship with Rex to her mother but has no words to explain it to her. The girl is unable to accept the fact of her mother's disapproval of her live-in relationship.

The woman in the story 'The Disappearance' (*Arranged Marriage*) is another typical example of a woman opting out of wedlock to find her authentic self and identity that has been eroded by the traumatic conditions of diaspora and the influence of new society. 'Silver Pavements, Golden Roofs' continues with Divakaruni's intermittent theme of fascination for the American dream. A young girl, Jayanti, secures admission to a college in Chicago and gets a chance to escape from the dismal streets of Calcutta. She puts herself with her mother's sister there and sees that America has its own set of problems for immigrants. Soon enough, she came face to face with the reality of America when she went for a walk with her aunt. She observed that roads were less crowded and cleaner, unlike the hustle and bustle of Calcutta streets, with hawkers and honking buses loaded with people and rickshaw pullers shouting to give them way. They were immersed in their talks about India and walking back to their apartment when they encountered four boys in the age group of eight to fourteen years playing in the middle of the street with cans and sticks. As they looked at these two women, they shouted "nigger, nigger" and started throwing handfuls of slush on them. The mud splashed on their coats and saris and even their face. This was a culture shock for Jayanti, as whenever she stepped out in her chauffer-driven car in Calcutta, people whispered and admired her beauty. This bunch of kids had racially abused them, and they could not retaliate instead, they hurried back home.

Divakaruni, in her novel *Queen of Dreams* (2004) too, has used a similar theme of reconciliation of familial ties, and the horrors of 9/11 exposed the feeling of hatred of the natives for the immigrants. In Divakaruni's another novel, *Queen of Dreams* (2004), a second-generation Sikh young man, Jaspal, is beaten mercilessly by a few American youths, though he says he is American like them. This creates an insecure situation where the diaspora fails to understand whether they belong to the country which their parents or grandparents left to settle in another country or the one they had adopted, which never accepted them. However, such hatred by the American youth makes one think, is it because of nationalism, mistaken identities, or the large number of diasporas entering their country and taking up their job opportunities due to easy immigration policy.

Divakaruni has presented myth, magic, and romance to create a perfect background of immigrants' experiences and their longing for Indian culture and traditions. They feel alienated, so they long silently for home as they face various existential problems in their new foreign land. Tilo's occupation of selling groceries, lentils, and oil from her store allows her to meet and help different sections of Indian immigrants. She understands their longing for what they have left when they choose America. She observes them, listens to their stories, sees into their secret fears, and sometimes slips a special spice in their grocery bags to help them in their adversity. *The Mistress of Spices* showcases the intermingling of realism, fantasy and mysticism through the representation of different characters in the novel. It portrays Indians living in America who have immigrated to America in search of jobs due to lack of it in their own country or for better living conditions and education facilities for their children or better professional opportunities or to increase their financial position.

Divakaruni presents Indian and American experiences and differences in the cultures through the protagonist, Korobi Roy. *Oleander Girl* is a combination of tradition and modernity. The reader gets an insight into the novel with reference to the patriarchal attitude towards vulnerable female characters. The inviolable strength of Divakaruni as an innovative writer arises from her treatment of women protagonists who were initially like normal girls but take a tough stance when their very existence is shaken by certain circumstances that are forced on them. Divakaruni skilfully works with different aspects of women's lives that portray her literary creativity. The feminist themes of man-woman relationship in marriage with differences in their cultures, female bonding or sisterhood, distress of the older generation due to migration, difficulty women face as they settle in a foreign land, the quest to know one's own identity, differences in the perception of first-generation immigrants and their children, female opposition against patriarchal oppression explicitly find space in her fiction.

Being a contemporary writer, Divakaruni has developed a niche of blending tradition and modernity. In almost all of her novels, discords come into existence when the protagonists try to coexist with traditional and modern values to create an identity of their own. The affliction and anguish that comes with the ordeals of following the traditional values and combining these values with the modern values of the present time make them strong female characters. She has not out-rightly rejected either the traditional or modern value system but has focused on harmonizing these two different trends. Though she is living in modern times and settled in America, there is a feeling of belongingness and rootedness in India, and her interest in women makes her feel that women should be free from the patriarchal mindset. According to *Booklist*, "Divakaruni's books possess a power that is both transporting and healing... serious and entrancing".

References

- Desai, Anita. *Bye Bye Blackbird*. New Delhi: Orient Paper backs, 3rd Printing 2008.

- Desires and Conflicts in Female Bonding in Chitra Banerjee Divakaruni Novels: *Sister of My Heart* and *Vine of Desire* search. ebscohost.com

- Divakaruni, Chitra Banerjee. *Arranged Marriage*. London: Black Swan edition, 1997.

- Divakaruni, Chitra Banerjee. *Oleander Girl*. United Kingdom: Penguin, 2013.

- Divakaruni, Chitra Banerjee. *Sister of My Heart*. U.K: Black Swan edition, 1999.

- Divakaruni, Chitra Banerjee. *The Mistress of Spices*. U.K: Black Swan edition, 1997.

- Diasporic Consciousness in the Novels of Bharati Mukherjee www.ijelr.in

- Diasporic Discourses in the fictions of Jhumpa Lahirid space. bracu.ac.bd: 8080

- Diasporic Narratives in Bharati Mukherjee's *The Tiger's Daughter* by Dr. Sadashiv Pawar www.academia.edu

- Emergence of New Woman in Chitra Banerjee Divakaruni's "Arranged Marriage" www.ijelr.in

- Home and Abroad: Woman Centred Fiction of Chitra Banerjee Divakaruni. shodhganga.inflibnet.ac.in

- Review: The Inheritance of Loss by Kiran Desai. The Guardian www.theguardian.com

- Scroll.in.In Literary Tribute by Sandip Roy. TOI 5th February 2017

- "Unbraiding Tradition: An interview with Chitra Divakaruni". Interview by Frederick Luis Aldama.www.jstor.org

- Writing on the immigrant experience is a political act, especially now in US Sunday Times of India, Lucknow: December 10, 2017.

Chapter 10

Diasporic Education:
Challenges and Possibilities

Dr. Kotra Balayogi

Assistant Professor, Unity College of Teacher Education,
Dimapur, Nagaland – 797112
Email Address- drkotrayogi@uctedimapur.org

Abstract

The educational activities of migrant andminoritized communities, the disadvantages, etc., faced in education have been of interest to sociologists for a long time. The concept of diaspora is a powerful and generative analytical tool with which we can approach the complex dynamics of racially, ethnically, and religiously diverse educational contexts. Traditionally, 'diaspora' refers to the migration of groups/communities of people from a place of origin (a 'homeland') and their subsequent settlement in different parts of the world. Importantly, however, it also refers to a set of complex and ongoing dynamics related to settlement, transnationality, and hybridity, which are significant for unfolding understandings of social relations and collective and individual identities generally and but also specifically around educational practices in institutions.

Diasporic education refers to "concrete educational practices that come to exist through the transnational connections of diasporic communities", engage and problematise notions of 'home' and 'host' and are aimed at improving the lives of diasporas as settled citizens of 'host' nation-states, usually in ways that fall outside the ability towards mainstream education, prevent the 'closure' of essentialist hegemonies at national and ethnic/denominational levels and cannot be ultimately regulated by national/ethnic/denominational policies and ideologies. The Indian diaspora consists of low and semi-skilled migrants, mainly to the Middle East and migration of the highly-skilled to developed countries, and cross-border students who seek employment and remain in their host countries. India initially viewed the migration of the best educated from its prestigious institutions as a 'brain drain.' However, with the reverse flow of these professionals, the diaspora came to be seen as 'brain gain'. The highly skilled Indian diaspora assumed positions of responsibility in the corporate world, in academia, and in the political and social spheres in some host countries, thereby enhancing 21st-century India's image abroad.

Keywords: Challenges, Diasporic, Disadvantaged, Education, India, Migrants, Minoritized Communities, Possibilities, Students, Teachers

Introduction

A growing number of people no longer live in their place of birth but move within their country/to another country. Nearly 12% of the global population falls within the former category and 3.3% in the latter (UNESCO, 2018). With more than a billion people living outside their place of birth, migration has become an integral part of the development process. "Migration is an expression of human aspirations for safety, dignity and better future" (UNESCO, 2018, p. 2), and in general, people move from resource-poor locations to resource-rich areas. Such movement can be voluntary/ involuntary and driven by political, ethnic, religious, and other factors. Involuntary migration and displacements have traditionally been referred to by the term diaspora (UN, 2000); however, given that a fair share of cross-border movement has not been associated with traumatic events/disasters (Reis, 2004) and is voluntary in nature, the meaning of the term was expanded to signify all forms of cross-border movement, leading to people living outside their homeland. Nearly 98 million people have migrated in this century, mainly from developing to developed countries (UN, 2019).

India has experienced large-scale internal and international migration. The former is mostly from rural to urban areas, and it is estimated that nearly nine million Indian people migrated annually from one of the country's states to another during the period 2011 to 2016 (UNESCO, 2018). International migration from India is mainly to developed and Middle Eastern countries that promise employment opportunities, better wages and working conditions. India accounted for the largest proportion of total global migration, 272 million as of 2019, with more than 17.5 million migrants (UN, 2019), and the present study discusses the transformation of the Indian diaspora from illiterate plantation labourers to highly educated and skilled knowledge workers that are highly valued in economically advanced countries.

The expansion of the Indian diaspora takes place through the migration of the highly educated for employment and cross-border student mobility to seek higher education in the host countries, and the diaspora's recognition and professional respectability in their host countries have enhanced their status with the Indian government which has acknowledged their role in promoting India as a global force.

Objectives of the Study

- To study the concept of diasporic education and its significance

- To analyse migration and development in the context of economic growth

- To highlight diaspora guidelines and policies in India

- To discuss diasporic education challenges and their possibilities

Methodology

The study has been conducted based on the method of document review in accordance with the qualitative approach of research and has been done on the basis of the secondary sources of data like books, research journals, newspaper articles, websites, etc., towards "Diasporic Education: The Challenges and Possibilities."

Diasporic Education

Diasporic education also opens up spaces for questioning methodological approaches, as well as the very politics of research, which problematically often results in national and social-scientific interests being conflated, while 'global' research becomes reduced to a comparison of national data sets and trends. It is clear that in a political context where educational problems and their potential solutions are only ever framed and studied in national terms, the voices of minoritized communities are likely to be silenced and their educational questions, ideas, and innovations glossed over.

The diaspora concept has a tendency to challenge nation-centric and generally essentialist assumptions, and there are important conversations to be had around how research on diasporic education can contribute new or 'refurbished' research methodologies while engaging critically with the politics and policies of research at governmental and institutional levels. These conversations might build on existing, but in addition to their global orientation, they must be attuned to the fact that on the ground, diasporic communities pose different questions and raise different concerns that their everyday empiricalreality does not neatly map onto the nation-state's imagination of itself. The diasporic sites of education, which have for decades fought against racism, misrepresentation, and systematic exclusion, it is crucial for scholars and researchers of diasporic education to remain explicitly committed to the cause of social justice.

Among diasporic and/or migrant communities, there are many groups and individuals who adopt dangerously myopic, exclusivist, and exploitative ideologies. At one level, such groups have as much claim as anyone else to 'being diasporic,' and in fact, they will often assert that they are the 'true' representatives of their homeland and thus the 'true' diaspora. These groups will also engage in educational activities aimed at furthering their ideological projects and an interest in studying the educational efforts of such groups,we should always do so critically so as not to be complicit in their exploitative endeavours, researching and writing about diasporic education not as politically neutral but rather as a form of activism or advocacy in itself. The need for scholars/activists to, among other things, 'bear witness to negativity' and act as 'critical secretaries' to people and organisations fighting for justice and studying diasporas in general, and 21st-century diasporic education specifically, positions researchers and authors ideally to do this.

Migration and Development

Migration has become an integral part of the development process and has been influenced by various factors in different regions and at different points in time. The slave trade marked the beginning of the largest labour migration in history. The flow of slaves was mainly from Africa to America, Europe, and the Caribbean. Job losses due to industrialisation and the potato famine encouraged large-scale migration from Europe to the US, Canada, Latin American countries, Australia, New Zealand and South Africa (UN, 1997). In all these instances, the economic benefits accruing to the host countries defined the rationale for and the direction of the flow of migration. Family reunion, asylum-seeking, employment and studying are important reasons for migration (UN, 1998). It can be argued that the economic rationale remained the driving force behind voluntary migration in most instances.

During the colonial period, the economic needs of the imperial powers determined the direction of the flow of migrants. The movement of people during the post-colonial period has been influenced by the economic benefits accruing to both migrants and their hosts in the country of destination. Employment is a major factor influencing voluntary migration, with wage differentials and currency exchange rates promoting this phenomenon. Furthermore, in many instances, employing natives is more expensive than engaging migrant workers. Migrants' low wages and high productivity increased employers' willingness to engage them. Migrants are better educated, their productivity is higher, their salaries are relatively lower, and they make substantial contributions to research. In 2018, India received the highest level of remittances at USD 79 billion, followed by China ($67 billion), Mexico ($36 billion), the Philippines ($34 billion), and Egypt ($29 billion).

While they accounted for 2.7% of India's GDP, the percentage is much higher in some smaller countries.

Most migrants were of working-age and became a positive asset to their host countries. Indeed, the migrant population has helped many greying economies grow in recent decades. It is estimated that migrants accounted for nearly half of the increase in the workforce in the US and nearly 70% in Europe in the current century (OECD, 2012). Europe hosts the largest number of international migrants (82 million), while North America is home to 59 million (UN, 2019). It was previously believed that the brain that migrates is a brain lost for the country of origin. It is difficult to make a conclusive statement on this issue. It may be more realistic to argue that the host country benefits from the higher educational levels and the resultant increased productivity of migrant workers and professionals, while their countries of origin benefit from the remittances and technology transfer facilitated by the diaspora. In other words, if managed well, migration becomes mutually beneficial to the countries of both origin and destination.

Diaspora Policies in India

The Indian government was a dormant player rather than an active agent of change in migration policies until the 1990s. Moreover, Indian IT professionals, bio-technologists, financial managers, scientists, architects, lawyers, teachers, and professors have become successful figures in all the countries where they have settled. The German Green Card, the American H1-B visa, the British work permit, the Canadian investment visa, the Australian student visa, and New Zealand citizenship all attracted Indian talent in the form of employees as well as students.

The Indian government's new approach and positive attitude to the Indian diaspora are reflected in many of its recent initiatives. In 1999, India introduced the Person of Indian Origin Card (PIO card) for Indian citizens and their non-Indian-born descendants up to four generations. In 2005, the government introduced Overseas Citizenship of India (OCI) for those whose parents or grandparents were citizens as of January 26, 1950. India established a Ministry of Non-Resident Indians' Affairs in May 2004 (renamed the Ministry of Overseas Indian Affairs (MOIA) in September 2004). Its main objective is to connect the Indian diaspora community to India. The Ministry launched several programmes in this regard, including the 'Know India Programme' (KIP), which aims to familiarise Indian diaspora youth with their ancestors. Thousands of young people in the diaspora aged 18 to 26 have visited India under this programme. In 2007, the government established the Overseas Indian Facilitation Centre to promote investment in India by the Indian diaspora. A scholarship programme for diaspora students to study in India was started in 2007. Another programme, 'Tracing the Roots,' was launched in 2008 to help PIOs to trace their roots in India. In 2015, the PIO and OCI cards were merged under the OCI.

Furthermore, from 2015 onwards, the government decided to treat NRI/OCI holders' investment as domestic investment rather than FDI. In 2016, the MOIA merged with the Ministry of External Affairs. The attitude of the diaspora towards India also changed, and they became eager to establish ongoing relationships with their homeland for various reasons. The Indian diaspora promotes technology and knowledge transfer through trade and FDI and also by means of informal networks that are interested in promoting scientific and economic development in their home country. Skilled migrants also facilitate the adoption of foreign technologies in their home country. Many governments are keen to exploit these opportunities provided by the diaspora. The government of India launched the Global Initiative for Academic Network (GIAN) in 2017/18 to attract foreign faculty members, including the Indian diaspora, to teach for short periods in Indian universities. The Scheme for Promotion of Academic Research and Collaboration (SPARC) was launched in 2018 to promote research collaboration between reputed institutions abroad and Indian institutions.

Education and the Diaspora

The new generation of young migrants is generally better educated than older settlers, and the number of immigrants with tertiary qualifications in Western countries increased by 70%, reaching a total of almost 30 million in 2010 and 2011. This trend is mainly driven by Asian migration, with more than two million migrants with such qualifications originating from the Asian region having arrived in the OECD in the first decade of the current century (OECD, 2012). These migrants have become part of the highly educated workforce in Canada, the US, and Europe (OECD, 2014), especially in the healthcare sector and science, technology, engineering, and mathematics (STEM) based occupations.

One of the characteristics of Indian students abroad is that they prefer to work in the host country after graduation. The return plans of doctoral graduates from US universities revealed that nearly 90% of Indian students would prefer to stay in the USA.Furthermore, students from India accounted for 14% of all temporary visa holders earning doctorates at U.S. colleges and universities in 2015. In 2017, nearly 44% of Indian cross-border students studied in the USA, and they accounted for 16% of international students in the country. Nearly 80% of Indian immigrant students are enrolled in STEM disciplines. Employment is one of the top reasons why Indian students pursue a degree abroad. Countries like the USA and Canada offer attractive job prospects for postgraduates, and their flexible immigration policies allow them to seek employment upon completion of their studies.

Admission to India's top-ranking institutes is highly competitive, given the large number of prospective students and few places. Study abroad programmes are safety valves for students from well-to-do families who may not be admitted to these prestigious Indian institutions (Choudaha, 2019). The USA hosts the largest share at nearly a million cross-border students, followed by the UK, Australia, France, and Germany. The most important sending countries are China, India, Saudi Arabia and the Republic of Korea, and nearly 305,000 Indian students were pursuing higher education abroad in 2018, with the country's share of international students increasing from 2.3% in the year 2000 to 6% in 2015. The USA, Australia, Canada, the UK, UAE and New Zealand host more than 70% of Indian students abroad. Post-study visa facilities and employment opportunities are the main factors influencing students' decisions in choosing a destination country and this is evident from the decline in the student flow to the UK.

Diaspora's Contributions to India

The diaspora makes significant contributions to India's development in many respects. The most visible form is remittances. Global remittances reached USD 689 billion in 2018, with India accounting for USD 79.0 billion (World Bank, 2019). Although India accounts for only 6% of the global diaspora population, it receives nearly 11.5% of global remittances. On average, remittances by the Indian diaspora increased by nearly USD 2.9 billion annually in the past three decades. This reflects the high levels of income of the skilled Indian diaspora. In 2017, three states accounted for 65% of remittances to India. Kerala received 40%, Punjab 12.7%, and Tamil Nadu 12.4% (World Bank, 2019). The state of Kerala, which has the largest migrant population in India, experienced an increase in remittances in the second decade of the 21st century, even though the number of people migrating declined, especially to the Gulf countries. Once again, this is due to the high remuneration received by highly skilled migrants, and technology transfer is another major aspect of the Indian diaspora's contributions.

The success of Indian IT professionals globally and in the US, in particular, created credibility and trust in India's intellectual abilities. Indian IT professionals, biotechnologists, financial managers, scientists, architects, lawyers, professors, etc., have helped to create an image that brands Indians as well-educated, hard-working professionals with a global outlook. This has also enabled Indian graduates to take up leadership positions in renowned companies and outsource to companies located in India. The Indian diaspora has also boosted India's social and political image. As noted earlier, members of this diaspora have become Prime Ministers, Presidents, and Vice Presidents in some of their host countries and occupy high positions in the corporate world. The contribution of these 'social remittances' (Levitt, 1998) has been substantial.

The diaspora has influenced political decision-making in India, with the introduction of market-friendly reforms in the 1990s reflecting such influence. The Indian diaspora's socialisation in mature market economies influenced pro-market economic policies in their home country, including in the education sector. India started establishing private universities in the year 2000, and the private sector currently accounts for nearly 78% of higher education institutions and nearly two-thirds of student enrolment, and many private universities in India collaborate with institutions abroad.

Conclusion, Discussion and Summary

The Indian diaspora has a long history and it includes involuntary migration during the colonial period and voluntary migration in post-colonial times. Post-independence, there were three major channels of migration, namely, lowand semi-skilled migration, mainly to the Middle East and migration of the highly skilled to developed countries, especially to the USA and cross-border student mobility to seek higher education and to remain in the host countries to become part of the Indian diaspora. India initially regarded the diaspora from the perspective of a 'brain drain' since the best educated from prestigious public higher education institutions were the first to migrate to developed countries. However, it now regards this phenomenon as an asset that is part of 'brain gain.'

Highly skilled Indian diaspora have assumed positions of responsibility in the corporate world, in academia and in the political and social spheres in some of their host countries. They have also promoted technology transfer and invested in many sectors of the Indian economy. India receives the highest share of remittances, which have increased substantially in the past decades, reflecting the high levels of income of skilled Indian diaspora. Such migration is dominated by IT professionals who have contributed to the development of technology-based economic sectors. The technological hubs in Bangalore, Gurugram, Hyderabad, etc., are visible examples of the diaspora's contributions. Indian professionals' success at the global level has created a new image of 21st-century India and enhanced trust in the country's intellectual abilities and professional competencies, and the social and political roles played by the Indian diaspora have also helped to improve India's global image.

References

- Anthias, F. Evaluating "Diaspora": Beyond ethnicity? *Sociology*, 32(3), 1998. 557–580.

- Brah, A. *Cartographies of Diaspora: Contesting Identities.* Routledge, 1996.

- Cela, T. Higher education reform and diasporic engagement in post-earthquake Haiti. *International Studies in Sociology of Education*, 2021. 1–28.

- Choudaha, R. "Study abroad trends of Indian students to USA, UK, Australia and Canada."*Dr Education: Global higher education trends and insights*, 29 January. 2019.

- Gholami, R. "The sweet spot between submission and subversion: Diaspora, education and the cosmopolitan project." D. Carment& A. Sadjed (Eds.), *Diaspora as Cultures of Cooperation: Global and Local Perspectives* (pp. 49–69). Palgrave. (2017)

- GOI: Government of India. High Level Committee on Indian Diaspora. New Delhi: MHRD. 2002.

- Reis, M. Theorizing Diasporas: Perspectives on 'classical' and 'contemporary' Diaspora. *International Migration* 42(2), 2004. 41-56.

- Tölölyan, K. The contemporary discourse of diaspora studies. *Comparative Studies of South Asia, Africa and the Middle East*, 27(3), 2007. 647–655.

- UNESCO: United Nations Educational Scientific and Cultural Organization. Migration, Displacement and Education: building bridges, not walls, Global Education Monitoring Report. Paris: UNESCO. 2018.

- Xu, C. L. "Diaspora at home": Class and politics in the navigation of Hong Kong students in Mainland China's Universities. *International Studies in Sociology of Education*, 2019. 1–18.

Chapter 11

Unveiling Diaspora Powers: Globalisation of the Indian Identity

Ms. Monika Vishwakarma

Research scholar
University of Lucknow, Babuganj,
Lucknow (U.P.), India
Email Address- vmona384@gmail.com

Abstract

The term "Indian diaspora" describes an international group of people who are of Indian ancestry or heritage and have made their homes in nations other than India. This diaspora consists of people and their offspring who have migrated for a variety of reasons, including employment possibilities, educational opportunities, and historical developments like indentured labour during the British colonial era. The Indian diaspora, as a global network, continues to have a significant influence on social advancement in their host nations and on India's development. Their contributions range across the fields of economics, culture, healthcare, technology, politics, and education.

The Indian diaspora's importance in creating a more connected and affluent globe is highlighted by this continual engagement. The Indian diaspora is a thriving, multifaceted worldwide group that has not only managed to retain its cultural heritage but also made a significant contribution to the socioeconomic advancement of the nations they call home. The Indian diaspora represents the idea of unity in variety by uniting people from various backgrounds. The future of social development, fostering understanding, and improving the world for everyone will all be shaped by the growth and evolution of this global community, which will definitely become even more important. This paper intends to examine the Indian diaspora's enormous and enduring effects on social development.

A remarkable force with an impact that transcends national boundaries is the Indian diaspora. The Indian diaspora contributes intangibly as well as materially to society's development; therefore, its influence on that process is not just limited to outward manifestations. The Indian diaspora will remain a potent force for good change, linking cultures, fostering advancement, and improving the globe for all as it expands and changes. Their tale exemplifies the resilience of the human spirit and the limitless potential of global citizenship.

Keywords: Indian diaspora, development, society, power, motherland, globalisation

Introduction

The term "diaspora" comes from the Greek Hebrew word "Halut", which means "migration and colonisation". Migration frequently arises as a consequence of colonisation, where people from settled regions move to new homes. This dynamic plays a central role in the conformation of diaspora communities as individualities and groups dispersed from their motherland to colourful corridors of the world, maintaining artistic and literal ties to their origins. The heritage of colonisation, through migration and its goods, continues to shape the identity, social connections, and engagement of diaspora populations. It represents several ages in the history of the Jewish people. It explained the situation of the Jews in the sixth-century B.C. sumptuous prison and the thriving Jewish community in Alexandria prior to the arrival of Christianity. The further ultramodern operation alludes to the situation of the Jews following their unprofitable insurrection against Roman power in the first century, which culminated in the destruction of the Jerusalem Temple in 70 A.D. As a result, Jews were extensively dispersed around the world.

The Indian diaspora, one of the most vibrant and dynamic, is the largest in the world, with 18 million people from the country living outside their motherland in 2020, the UN has said. Another point that is veritably intriguing about the Indian migratory population is that they are really distributed across the globe. Diaspora denotes migratory communities abiding overseas while retaining connections to their country of origin. The Indian Diaspora comprises people with Indian roots who have established themselves abroad. They carry significance on multiple fronts, making contributions to the welfare of both their host nations and India. Beyond its profitable value, this diaspora exerts social influence by propagating ideas, values, beliefs, and customs. As one of the world's largest, the Indian Diaspora functions as a pivotal tool of soft power, enhancing India's global influence and development. It warrants devoted recognition and attention for its significant impact.

Chitra Banerjee Divakaruni, the Indian-American author famed for novels like *"The Mistress of Spices"* and *"Family of My*

Heart," offers a perceptive perspective on the Indian diaspora. She characterises it as a vast and intricate shade, interwoven with rudiments of culture and tradition and a deep hankering for their motherland. This mosaic of individualities is a beautiful and multifaceted representation where the substance of India resonates in accentuations, shines through carnivals, and resides within the hearts of individuals scattered across the world.

The Indian diaspora is a multifaceted and vibrant global community characterised by remarkable diversity, a wide presence across the world, and significant achievements in colourful fields. These individualities represent a rich shade of verbal, religious, and indigenous backgrounds, laboriously conserving and celebrating Indian traditions within their host nations.Indian migration has taken place in three crucial phases: ancient, classical, and ultramodern. In ancient times, people travelled for trade and the exchange of ideas along the Silk Route. Religious numbers, like Buddhist monks, also spread their training. India saw immigration from places like China. In the ultramodern period, British colonialism led to significant migration, including the British Army labour force, retainers, slaves, dealers, and labourers. After slavery ended, indentured labour migration transferred numerous Indians to British colonies worldwide. In this way, diasporas are different groups of people who share a common artistic and indigenous origin but live away from their traditional motherland. They can be categorised into victim, Homeric/coloniser, trade, or labour diasporas based on the reasons for their migration. Post-independence migration brought a new surge of Indian professionals and labourers seeking better openings worldwide.

Numerous diaspora communities are international, and it is important to save their artistic connections to maintain the diasporic identity. According to Vertovec (1997), the term "diaspora" is frequently applied to describe virtually any population that is considered "reterritorialized" or "international"—that is, which has begun in land other than that in which it presently resides and whose social, profitable, and political networks cross the borders of nation-states or, indeed, gauge the globe. It is thus apparent that, geographically, diaspora involves a radical redefinition of place. Diaspora populations frequently maintain strong ties to their motherland, emphasising their artistic or religious heritage. Still, they also produce connections within the culture of their new home, performing in a binary identity where both surroundings impact how they perceive themselves.

Thus, the present research paper attempts to highlight the idea that the Indian diaspora plays a significant rolein shaping the global perception of the Indian identity and its contribution to various aspects of society.

The Global Economic Impact of the Indian Diaspora

The Indian Diaspora plays a pivotal role in building trust on an international level and fostering innovation and knowledge creation. Premier institutes like IITs and NITs have consistently contributed to skill enhancement and innovative ideas. This community strengthens relations between nations, benefiting India and facilitating foreign investment. Globalisation and liberalisation policies have opened up the Indian economy to international investors, with Indian Diaspora communities abroad playing a significant role in driving innovation and technology transfer. Their impact on both economic and non-economic aspects is commendable.

The seamless integration of Indian culture and traditions into the globalised world is evident. PIO (person of Indian origin) associations play a vital role in bolstering the social cohesion of the Indian Diaspora on Reunion Island. They are dedicated to upholding the distinct ethno-cultural identity of Indo-Reunionese, encompassing language, attire, religious rituals, and customs. This dedicated preservation work guarantees the continued existence of Indian cultural elements in their social and cultural existence.

The Indian diaspora is a significant global community that plays a crucial role in enhancing social development in both host countries and India. This abstract delves into their diverse contributions and influence on social development. They excel across diverse domains, stimulating local economies and providing remittances to their homelands. As cultural ambassadors, they spread Indian culture, promoting intercultural understanding. Engaging in philanthropic endeavours, they back various projects. Their advocacy for social justice and human rights influences policies. In the realm of education, they establish institutions, provide scholarships, and foster knowledge exchange. Therefore, the Indian diaspora's diverse roles drive social development and positive transformations in both host nations and India.

Economic Progression

By encouraging its thriftiness, investing, and fostering innovation, the Indian Diaspora plays a crucial role in India's development. Through foreign portfolio investment (FPI, or foreign portfolio investment) as well as foreign direct investment (FDI, or foreign direct investment), they increase India's capacity for investment while fostering new ventures, enterprises, and risks. They promote trade and entrepreneurial pursuits by acting as a bridge between India and the rest of the globe. Along with knowledge and education, this diaspora fosters trust among international investors and enhances India's worldwide standing. Similarly, the money they send home in the form of remittances aids in promoting social integration and alleviating poverty. Their influence extends to the economic world as well, influencing governments and forging lucrative ties with India.

The Indian diaspora's remittances have a positive systemic impact on the Balance of Payments (BOP), which helps to offset a larger trade deficit. The decline in concealed severance in India can be attributed in part to the exodus of lower-class labourers, particularly to West Asia. Additionally, the migrant labourers facilitated the entry of technologies, lucrative commercial ideas, and informational knowledge into India.

Education Enrichment

The Indian Diaspora plays a crucial role in education, health, and various productive activities. They contribute significantly to India's GDP through remittances and also offer knowledge, direct or indirect investment, technical expertise, and consulting services, aiding in the country's development efforts. Their contributions extend beyond financial support, providing valuable insights for India's betterment. Early education is vital, and investing in early learning efforts increases the chances of success for everyone in society. Providing children with a strong educational base significantly boosts their future opportunities for achievement.

A cost-effective, excellent childcare system is essential for societal success. When parents are confident in their children's well-being, they can be more productive at work. Productive employees benefit businesses, leading to improved community economics. Investing in quality childcare programmes today can yield substantial long-term economic advantages for society.

Social Welfare and Healthcare

When people from colonised regions migrate to new territories, migration frequently results from colonisation. As people and groups leave their native country for other regions of the globe while retaining cultural and historical ties to where they came from, this dynamic is crucial to the development of diaspora communities. Diaspora people's identities, social ties, and engagement are still being shaped by the colonial history of migration and its ramifications. When people from colonised regions migrate to new territories, migration frequently results from colonisation. As people and groups leave their native country for other regions of the globe while retaining cultural and historical ties to where they came from, this dynamic is crucial to the development of diaspora communities. Diaspora people's identities, social ties, and engagement are still being shaped by the colonial history of migration and its ramifications. Other investments in people that contribute to the economic prosperity of society include youth programmes and services, post-secondary education, job creation, the promotion of healthy, active living, and safe and secure communities.

To address poverty effectively, we should embrace a social development strategy and focus on investing in our people. This entails working together with a range of stakeholders, including the government, community organisations, businesses, universities, and municipalities, to improve the welfare of New Brunswick's residents and combat poverty. Additionally, the diaspora serves as a crucial link for trade and investment, promoting economic connections that contribute to India's economic growth, which is fundamental for reducing poverty and fostering social development.

The Indian diaspora has a noteworthy impact on social development, primarily in healthcare and technology. A considerable number of Indian healthcare professionals work worldwide, enhancing the health of their host communities and participating in medical missions. In the technology sector, Indian entrepreneurs and engineers lead innovation, generate employment, and improve access to information, resulting in an overall enhancement of quality of life. Within politics, the Indian diaspora has established a presence in various countries, actively promoting issues related to immigration, diversity, and human rights. Their influence is pivotal in crafting inclusive, progressive policies that champion social justice and protect the rights of minority communities.

Cultural Preservation and Philanthropy

The Indian diaspora actively supports cultural and educational exchange initiatives that enable the exchange of students, artists, and professionals between India and their host nations. These endeavours promote better cross-cultural comprehension and inspire academic and artistic collaborations, ultimately driving social development by boosting global cooperation and enriching cultures. The Indian diaspora includes individuals of Indian origin living overseas, stemming from migrations due to reasons such as economic opportunities, education, and historical occurrences like British colonial era indentured labour. While residing in different regions, they maintain connections to India, encompassing cultural, social, and sometimes economic bonds.

The Indian diaspora is a diverse global community known for its cultural richness, global presence, professional excellence, entrepreneurial spirit, cultural preservation, philanthropic endeavours, and political engagement. They serve as cultural bridges, maintain strong ties with India, possess multilingual abilities, and contribute to education and research. Additionally, many are dedicated human rights advocates, actively championing justice and equality. As a global network, they wield substantial influence in driving social progress in their host nations while simultaneously contributing to India's growth. This continuous engagement underscores the pivotal role of the Indian diaspora in forging a more interconnected and prosperous world.

Increasing the Soft Power of India

People from the Indian diaspora have made a huge impact on the political landscape of their host countries by supporting various causes and serving as artistic ambassadors. The Indian diaspora, which is estimated to number 18 million individuals globally, has significantly influenced social progress. They are known for their tireless efforts to preserve and spread Indian culture through artistic events, community centres, and the development of traditions like yoga and Indian cooking. They have excelled in a variety of professions, including business, technology, medicine, and academics, which has stimulated progress in the nations they support. Their "diaspora tactfulness," or their ability to serve as "ground-builders" between their home country and the one they have embraced, is evident. Not only does the Indian diaspora contribute to India's soft power, but it also serves as a fully transferable political vote bank. Additionally, a large number of individuals of Indian descent occupy prominent political posts across multiple nations, augmenting India's political clout at transnational establishments such as the United Nations. In difficult times, the Indian diaspora is essential, supporting both India and their host communities. Their disparate upbringings encourage intercultural understanding by serving as creative ambassadors, shattering stereotypes, and igniting community through artistic endeavours, which in turn cultivates tolerance and respect for variety.

The Indian diaspora is a worldwide force that traverses the shifting transnational landscape, demonstrating the resilience of the human spirit, intercultural peace, and boundless potential for progress. Its evolution bears witness to relationships that withstand physical barriers, adapting and expanding with time. In a world where boundaries are becoming less permeable, the Indian diaspora stands for advancement, unity, and the universal human spirit. The story is a patchwork of optimism, flexibility, and opportunities that present themselves when disparate nations come together to create a better future.

Conclusion

To sum up, the Indian diaspora plays a multifaceted role in social development. They engage in educational and research collaborations, elevating academic standards and research outcomes. During crises, they provide humanitarian assistance, contributing to disaster relief and social recovery. They serve as a bridge for diplomatic and cultural exchanges, fostering understanding between host countries and India. Additionally, they take on leadership roles and mentor the next generation, enhancing the workforce. The Indian diaspora's impact extends beyond economics and culture, encompassing community support, education, crisis response, and diplomacy, shaping global social development. Members of the Indian diaspora have left a substantial imprint on the educational landscape, enriching academia and aiding students with scholarships and mentorship.

Their global impact in areas like cultural preservation, philanthropy, and facilitating connections between cultures is evident. This diverse community exemplifies unity within diversity, forging connections among people and cultures across the globe. Within the healthcare sector, diaspora individuals, including doctors and researchers, have not only enhanced medical services but have also spearheaded pioneering research, furthering our comprehension and treatment of various diseases. They have influenced the economies, cultures, and societies of their host countries, excelling in diverse fields like technology, medicine, and academia. They have maintained strong connections with India, promoted Indian culture, and increasingly engaged in politics, advocacy for human rights, and philanthropy.

The Indian diaspora is a global citizenship movement that promotes advancement and strengthens linkages across societies. It highlights the resilience of the mortal spirit, appreciation of diverse artistic backgrounds, and opportunities for advancement in a less interconnected world. This paper emphasises the importance of relationships beyond geographic boundaries, progress, belonging, and the unchangeability of the mortal soul. Itwill remain a potent force for good as it develops and adapts, encouraging creative unity, advancing technology, and improving the world for everybody.

References

- Kumar Mishra, Parmendra. "Diasporic identity: Mirroring Chitra Banerjee Divakaruni." *International Journal of Advanced Research*, vol. 8, no. 8, 2020, pp. 1223–1226, doi.org/10.21474/ijar01/11606.

- Meyer, Jean-Baptiste. "A Sociology of Diaspora Knowledge Networks." *The Migration-Development Nexus*, 2011, pp. 159–181, doi.org/10.1057/9780230305694_7.

- Pellerin, Hélène, and Beverley Mullings. "The 'Diaspora Option,' Migration and the Changing Political Economy of Development." *Review of International Political Economy*, vol. 20, no. 1, 2013, pp. 89–120, doi.org/10.1080/09692290.2011.649294.

- Sahoo, Ajaya Kumar. "Issues of identity in the Indian Diaspora: A transnational perspective." *Perspectives on Global Development and Technology*, vol. 5, no. 1–2, 2006, pp. 81–98, doi.org/10.1163/156915006777354482.

- Varma, N. Shradha. "Indian Diaspora: Analysis of its advantage to the home country and to the world." *International Review of Business and Economics*, vol. 4, no. 2, 2020, pp.433–439, doi.org/10.56902/irbe.2020.4.2.2.

- Varrel, Aurelia. "Bhikhu Parekh, Gurharpal Singh, Steven Vertovec (eds), culture and economy in the Indian diaspora." *Revue Europeans Des Migrations Internationals*, Vol. 22, no. 2, 2006, pp. 179–180, doi.org/10.4000/remi.4097.

Chapter 12

Psychological Issues and Challenges of Integrated Identity of Indian Diaspora

Ms. Daksha Kala

M.A., IGNOU, National P.G. College, Lucknow
Email Address- jyotikala2010@gmail.com

Abstract

People leaving their homeland due to aspirations, war, hunger, manmade or natural disasters, etc., retain a strong identification with the culture of their home country. A number of such migrants experience problems such as homesickness, loss of friends, different working environments, high cost of living, alienation due to smaller social circles, and above all, inability to stay besidefamily members during their adverse and critical situations. Along with these cultural differences, they also present a serious issue regarding their acceptance ofassimilation and integration into the socio-cultural matrix of the host country. Hence, these migrants struggle, face stress, and undergo the trauma of identity crisis and the construction of their diasporic self. Though the concept of 'integration strategy' as developed in cross-cultural psychology does provide some help, during the initial years, the adjustment and self-development in a culturally different new environment becomes quite a substantial challenge."Thriving in the diaspora as a "model minority," the South Asian migrant in the context of Western orientation to individualism, autonomy and confidentiality, independent consent often "accommodates rather than assimilates" (Gibson, 1988). Consequently, there emerge psychological problems due to the burden and stress of accommodating, adjusting and struggling with different socio-cultural values, practices, and ideologies. "The stigma of mental health problems and experiences or fears of racism have been recurrent themes as mental health risk factors in psychiatric literature for the UK." (Fernando, 2002)

The present paper aims to analyse the assumption that all immigrants undergo the same kind of psychological acculturation process and identity crisis and will attempt to bring forth the challenges and effective measures in the construction of their diasporic integrated personality.

Keywords: Integration strategy, acculturation, identity crisis.

Introduction

Diaspora means the scattering of a particular group or individual from one socio-cultural setting to another socio-culturally different country. The pangs of separation from one's nativity start formulating once the migration takes place from one socio-cultural setting to another socio-cultural setting, and this is because socio-cultural aspects dwell deep into the consciousness of an individual from the primary stage of his or her life. It becomes an integral part of an individual's psyche, encompassing feelings, memories, and familiarities with the things experienced from the formative years of life. The levels of similarity can be understood by social category and the dominance of that particular category,be it culture, religion, race, ethnicity, or language spoken. The pre-migration feelings of hope, dreams, and a better life vary in the migratory patterns. A migratedperson experiences a difference in the host society, and this experience of being different in another socio-cultural setting is called the post-migration feelings and diasporic sense.

The issue of Indians migrating to foreign countries worldwide for economic, academic or other purposes has been studied by a number of economists, sociologists, historians, anthropologists, and geographers.Psychological research is also one of the important aspects, considering that people leaving their homeland due to aspirations, war, hunger, manmade or natural disasters, etc., retain a strong identification with the culture of their home country.

Hence, it is pertinent to understand and analyse their socio-cultural and political experiences in the host land that affect the identity development and mental health of these migrants. A number of such migrants experience problems such as homesickness, loss of friends, different working environments, high cost of living, alienation due to smaller social circles, and above all, inability to stay beside family members during their adverse and critical situations. Along with these cultural differences, they also present a serious issue regarding their acceptance ofassimilation and integration into the socio-cultural matrix of the host country. Hence, these migrants struggle, face stress, and undergo the trauma of identity crisis and the construction of their diasporic self. Scholars like Robin Cohen, in his *Global Diaspora: An Introduction*, refer to different forms of migrations as diasporas, such as the "victim/refugee diaspora," "labour/service diaspora," "imperial/colonial diaspora," "the trade diaspora," and "cultural diaspora" because these migrants also face the post immigrant feelings, diasporic sense, and experience of difference. (R. Cohen)

Mental Health Challenges in the Indian Diaspora

-The primary challenge faced by the Indian diaspora is the process of acculturation, which is adjusting to and integrating into a new culture while preserving their own. The process of maintaining a balance between their Indian identity and the culture of the host country may cause feelings of alienation, hence exerting stress and anxiety.

-The pressure to assimilate into the mainstream culture while maintaining a connection to Indian values and traditions can be emotionally conflicting, leading to conflicts in personal and cultural identities.

-Indians migrating from joint family systems to countries having nuclear families face a different socio-cultural environment. The lack of a familiar social circle can lead to feelings of isolation, depression, and anxiety. Cohen writes,

Diaspora signified a collective trauma, a banishment, where one dreamed of home but lived in exile. Other people abroad who have also maintained strong collective identities have, in recent years, defined themselves as diasporas, though they were neither active agents of colonization nor passive victims of persecution. (ix Introduction, R. Cohen)

- Mental health issues are still stigmatized in many Indian communities. Seeking professional help in the case of a psychic problem is often avoided. This attitude of diasporacandeter them from seeking the support they need to cope with their mental health challenges.

Well-being and Life Satisfaction

World Health Organization defines mental health as a "state of well-being in which every individual realises his or her potential, can cope with the normal stresses of life, can work productively and fruitfully, and can contribute to her or his community" (World Health Organization [WHO], 2005) (springer.com).To live happily with satisfaction fulfils the objective of mental health. Happiness can be defined in many ways. In psychology, there are two popular conceptions of happiness: hedonic and eudaimonic. "Hedonic happiness is achieved through experiences of pleasure and enjoyment, while eudaimonic happiness is achieved through experiences of meaning and purpose. Both kinds of happiness are achieved and contribute to overall well-being in different ways… psychological well-being is measured with six constructs related to self-actualization: autonomy, personal growth, purpose in life, self-acceptance, mastery, and positive connections to others."(thoughtco. com)The three core components of the WHO definition are well-being, effective functioning of the individual, and effective functioning of the society. In line with this definition, Keyes proposed a model of mental health that included three domains:emotional, psychological, and social well-being. "Emotional well-being is comprised of avowed quality of life (viz., satisfaction andhappiness with life) and positive affect. Psychological well-beingis the extent to which people are thriving in their personal lives, forexample, self-acceptance and a sense of purpose in life."(C.D. Ryff)

Social well-being is the extent to which people thrive in their social lives in local and broader communities(C.L.M. Keyes). With reference to the mental healthof adiaspora, both hedonic and eudaimonic aspects, that is, their experiences of pleasure and enjoyment and meaning and purpose, ought to be considered.

Positive mental health is guided and shaped by socio-demographic factors such as age, gender, caste, and even lived experiences. "These six dimensions: a positive evaluation of oneself and one's past (self-acceptance), a sense of continued growth and development (environmental mastery), the belief that one's life is purposeful and meaningful (purpose in life), quality relations with others (positive relationships), a sense of capacity to manage one's life and the surrounding world effectively (personal growth), and a sense of self-determination (autonomy)tap into the individual's ability to function and fulfil their potential." (C.D. Ryff and C.L.M. Keyes)

Conflict and Challenges of "Hybrid Identity" ofthe Indian Diaspora

The Indian diaspora has long been migrating and settling down in foreign countries. India has the most extensive diaspora, followed by Mexico in second place. Among the Indian diaspora, women make up a significant percentage, and they contribute to the development and growth of their host country as well.

> Although the immigrant community settled in the "new sociocultural setting" long back, might have assimilated or become the citizens of this "newly old" sociocultural setting, continues to have connections and idealized imagination of the culture left behind. The dilemma whether to accept the values of "the other" creates what Homi Bhabha calls "third space"–"hybrid" identity. Therefore, diaspora identities are constantly producing and reproducing themselves anew through transformations and difference.(doi.org)

The new settlers in host countries undergo myriad conflicting situations resulting in mental disturbances. The concept of 'integration strategy' in cross-cultural psychology does provide some help, but it is quite a substantial challenge during the initial years to make adjustments and self-development in a culturally different new environment. "Traditionally, mainstream psychology has been primarily occupied with developing universal, linear models and theories of immigrant identity, acculturation, and adaptation. For instance, cross-cultural psychologists have studied topics such as acculturation and acculturative stress (Berry, 1998), socialization and enculturation (Camilleri &Malewska-Peyre, 1997), and bicultural identity (LaFromboise, Coleman, &Gerton, 1998)" (sciencedirect.com).

The migrants making efforts for assimilation and acceptance to the new socio-cultural settings may face a long problematic way to the satisfactory integration of the self to the new environment. Integration implies both the preservation of home culture and an active involvement with the host culture. Central to the theory of integration strategy is the assumption of universality. Berry and his colleagues take up the position that although there are "substantial variations in the life circumstances of the cultural groups that experience acculturation, the psychological processes that operate during acculturation are essentially same for all the groups; that is, we adopt a universalist perspective on acculturation." In other words, immigrants' acculturation strategies reveal the underlying psychological processes that unfold during their adaptation to new cultural contexts."(sciencedirect.com)

Mental Health Issues and Support System

A large number of studies on the Indian Diaspora relate to the socio-cultural'bearings' that the 'emigrating' Indians carry to the host land. Jaswant Guzder and Meenakshi Krishna, in their research work entitled *Mind the Gap: Diaspora Issues of Indian*

Origin Women in Psychotherapy, have explored how the traditional Indian Hindu diaspora women face the conflict while trying for internalization of host countries' paradigms of individuation. The traditional background of hierarchies, caste system, and particularly, the difference between South Asian Cultural aspects and that of Western Feminism exerts excessive pressure on them to reconcile in a different cultural setting.

> Diaspora women, with origins in Hindu Indian cultural spaces, are seeking psychotherapy to address mental health and personal identity issues within the North American context.... Older diaspora women may carry many worlds within them that shape their marital life, parenting and other role changes related to the migratory reality. (Jaswant Guzder and Meenakshi Krishna)

Though the concept of 'integration strategy' as developed in cross-cultural psychology does provide some help but, during the initial years, the adjustment and self-development in a culturally different new environment becomes quite a substantial challenge. "Since psychotherapy literature is dominated by ethnocentric Euro-North American paradigms, the challenge to analysts and therapists working in the diaspora is to widen bedrock questions of counter-transference, neutrality, identity and psychotherapy processes to accommodate the cross-cultural realities of Hindu women" (Jaswant Guzder and Meenakshi Krishna).

Therefore, Keyes (1998) argued the importance of optimal social functioning of individuals and theorised about social well-being. Keyes' model consists of five dimensions: "the quality of one's relationship to society and community (social integration), a construal of society based on the qualities of the people (social acceptance), a belief that one is a vital member of the society (social contribution), a belief in the evolution of society realised through its institutions and citizens (social actualisation) and a belief that society is discernible, sensible and predictable (social coherence). These five components positively correlate with measures of happiness, life satisfaction, generativity, optimism, feelings of neighbourhood trust and safety, subjective perceptions of people's physical health, and the degree of past community involvement (Keyes, 1998). Hence, these five factors, taken together, indicate how structural influences impact individual functioning and social well-being."(springer.com 10.1007)

Indian migration to the Gulf has served as the backbone of the economies of high-migration states such as Kerala. The gender dimension of Indian migration, such as female nurses and housemaids in the Gulf, posits them in a very different socio-economic environment. "However, the increasing international scrutiny and condemnation of the treatment of blue-collar and domestic expatriate workers in the region in recent years has cast India-Gulf migration in a far less favourable light, prompting greater attention by the Government of India (GoI) to diaspora affairs and worker welfare issues. Yet, complaints received from and on behalf of migrant workers regarding various forms of abuse, exploitation, and hardship persist."(John Calabrese)

Sonia Amin and Priya Bansal, in their book *Understanding the Asian Indian Diaspora and Mental Health: Liberation from Western Frameworks,* have presented the lived experiences and subtle concerns of Asian Indian people trying to survive and thrive in American society. The book presents and examines patterns of oppression influencing the mental health status of Asian Indians in the U.S. It has also critically analysedthe shortcomings of Western models of psychological healing (titles.cognella.com).To be considered as 'other' by the dominant socio-cultural setting of the host land gives vent to challenges related to ethnicity, race, gender, and culture. "The stigma of mental health problems and experiences or fears of racism have been recurrent themes as mental health risk factors in psychiatric literature for the UK"(S. Fernando, 2002). Racial groups are not all stigmatised, but most often, the words used in racial descriptions have implicationsof the context in which they are used.

When people are referred to as 'white' and 'non-white' the implication is that the latter lackssomething that the former have, that the non-white isdeficient in some way –… Racism like psychiatric stigma, involves discrimination – in this case usually on the basis of skin colour, rather than diagnosis. Both discriminations may be expressed overtly in terms of personal prejudice or subtly through institutional processes. When a racial group is stigmatised people perceived as belonging to thatgroupalsoface problems of social exclusion and in extreme instancestheyareseenasalientosocietyinthe same way as schizophrenics are.… About four years ago, the Royal College of Psychiatrists in the UK embarked on (what it called) an 'anti-stigma campaign'… The medicalisation of social problems, the drug-peddling of pharmaceutical firms, stereotyping of certain groups via racist perceptions of people, all these and perhaps much else are involved in the power that is exercised over people through the psychiatric system. (S. Fernando, 2006)

In the case of the Indian diaspora, obstacles in obtaining appropriate professional psychiatric help or treatment can be from both ends. The discriminatory biases, prejudice, or power and control over the 'other' immigrantsby the psychiatric system of the host land on the one hand, and the traditional socio-cultural nuances of the diaspora on the other. Bagmi Das, The George

Washington University, did research to understand the relationship between acculturation and support seeking, both informal and formal support, for sexual violence survivors. Das found that there were differences in support-seeking depending uponthe immersion of the survivors in either dominant or ethnic societies. The research focused on understanding cultural norms as opposed to acculturation and integrating informal supports in the treatment of survivors. Indian diaspora in the United States faces the conflicting influence of carried Indian culture and ideologies and those cultures and ideologies that exist in the United States. Patriarchal notions pervade Indian culture, which often blame the survivor of the sexual violence.Indian culture also emphasizes that women's experiences influence the reputation and honour of the family.

> Women in the Indian diaspora, especially, may hear messages of blame in their cultural atmosphere, and then may refrain from seeking support for any experiences of sexual violence.... The data showed that acculturation has some impact on amount of support sought; however, it did not go in-depth to understand the phenomenon of acculturation in how each survivor understands the supports around them, receives messages regarding their experience, and then seeks support from their community.... It is powerful to note that many of the survivors (26.5%) identified seeking support from brothers, male friends, and male professors/teachers. (Sexual Violence...orcid.org).

Present Context

Online therapy has emerged as a valuable tool in providing convenient mental health support and offering accessible and culturally sensitive solutions.

"Online therapy platforms often have a diverse pool of mental health professionals, including those who are culturally sensitive and familiar with the challenges faced by the Indian diaspora. This allows individuals to seek support from professionals who can understand their cultural background and experiences better.… provides a level of anonymity that can be appealing to individuals who may feel hesitant about seeking help due to the fear of judgment and/or stigma. This privacy can encourage more people to open up about their mental health struggles.… India is a diverse country, with a plethora of languages. Many online therapy platforms cater to clients who speak various languages. This ensures that language barriers do not hinder individuals from seeking help.… it can be a more cost-effective alternative to traditional in-person therapy." (Abhishek Annappa)

Conclusion

Indian diaspora has a long history and has strengthenedthe economy of both India and the country they settled in with their hard work and expertise. Starting from indentured labourers to scientists and technocrats today, they have come across conflicting challenges from different kinds of socio-cultural aspects. Due to the complexities of multiple cultural identities, social isolation, and the stigma attached to mental health, the Indian diaspora faces distinct mental health challenges. Many studies have been done to address the psychological issues and challenges of developing an integrated identity for the Indian diaspora. Presently, in the age of technology and the digital world, online therapy has emerged as a valuable tool for addressing such challenges.

The Indian diaspora can break the barriers preventing them from seeking help towards improved well-being and emotional resilienceby embracing online therapy to access mental health services. The Internet can connect anyone with qualified therapists and mental health professionals, irrespective of geographical barriers. Online group therapy sessions can give a sense of community feeling and be immensely comforting and empowering at the same time where individuals can connect with others and share similar experiences and challenges. With online therapeutic support, the Indian diaspora can find the guidance they need to thrive in their socio-culturally different host country and stay connected to their roots at the same time.

References

- Annappa, Abhishek. Psychologist and Center Head, Veda Rehabilitation and Wellness Pvt. Ltd. Bengaluru vedawellnessworld.com/mental-health-challenges-in-the-indian diaspora-the-role-of-online-therapy/

- Calabrese, John. "India-Gulf Migration: A Testing Time." April 14, 2020, www.mei.edu/publications/india-gulf-migration-testing-time

- Cohen, R. "Global Diasporas: An Introduction." London: UCL Press.David A. Leeming (Ed), *Encyclopedia of Psychology and Religion.* 1997. doi.org/10.1007/978-3-030-24348-7

- digitalcommons.unf.edu/cgi/viewcontent.cgi?article=1059&context=jcssw

- doi.org/10.1007/978-3-030-24348-7

- Fernando, S. *Mental Health, Race and Culture.* 2nded. Basingstoke: Palgrave, 2002.

- Fernando, S. "Stigma, Racism and Power." *Aotearoa Ethnic Network Journal* Volume 1, Issue 1. June 2006.

- Guzder, Jaswant and Krishna, Meenakshi."Mind the Gap: Diaspora Issues of Indian Origin Women in Psychotherapy"*Sage Journals, Psychology and Developing Societies*. Vol. 17, Issue 2, journals.sagepub.com/doi/abs/10.1177/097133360501700203

- Keyes, C. L. M. "Social well-being."*Social Psychology Quarterly*, 61, 1998. 121–140.

- link.springer.com/article/10.1007/s12646-022-00667-6

- Ryff, C. D. "Happiness is everything, or is it? Explorations on the meaning of psychological well-being."*Journal of Personality and Social Psychology*, 57, 1989. 1069 –1081.

- Ryff, C. D., & Keyes, C. L. M. "The structure of psychological well-being revisited."*Journal of Personality and Social Psychology*, 69, 1995. 719 –727

- Sexual Violence Survivors in the Indian Diaspora: The Impact of Acculturation on Support-Seeking BehaviorBagmi Das The George Washington University. orcid.org/0000-0002-0765-9217

- titles.cognella.com/understanding-the-asian-indian-diaspora-and-mental-health-9781793521149

- www.sciencedirect.com/science/article/abs/pii/S0147176709000030

- www.thoughtco.com/eudaimonic-and-hedonic-happiness-4783750

Others-

- Berry, J. W."Acculturative Stress." In P. B. Organista, K. M. Chun, & G. Marín (Eds.), *Readings in Ethnic Psychology*. Taylor & Frances/Routledge, 1998,pp 117–122.

- Camilleri, C., &Malewska-Peyre, H. "Socialization and Identity Strategies" (A. Anugraham, C. Dasen, et al., Trans.). In J. W. Berry, P. R. Dasen, & T. S. Saraswathi (Eds.), *Handbook of Cross-cultural Psychology: Basic Processes and Human Development.* Allyn& Bacon, 1997, pp. 41–67.

Chapter 13

Experiences of the Indian Diaspora: A Literary Perspective

Dr. Shalini Srivastava

Associate Professor
Department of English
NSCB Govt. Girls' Degree College, Aliganj
Lucknow.
Email Address- shaliniatulsrivastava@gmail.com

Abstract

This paper provides a comprehensive exploration of the multifaceted experiences of the Indian diaspora, with a specific emphasis on the roles and identities of women within this expansive global community. The Indian diaspora, marked by its considerable size, widespread geographic distribution, and rich cultural diversity, has attracted significant attention from scholars, policymakers, and the general public across various academic disciplines.

The study delves into the intricate dimensions of diasporic experiences, shedding light on the intricate interplay of factors such as caste, culture, gender, and multiple identities. It diverges from traditional anthropological research methods by adopting an interpretive approach that centres on artistic expressions like literature and cinema to vividly portray the life-world of diasporic Indians. The paper presents a nuanced examination of how literature and the silver screen capture the essence of diasporic life and transnational existence. Through these artistic mediums, it discerns the advantages and challenges faced by individuals navigating a transnational context. This approach offers a fresh perspective on the intricate dynamics of migration. The literary contributions of diasporic Indians offer a rich tapestry of narratives that reflect their diverse histories, experiences, and aspirations. These narratives, ranging from creative writing to academic endeavours, become conduits for expressing the intricacies of everyday life and contribute to the creation of cultural artefacts. The paper underscores the deep connection between the authors and the broader diaspora community.

Moreover, the paper delves into the representation of women within diasporic literature. It unveils how these narratives serve as a lens through which the challenges confronted by women in patriarchal societies are exposed. The paper emphasizes the transformative journeys of Indian women within the diaspora, underscoring their resilience, adaptability, and success and how they have played a pivotal role in reshaping the narrative of migration and cultural preservation.

Keywords: Diaspora, migration, lived experiences, women in diaspora, diasporic Literature

The Indian diaspora has a broad appeal as a subject of study, spanning various academic disciplines such as anthropology, history, literature, cultural studies, and sociology. This widespread interest is not surprising, given the sheer size, geographical distribution, and diversity of the Indian diaspora. It captivates the attention of scholars, the general public, policymakers, and those interested in popular culture. Diverse experts from different fields have delved into the exploration of the Indian diaspora. Several social scientists from India have dedicated a significant amount of time immersing themselves within the Indian diaspora, aiming to unravel the intricate threads of diasporic existence. Their interest is often influenced by their own "Indian" identity, and their unique perspective as outsiders provides them with a deep understanding of the subtle dynamics at play. Their objective is to comprehend the lives of Indians in the diaspora while positioning themselves as Indians amid this community. Their contributions to the literature on the Indian diaspora shed light on the complexities of caste, culture, gender, and multiple identities. These works facilitate our understanding of the complex relationship that diasporic Indians maintain with their ancestral homeland and with other Indians.

To grasp the nuances of diasporic Indian experiences, one must engage with the intricacies of their "lifeworld." While classical anthropological tradition often employs ethnographic studies for this purpose, the approach in this paper diverges from the beaten path and leans more toward interpretive research. Interpretive research encompasses the interpretation of various forms of artistic expression, including cinema, literature, and music. In the context of diasporic Indians, the rich tapestry of their "life-world" finds its most vivid representation through literature and the silver screen. The experiences and nuances of life within the Indian diaspora have been eloquently portrayed through these artistic mediums. It is undeniable that the visual medium, especially cinema, has a wide-reaching impact, connecting with a diverse audience that includes both diasporic communities and others. Through the lens of cinema, the pros and cons of living in a transnational context have been thoughtfully explored and depicted. Additionally, literature serves as another valuable portal into the intricacies of the diasporic Indian "life-world."

Diasporic Indians have made significant literary contributions, offering a rich tapestry of narratives. The various components of the diaspora carry their distinct histories, experiences, and aspirations. Despite this diversity, a shared sense of pathos and orientation binds them together, albeit with different manifestations. The reasons underlying these variations in expression find their most insightful exploration within the literature of the Indian diaspora.

For many within this diaspora, their experiences find expression through creative writing, becoming a vital channel for their manifestations. For others, it sparks a quest to explore their histories, leading to academic endeavours. Being part of the diaspora presents common challenges felt across its diverse sections, driving many to engage with these ideas. Consequently, numerous diasporic Indians document their experiences and frustrations of living in the diaspora, typically in the form of fiction or non-fiction works. These writings often encapsulate everyday life facts that contribute to the creation of cultural artefacts.

It is fair to say that these literary pieces are deeply rooted in the life experiences of diaspora members or those who share their "life-world." These writings reflect a connection between the writer and the broader diaspora community. In delving into the everyday life of diasporic Indians, one encounters the complex concept of "home." This term carries ambiguity for both the diasporic Indians and those seeking to understand their experiences. The notion of "home" presents a multifaceted challenge, not only in its literal sense but also metaphorically. The yearning for a sense of "home" is poignantly conveyed in the works of diasporic Indian writers. Nevertheless, similar to many within the Indian diaspora, the concept of "home" holds diverse connotations for these writers, adding to the complexity of their narratives.

Indian Literature and Diaspora

Contemporary Indian writing in English often delves into the challenging aspects of dislocation, unfriendliness, rootlessness, fragmentation, racial discrimination, marginalization, identity crises, and cultural clashes experienced by migrants and the diaspora. However, the history of Indian migration goes back centuries. In the 17th century, V. S. Naipaul's early works, "The Mystic Masseur" and "The Mimic Men," captured the yearning and desires of people who had been uprooted due to forced labour and were returning to their homelands. The 18th and 19th centuries saw mass migrations of people from India to serve the British Empire in various parts of the world. These displaced individuals longed for their homelands, which hinted at a desire for political independence. Notably, many Hindus, Muslims, and predominantly Punjabi Sikhs ventured to Canada to work as lumberjacks in sawmills during the early 20th century. They faced lower wages, racism, and prejudice due to their ethnicity. In response to such injustices, the Indian diaspora in Canada formed the 'Gadar Party,' which played a significant role in India's struggle for independence. Sadhu Singh Dhami's work, "Maluka-1997," depicts this period.

Post-independence India witnessed a new dimension of asylum life, with people from the 16th and 17th centuries moving to developed countries to escape political or financial difficulties in their homeland, a phenomenon Gayatri Chakravorty Spivak terms "brain drain." Migration to other countries continued, with immigrants experiencing a sense of belonging and mobility in their new homes, regardless of their motivations. In literature,

Anita Desai's *Bye-Bye, Blackbird* and Kamala Markandaya's *The Man from Nowhere* were among the first novels to vividly portray diasporic Indian characters, revealing the isolation and dislocation faced by Indians in the United Kingdom in the 1960s due to racial prejudice. Bharati Mukherjee's *Wife* and *Jasmine* portrayed Indians in the United States, a place teeming with both legal and illegal immigrants before the era of globalization.

Salman Rushdie used magic realism in *The Satanic Verses* to metaphorically explore the experience of migration. Chitra Banerjee Divakaruni's *The Mistress of Spices* presents Tilo, the protagonist, as a mysterious character who unravels the pain of migrants. Amitav Ghosh's *The Shadow Lines* delves into the deep sense of rootlessness experienced by characters born and raised in foreign lands. Amit Chaudhary's *Afternoon Raag* sheds light on the lives of Indian students in Oxford. These authors also discuss the advantages of dislocation, such as gaining a dual perspective and experiencing various cultural forms. It is often this very advantage that allows diasporic Indians, particularly those of the second generation, to navigate the challenges of dual identities, even though it may result in existential turmoil in their psychology.

Representation of Women in Diasporan Literature

Literature often serves as a reflection of life, and the experiences of diasporic Indian women have been a recurring theme in the literary works of various Indian authors, falling within the broader category of diasporic literature. Diasporic literature encompasses a wide range of texts created by authors who write from outside their native countries, sharing common themes of alienation and identity. In particular, literary works focusing on the lives of women in the diaspora shed light on the challenges faced by the female community in patriarchal societies. For instance, Anita Desai's *Clear Light of Day* delves into the roles women play in society through the protagonist, Bimla Das. Desai's portrayal of the novel highlights the dynamics of male-female relationships and exposes the feelings of alienation, loneliness, isolation, and communication barriers experienced by emigrant women in a foreign land. It underscores the disparities in opportunities and treatment between men and women in Indian culture.

Not all immigrant women become part of the working class; some migrate to be with their families. Chitra Divakaruni's *The Unknown Errors of Our Lives* features a collection of short stories that illuminate the lives of these women. Set in India and America, Divakaruni's stories explore themes such as solitude, alienation, expectations, love, and betrayal. The stories introduce vivid characters like Mrs. Dutta, Aparna, and Meera, each representing different facets of migrant Indian women. The author's narratives capture the collective diaspora's reflections on their lives before migration and the simpler times they left behind.

In diasporic writings, Indian women are not always cast as the central characters. Sometimes, they take on roles as antagonists, accused of abandoning their duties as mothers or wives. Jhumpa Lahiri's *The Lowland* introduces such a character in Gauri, the widow of Udayan and the novel's antagonist. *The Lowland* delves into the experiences of the Indian diaspora, with a specific focus on the lives of two brothers, Subhash and Udayan, and their families. Gauri is portrayed as a complex character who grapples with unresolved grief over her husband's death and feelings of inadequacy as a mother, leading to her detachment from her former life and severing all contact with her second husband and daughter. Initially, Gauri, as a woman, has limited choices beyond conforming to the decisions of the men around her. Her act of fleeing from her reality mirrors the experiences of many women in foreign lands. The novel subtly reveals the struggles faced by migrant women as they navigate their new lives in foreign countries, exposing the impacts on their relationships, cultural identity, and mental well-being.

In India, women are deeply entrenched in the sociocultural fabric, shaped by historical traditions and religious narratives. These narratives are rooted in patriarchy, power hierarchies, and gendered perceptions. While Indian culture is incredibly diverse and lacks a uniform template, the patriarchal social order often dominates the overarching framework. Paradoxically, within this context, women have played a pivotal role in upholding Indian culture and tradition. They serve as focal points in the patriarchal family structure.

Despite occupying a subservient position in a culture marked by patriarchy, women have been custodians of tradition and culture, passing them down to the next generation. They have exhibited and enjoyed a form of power, agency, space, and rights, sometimes drawing from the very sources that sustain the patriarchal order and sometimes forging these on their own. An illustrative example of this paradox can be found in the character of Sita in *Ram Charit Manas*. She embodies the ideal woman, displaying grace and character as she moves from her father's home to her husband's, resists advances from powerful figures, and undergoes a "trial by fire" to prove her fidelity. However, she also accepts her fate when abandoned by her husband. Within this patriarchal structure, Sita remains the centre of Rama's life, and he never remarries. Her character serves as a metaphor presented to Indian women, sometimes selectively to reinforce patriarchal power structures.

Over millennia, women's status in India has experienced significant shifts, with women facing extreme forms of exploitation such as widow immolation (*sati*), veiling (*purdah*), dowry issues, female infanticide, and limited access to education and public activities. However, with modernization, economic independence, education, and state intervention, Indian women have improved their position in society and challenged patriarchal norms successfully. These dynamics also extend to the context of migration. The cultural baggage that women carry is incredibly diverse and complex, rooted in centuries-old civilisation- consciousness. Migration and diasporic conditions can alter women's authority and power within families and modify patriarchal structures, depending on the socio-economic contexts of both home and host countries. These changes are not uniform and can lead to both greater equality within families and increased agency and opportunities, but they can also, in some cases, reinforce and rigidify gender hierarchies, especially in perceived hostile or morally different host societies.

On one hand, migration can be liberating and provide opportunities for women to negotiate and establish new cultural practices. On the other hand, it can sometimes result in physical abuse, honour killings, and other forms of cruelty due to a perceived loss of control over women in an unfamiliar, potentially threatening host society. Moreover, issues like marital disputes, difficulty adapting to new environments, dowry demands, nostalgia, insecurity, and complex dual belongingness between home and host countries can persist. The feminist and civil rights movements in various countries have not always prioritized migrant women's rights, but these movements have had a generally positive impact on the rights and status of migrant women.

Conclusion

In conclusion, the experiences of the Indian diaspora represent a rich tapestry of narratives that illuminate the intricate interplay between tradition, identity, and adaptation in a globalized world. The Indian diaspora, spanning the corners of the globe, is a testament to the enduring spirit of a diverse and culturally rich community. As we have explored in this paper, these experiences are shaped by a multitude of factors, including historical legacies, economic opportunities, educational pursuits, and the ongoing quest for identity. The Indian diaspora, while geographically dispersed, maintains a deep and abiding connection to its cultural roots. This connection is reflected in the preservation of traditions, languages, and customs that have been passed down through generations. At the same time, the diaspora has evolved, with its members embracing new cultures, forging unique identities, and contributing to the enrichment of their host societies. The stories of the Indian diaspora are not only tales of migration but also of resilience, adaptability, and success. Across the world, Indian diaspora communities have made significant contributions to various fields, from business and technology to the arts and academia. These success stories exemplify the resourcefulness and determination that are often born out of the challenges of migration.

The experiences of the Indian diaspora, whether in search of better opportunities, economic independence, or educational pursuits, have had a profound impact on the roles and identities of women. Migration and diasporic conditions, however, do not follow a linear trajectory; they can liberate and empower women or reinforce rigid gender hierarchies, depending on the social, economic, and cultural contexts of the host country. As explored in this paper, the stories of Indian women in the diaspora are a testament to their strength, resilience, and adaptability. Over the years, they have navigated complex dual identities and, in many cases, succeeded in challenging and transforming patriarchal norms. The feminist and civil rights movements have played a role in shaping these experiences positively, providing a platform for migrant women to advocate for their rights and agency. The evolving narratives of Indian women in the diaspora offer valuable insights into the dynamic relationship between tradition and change, culture and adaptation, and gender roles and empowerment. They illuminate the diverse and transformative journeys of women within the Indian diaspora, underscoring the significance of their experiences in reshaping the narrative of migration and cultural preservation.

The stories of the Indian diaspora are not only tales of migration but also of resilience, adaptability, and success. Across the world, Indian diaspora communities have made significant contributions to various fields, from business and technology to the arts and academia. These success stories exemplify the resourcefulness and determination that are often born out of the challenges of migration.In the contemporary world, the experiences of the Indian diaspora offer valuable insights into the dynamics of globalization, transnational identities, and the enduring connection between people and their cultural heritage. The Indian diaspora, with its rich history and vibrant present, represents a dynamic force that contributes not only to the enrichment of its host societies but also to the broader narrative of human migration, adaptation, and cultural diversity.

References

- Fludernik, Monika. *Diaspora and Multiculturalism Common Traditions and Developments*. Overseas Press India Limited, 2009.

- Iyengar, K.R. Srinivasa. *Indian Writing in English*. Sterling Publishers Pvt. Ltd., 1995.

- Lahiri, Jhumpa. *The Namesake*. Harper Collins, 2010 (Print).

- Lal Brij V. Ed. *The Encyclopaedia of the Indian Diaspora*. Oxford University Press, 2007.

Chapter 14

Role of Indian Diaspora in Spreading the Traditional Botanical Knowledge and Agricultural Practices

Dr. Richa Pandey

Assistant Professor,
Department of Botany
Pt. D.D.U. Govt. Girls' PG College,
Rajajipuram, Lucknow
Email Address: richa11tripathi@gmail.com

Abstract

The Indian Diaspora has played a significant role in spreading traditional Indian knowledge, ranging from spices, to medicines, dyes, fabrics, religion and literature. Even various dance forms across the world depict stories of Mahabharata and Ramayana, two great Indian epics in Indian Mythology propagated by migrant Indians. Indian slaves and immigrant Indians have played an important role in the spread of Indian values (Indianness) across the world.

India is the most populated country in the world (Population 2021-2022) with more than 1.4 billion people; it ranks first in the world in population (Wikipedia). Of this, 29 million people are residing outside India as NRIs (Non-Resident Indians), as PIOs (People of Indian origin), or as OCIs (Ministry of External Affairs).

They comprise about one-third of the total Indian population. Every year, 2.5 million Indians migrate overseas, which is the highest annual number of migrants in the world, and they are the focused lot that has triggered the transfer of Traditional Botanical knowledge from India to their respective countries in which the diaspora reside. It is these immigrants who play a significant role in communicating and transferring the ancient Indian Knowledge System to the rest of the world.

Keywords: Indian Diaspora, migrants, immigrants, botanical, Indian Knowledge System.

The Western Countries received the migrant Indians with a warm welcome as most of the migrant Indians were or acted as a workforce or fell in the employee category. In the early days, before Indian Independence, many Indians were taken by the British to England and its colonies that formed the British Empire as slaves (Global Slavery Index 2023) when the "Slave Culture" was practised whereby Blacks or Asians or Indians were treated as slaves, meant largely to serve the British officers; these slaves were denied their basic human rights and were treated or looked down upon as a commodity that could be sold or bought. These included people of the young age group from 16-45 years, be it children, men, or women. Britain used India to replace the Slave Labour as Indians served or proved to be cheaper in rates than the Africans.

After the so-called slavery abolishment, Britain looked towards India as a slave-rich country and exploited India through the provision of Indian slaves in its plantations. The British Empire ever since has gone to great lengths in History to forget how it indirectly created the World's largest diaspora, the Indian diaspora. Shipped in large cruises all across Europe, America, and their allied islands like New Zealand, Australia, Solomon Islands, Zanzibar Islands, Caribbean Islands, Mauritius, Indonesia, Thailand, Bali, Malaysia, etc., with the gradual passage of time, these slave Indians permanently resided in their respective migrant countries and became their permanent residents and no longer returned to their native country, India. These people amalgamated their Indian culture with the culture of their resident countries and, in the process, tried to Indian-ise everything, from cooking to medicines, to literature and so on.

This process led to the spread of traditional Indian knowledge, for instance, the use of turmeric in food, the making of South Indian delicacies, the use of pepper, cardamom, cashew, chillies, coconut, and other spices in culinary items, etc. The use of spices as medicines largely forms the base of the Indian Medicinal System. This tradition of using various spices to treat illnesses and recover from diseases was very lucrative and attractive and was easily accepted by the West. This inherited knowledge of using specific spices for which targeted disease was passed on from migrant slaves to their Western masters through successive generations was highly valued.

It was for these reasons that migrants depended upon India for the basic raw materials that were used as spices and medicines. Plants like "Vanilla and Cinnamon" became an inseparable part of cakes and ice-creams, which were largely a Western sweet delicacy. It was India that introduced Turmeric (*Curcuma longa*) as an antiseptic to the West. Indians popularised 'Neem' (*Azadirachta Indica*) as a natural antifungal and antiseptic medicine. The Indians used Neem twigs for cleansing their teeth and for cleaning their tongue as a 'Tongue-Cleaner'. It was Indians who familiarised the West with Sandal Wood (*Santalum album*) as a natural exfoliating agent. The West was not aware of the cooling medicinal effects of Mint (*Mentha sp.*) and Tulsi (*Ocimum sanctum*). They were introduced to the use of Henna (*Lawsonia inermis*) and Hibiscus (*Hibiscus rosa sinensis*) as hair conditioners other than colouring-agents. The British became aware of the use of Indigo (*Indigo sp.*) as a blue dye and Saffron (*Zephyranthus zeylanica*) for an orange colour. Turmeric was used for the yellow colour. *Bixa orellana* (Bixa) was used as a red and maroon dye.

A large number of Indians worked as slaves in plantations and orchards of the elite, and rich British owned large farmlands and pastures. Various agricultural practices were introduced to the West over a long period. Some important ones included cuttings for Rose, Bamboo, and Bougainvillea propagation. Jackfruits were cultivated through grafting bulbs, and corms plantation was operated in the case of Onion, Garlic, and rooting vegetables like Yam, Tapioca, Colocasia, Sweet Potato, etc. Potatoes or Potato tubers were directly planted in soil for their propagation. Just leaves with nodes were required for growing ornamental plants like Money Plant (*Pothos*), Monstera, ZZ plant, String of Hearts, Palms, etc. In Indonesia and Malaysia, it was Indian slaves who propagated Coconut, Phoenix, and other ornamentals from the Palmae family with whole rhizomes or Tubers or Corms or Bulbs. Dates were propagatedand cultivated through seeds, an ancient Indian traditional knowledge tracing back to 4000 BC. Dates were used (Ramzan Fast) by Muslims across Malaysia. Even Rubber plantations and rubber harvesting techniques were introduced to Indonesia, Malaysia, and the Philippines by enslaved Indians.

A large section of South Indians were taken as slaves by the Portuguese and French Generals to Southeast Asia to reap rich harvests of Rice and Tea. South Indians worked as slaves in tea plantations, rice fields, and rubber gardens, cutting down trees for lumbering, pelching, latex collection, and leaf plucking. These slaves, during their stay, formed small social groups to continue their rich cultural Indian tradition of offering prayers to their Indian Gods like Lord Murugan, Lord Ayyappa, Goddess Laxmi, Lord Ganpati, and Lord Venkateshwara. Instead of accepting the foreign Gods, these slave groups decided to perform their own social customs, rituals, and prayers in the same manner as inherited from India. These groups built large temples (e.g., Angkor Wat, the largest temple of the world in Cambodia; Angkor Wat, a large religious monument that was built in the 12th Century for King Suryavarman II) to follow Hinduism (when several generations grouped together to form a significant part of the citizens of the foreign country in which they reside in). Similarly, Mahendra and Sanghamitra, the son and daughter of King Ashoka, were sent to Sri Lanka to spread Buddhism. Sanghamitra carried a branch of the Bodhi Tree along with her to Sri Lanka (Mahavamsa, Buddhist texts written in Sri Lanka), and this spread of Buddhism made Sri Lanka (Ceylon in the past) a Buddhist country promoting non-violence. Hinduism gained popularity and became one of the prime religions, followed by Southeast Asians. It is through them (migrant populations) that Ramayana and Mahabharata stories are still depicted in the dance forms of Thailand, Bali, Indonesia, Mauritius, Zanzibar Islands, Malaysia, etc.

Sendratari Ramayana and Wayang Wong in Indonesia (Java and Bali), Ramakien dance (Thailand), and Reamker dance (Cambodia) also depict Ramayana Stories.

Some dance forms, or *'Natya Shastra'* as they call it, are similar to *'Kathakali'* of Kerala and *'Kathak* dance' of UP, which narrate stories from great Indian epics as acts or *Natyas*. Hence, the name *'Katha'* means stories.

These dance forms, though originally from different states, yet, gained their importance and recognition as Indian dances.

The use of Pepper (*Syzygium aromaticum*) and Tea (*Thea sinensis*) in food was introduced to Southeast Asians by the migrant Indians. India was the largest exporter of tea and indigo way back in the British era. Besides, plants like the Banyan Tree. (*Ficus benghalensis*), Jasmine (*Jasminum sp.*) Lotus (*Nelumbo nucifera*), Neem Tree (*Azadirachta indica*), and Indian Mahogany (*Swietenia mahagoni*) which originated in India, were introduced to the world. Similarly fruits or edible plants like Mango (*Mangifera indica*), Banana (*Musa paradiasica*), Citrus, Jackfruit (*Ficus sp.*), Aonla (*Emblica officinalis*), Jambolana (*Syzygium jambolana*), Ber (*Ziziphus jujuba*), Bael (*Aegle marmelos*), Chironji (*Buchanania lanzan*), Ker (*Caparis decidua*), Karonda (*Carissa carandas*) were native to India, were introduced to the world.

Similarly, the following vegetables originated in India and spread across the world, Potato (*Solanum tuberosum*), Onion (*Allium cepa*) and Okra (*Abelmoschus esculentum*), Cauliflower (*Brassica oleracea var. botrytis*), Taro (*Colocasia sp.*) were constantly used by the migrant Indian Arbi population.

Following trees like Kachnar (*Bauhinia variegata*) (britannica), Amaltas (*Cassia fistula*), Pink Cassia (*Cassia nodosa*), Dhak or Flame of the Forest (*Butea Frondosa*), Indian Coral tree (*Erythrina blakei*), Pride of India (*Lagerstroemia flos-reginae*) etc., all are the trees of native land and became popular by the constant use of their flowers by migrant Indians.

Thus, the migrant Indians have played a very constructive role in spreading Indian culture, traditions, and Indianness (qualities like humility and humanity). Despite staying away from India,they have held India in high spirits, in thought and mind, and today's multiculturalism, linguism, etc., is a testimony to this Indianness.

References

- Botanical Names of Plants.www.britannica.com
- Migrant Population of India, Ministry of External Affairs. mea. gov.in
- Population Census 2022, Census of India, Ministry of Home Affairs. censusindia.gov.in
- Slavery in India (Global Slavery Index 2023). freetheslaves.net.
- Wikipedia on Demographics of India. en.m.wikipedia.org.

Chapter 15

Political Engagement: Influence and Challenges of the Indian Diaspora

Dr. Nisha Dubey

Assistant Professor
(Human Resource Management)
Dr. RML Awadh University Ayodhya
Email Address- dubeydrnisha@gmail.com

Abstract

The present paper studies the historical overview of the Indian diaspora, along with the demographic analysis, cultural contributions and identity, economic impact and remittances, political participation, challenges and opportunities, technological connectivity, impact on foreign policy, case studies of successful political engagement, challenges to unity, and future trends and prospects. The historical overview of the Indian diaspora is a multifaceted narrative spanning centuries, characterized by diverse migratory patterns and the establishment of vibrant communities across the globe. Demographic analysis of the Indian diaspora encompasses a thorough exploration of its population distribution, age structure, socio-economic characteristics, and other key demographic factors. Culture plays a vital role in shaping the character and identity of individuals. It provides a set of shared beliefs, values, customs, and practices that guide behaviour, define relationships, and create a sense of belonging. The economic impact of remittances is complex and depends on a number of factors, including the size of the remittance flow, the way in which remittances are used, and the policies of the receiving country. However, there is no doubt that remittances can have a significant positive impact on the economy of the receiving country.

Keywords: Indian diaspora, demographic analysis, historical, culture, political participation

Historical Overview of Indian Diaspora

The roots of this diaspora can be traced back to ancient times, with early Indian traders and merchants venturing beyond the Indian subcontinent for commerce and cultural exchange.

The Indian Diaspora - Past, Present and Future

Ancient Migrations

One significant historical aspect involves the migration of Indian traders along maritime routes, fostering connections with

Southeast Asia, the Middle East, and Africa. The spread of Indian cultural and religious influences, particularly through the dissemination of Hinduism and Buddhism, played a pivotal role in shaping the early diaspora.

Colonial Era Migration

The colonial era witnessed substantial Indian migration driven by British imperial expansion. Indian indentured labourers were transported to various parts of the British Empire, such as the Caribbean, Africa, and Southeast Asia, to work on plantations. This migration not only contributed to the economic prosperity of colonial powers but also led to the establishment of diasporic communities with distinct cultural identities.

Post-Independence Migration

The post-independence period saw a surge in Indian migration for diverse reasons, including educational pursuits, employment opportunities, and the search for a better quality of life. The Indian diaspora expanded globally, with significant communities forming in North America, Europe, Australia, and the Middle East.

Tech Diaspora

The latter half of the 20th century witnessed a notable wave of Indian migration driven by technology. Skilled professionals, particularly in fields like information technology, sought opportunities abroad, contributing to the formation of a highly skilled and influential diaspora, particularly in the United States.

Cultural Preservation and Adaptation

Throughout these historical phases, the Indian diaspora has demonstrated resilience in preserving its cultural heritage while adapting to the local contexts of host countries. Religious practices, languages, festivals, and traditional arts have been sustained across generations, fostering a unique diasporic identity.

Challenges and Achievements

The historical journey of the Indian diaspora is marked by both challenges and achievements. Discrimination, cultural assimilation, and struggles for acceptance have been countered by success stories of individuals and communities making significant contributions in various fields, including politics, academia, business, and the arts.

In essence, the historical overview of the Indian diaspora is a tapestry woven with threads of migration, cultural exchange, economic endeavours, and the continuous evolution of identity. It reflects the dynamic interplay between the homeland and host countries, shaping a diaspora that is not only geographically dispersed but also culturally rich and globally interconnected.

Demographic Analysis

This examination serves as a comprehensive lens through which the diverse composition of the diaspora can be understood, revealing insights into its growth, challenges, and potential impact.

The Indian diaspora is notably widespread, with substantial communities established across the globe. Major hubs are identified in countries such as the United States, Canada, the United Kingdom, Australia, the Gulf nations, and various Southeast Asian countries. This distribution analysis unveils the geographical dispersion of the diaspora.

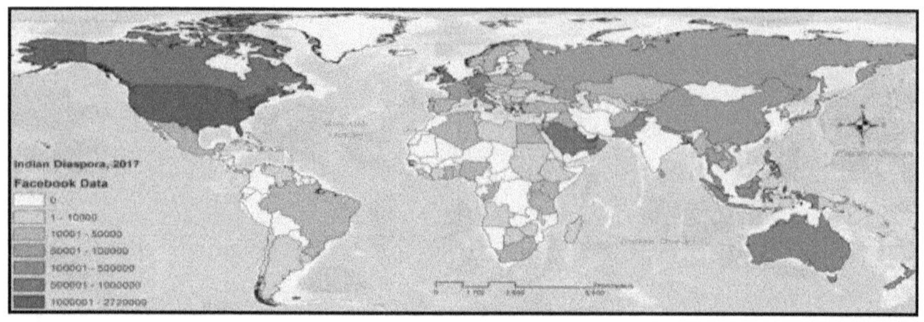

Delving into the age structure, the analysis distinguishes between different generations within the Indian diaspora. It explores the unique challenges and opportunities faced by first-generationmigrants, the experiences of second-generation individuals born in the diaspora, and the cultural transitions among subsequent generations. This generational lens proves crucial for understanding the evolving identity of the diaspora.

Educational attainment is a key focus, shedding light on the levels of academic achievement within the community. Many individuals from the diaspora have excelled in higher education, contributing significantly to fields such as science, technology, engineering, medicine, and business.

Socio-economic factors, including income levels, occupation types, and wealth distribution, are analyzed to gain a nuanced understanding of the Indian diaspora's economic standing. This encompasses both skilled professionals contributing to the knowledge economy and individuals engaged in entrepreneurial activities.

The diaspora is often characterized by a strong presence in specific professional fields, including information technology, medicine, academia, and finance. Examining these patterns provides insights into the economic contributions and influence of the diaspora.

Gender dynamics within the Indian diaspora are explored, encompassing an analysis of the roles and experiences of both men and women. This includes studying patterns of migration, educational and professional opportunities, and the evolving roles of women in diasporic communities.

Demographic analysis extends to the examination of diaspora networks and organizations. This involves analyzing the structures and activities of associations, community groups, and professional networks that connect individuals within the diaspora. These networks play a vital role in fostering a sense of community, providing support, and facilitating socio-economic collaborations.

The proficiency in language and the preservation of cultural practices within the diaspora are integral aspects of demographic analysis. This examination assesses the extent to which linguistic and cultural ties are maintained across generations and how these factors contribute to the overall identity of the diaspora.

Finally, migration trends over time are scrutinized. This involves studying patterns of immigration, emigration, and diasporic mobility, providing insights into the factors influencing these movements. In summary, a comprehensive demographic analysis of the Indian diaspora offers a nuanced understanding of its composition, challenges, and contributions. It provides a foundation for policymakers, researchers, and community leaders to make informed decisions and develop strategies that address the diverse needs of this global community.

Cultural Contributions and Identity

Culture refers to the collective characteristics and knowledge of a particular group of people, such as traditions, language, religion, food, music, norms, customs, and values. Culture can be represented in two ways: Material culture refers to physical objects or artefacts that symbolize or originate from a culture. Non-material culture refers to the intangible aspects of a culture, such as beliefs, values, and norms.

Our cultural identity is a critical piece of our personal identity (and worldview) that develops as we absorb, interpret, and adopt (or reject) the beliefs, values, behaviours, and norms of the communities in our lives. Our cultural identity can evolve, as culture is ever-evolving and dynamic.

Cultural identity is self-identification, a sense of belonging to a group that reaffirms itself. It is the extent to which one is a representative of a given culture behaviourally, communicatively, psychologically and sociologically. It consists of values, meanings, customs and beliefs used to relate to the world.

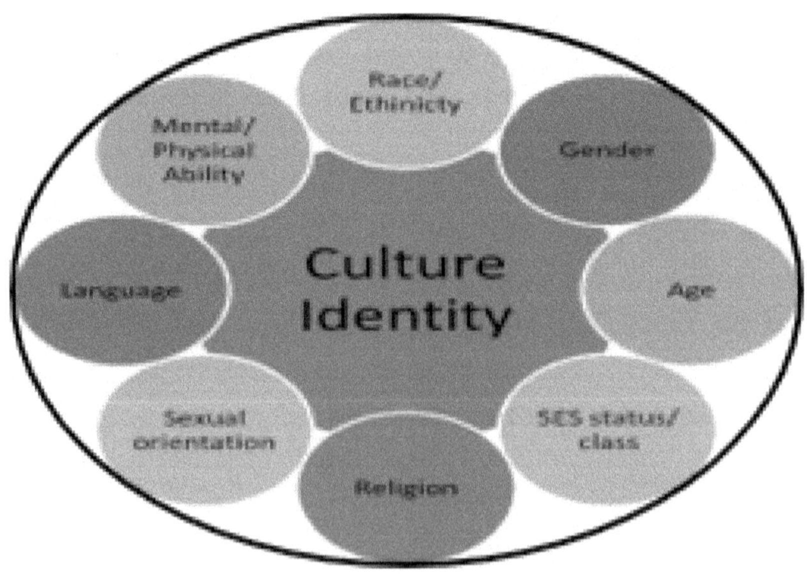

Cultural contributions are the ways in which a culture has enriched the world. They can take many forms, such as art, music, literature, science, and technology. Some examples of cultural contributions include the invention of the printing press, the development of democracy, and the creation of the Mona Lisa.

Cultural contributions are important because they help make the world more interesting and diverse. They also allow us to learn about different cultures and appreciate the unique perspectives that they offer.

Culture Fit
Culture Contribution

Here are some specific examples of how culture has contributed to society:

Art

Culture has produced some of the most iconic works of art in history, such as the Mona Lisa, the Taj Mahal, and the Great Wall of China. These works of art have inspired and fascinated people for centuries.

Music

Culture has also produced some of the most popular and enduring music in the world, such as classical music, jazz, and rock and roll. Music can bring people from all walks of life together and can help to create a sense of community.

Literature

Culture has also produced some of the most beloved and celebrated works of literature in the world, such as the Bible, the Quran, and the works of Shakespeare. Literature can teach us about different cultures and perspectives and help us better understand ourselves and the world around us.

Science

Culture has also made significant contributions to science. Some of the most important scientific discoveries in history, such as the discovery of gravity and the development of the theory of evolution, were made by people from different cultures. Science has helped us to understand the world around us and has led to many technological advancements that have improved our lives.

Technology

Culture has also contributed to the development of technology. Some of the most significant technological advancements in history, such as the invention of the printing press and the development of the computer, were made by people from different cultures. Technology has made our lives easier and more convenient and has helped us to stay connected with people all over the world.

These are just a few examples of the many ways in which culture has contributed to society. Culture is an essential part of what makes us human, and it is something that we should all be proud of.

Economic Impact and Remittances

Remittances are money that migrants send home to their families. They have a significant economic impact on both the sending and receiving countries. In many developing countries, remittances are a major source of foreign income. They can help to reduce poverty, improve living standards, and promote economic growth.

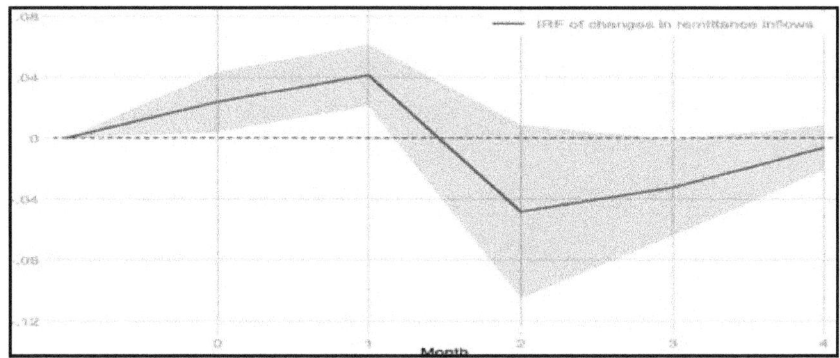

Remittances during the COVID-19 Pandemic

There are a number of ways in which remittances can have a positive impact on the economy of the receiving country. First, remittances can increase aggregate demand. When migrants send money home, their families spend it on goods and services, which boosts economic activity. Second, remittances can help to improve the balance of payments. When migrants send money home, it increases the foreign exchange reserves of the receiving country. This can help to stabilize the currency and make it easier to import goods and services. Third, remittances can help to promote financial development. When migrants send money home, they often use formal financial channels, such as banks or money transfer operators. This can help to increase access to financial services for the poor and unbanked.

There are also a number of ways in which remittances can have a negative impact on the economy of the receiving country. First, remittances can lead to inflation. When migrants send money home, it increases the money supply. This can lead to higher prices for goods and services. Second, remittances can lead to a brain drain. When skilled workers migrate, they can take their skills and knowledge with them. This can make it more difficult for the receiving country to develop its own economy. Third, remittances can lead to social problems. When migrants send money home, it can create a sense of dependence on remittances. This can make it difficult for the receiving country to develop its own economy.

Here are some specific examples of the economic impact of remittances:

- In the Philippines, remittances are a major source of foreign income. In 2017, remittances totalled $28.5 billion, which was equivalent to 9.9% of GDP. Remittances help to reduce poverty, improve living standards, and promote economic growth in the Philippines.

- In Mexico, remittances are also a major source of foreign income. In 2017, remittances totalled $28.3 billion, which was equivalent to 2.7% of GDP. Remittances help to reduce poverty, improve living standards, and promote economic growth in Mexico.

- In India, remittances are a significant source of foreign income. In 2017, remittances totalled $70.8 billion, which was equivalent to 2.2% of GDP. Remittances help to reduce poverty, improve living standards, and promote economic growth in India.

These are just a few examples of the many ways in which remittances can have a positive impact on the economy of the receiving country. Remittances are a vital source of income for many families around the world, and they play an important role in promoting economic growth and development.

Political Participation

Political participation within the context of the Indian diaspora encapsulates the engagement of individuals and communities in political processes, both within their host countries and in connection with India. This multifaceted involvement manifests through various avenues, ranging from active participation in local politics to influencing policies that impact their homeland. The exploration of political participation within the Indian diaspora chapter involves several key dimensions:

1. Local Political Engagement

   Delve into how members of the Indian diaspora actively participate in the local politics of their host countries. This includes involvement in civic activities, community organizations, and electoral processes. Understanding their roles in shaping local policies and contributing to the political landscape enhances the comprehension of their influence.

2. Lobbying and Advocacy Efforts

   Examine instances where the Indian diaspora engages in lobbying and advocacy to influence policies and decisions. This can involve addressing issues that directly impact the diaspora community or broader concerns related to India. Explore the strategies employed and the impact of these efforts on political outcomes.

3. Representation in Government

   Analyze the presence of individuals from the Indian diaspora in governmental bodies, such as elected officials, appointed representatives, or diplomats. Understanding their representation provides insights into the diaspora's visibility and influence within the political structures of host countries.

4. Transnational Political Connections

Explore how the Indian diaspora maintains political ties with India, contributing to transnational political engagement. This can include participating in Indian elections, supporting political causes in India, and fostering diplomatic relations between their host countries and India.

5. Political Activism and Social Movements

Investigate instances of political activism and involvement in social movements by members of the Indian diaspora. This can range from advocating for human rights to participating in movements that address issues affecting India and its global image.

6. Media and Communication Influence

Examine the role of the diaspora in shaping political narratives through media and communication channels. This includes diasporic media outlets, social media activism, and the impact of their voices on public opinion, both in host countries and globally.

7. Challenges and Opportunities in Political Engagement

Discuss the challenges faced by the Indian diaspora in actively participating in politics, such as navigating diverse political landscapes, addressing discrimination, and balancing dual allegiances. Highlight opportunities for increased political engagement and collaboration.

8. Electoral Contributions and Campaign Financing

Explore the role of the Indian diaspora in electoral contributions, campaign financing, and its impact on political candidates and parties in both host countries and India. Investigate the motivations behind such financial support and its implications.

9. Political Awareness and Education

Examine efforts within the Indian diaspora to enhance political awareness and education. This includes initiatives to inform the community about political processes, encourage voter participation, and foster a deeper understanding of political issues.

Challenges and Opportunities

Challenges and Opportunities in the Political Engagement of the Indian Diaspora:

Challenges

1. Cultural and Ideological Diversity:The Indian diaspora is characterized by a rich tapestry of cultural and ideological diversity. While this diversity is a strength, it also poses challenges in fostering unified political engagement. Negotiating differences in political perspectives and priorities can be complex.

2. Integration and Dual Allegiance: Balancing integration into host societies while maintaining connections to India presents a challenge. The diaspora may grapple with questions of dual allegiance, especially when political issues in host countries may differ from those in India.

3. Discrimination and Xenophobia:Instances of discrimination and xenophobia can impede the political participation of the Indian diaspora. Overcoming stereotypes and biases is a persistent challenge, influencing the extent to which individuals feel empowered to engage in political processes.

4. Limited Representation: Despite contributions, the representation of the Indian diaspora in key political positions may be limited. Overcoming barriers to political office, breaking through glass ceilings, and achieving proportional representation remain challenges for the diaspora.

5. Transnational Legal Barriers: Navigating transnational legal frameworks and understanding the nuances of political systems in both host countries and India poses challenges. Legal barriers, including voting eligibility and participation in political activities, vary and may hinder engagement.

Opportunities

1. Civic Empowerment through Education: Opportunities lie in enhancing civic education within the diaspora community. By promoting political awareness and understanding of democratic processes, individuals can be empowered to actively participate in politics, bridging gaps in knowledge.

2. Technology and Digital Activism: The digital age presents unique opportunities for the Indian diaspora to engage in political activism. Leveraging technology, social media, and digital platforms allows for effective communication, awareness campaigns, and mobilization of support.

3. Collaborative Advocacy: Collaborative advocacy on common issues provides opportunities for the Indian diaspora to amplify its political impact. Building alliances with other communities

and interest groups enhances the collective voice and influence in shaping policies.

4. Youth Mobilization: Recognizing the potential of youth engagement, opportunities exist in mobilizing the younger generation within the diaspora. Initiatives focusing on youth empowerment, education, and mentorship can cultivate future leaders and political influencers.

5. Diaspora Networks and Organizations: The existence of diaspora networks and organizations creates platforms for political engagement. These entities can serve as catalysts for collaboration, information exchange, and coordinated efforts to address challenges faced by the community.

6. Political Diplomacy and Bridge-Building: The diaspora's unique position as a bridge between host countries and India presents opportunities for political diplomacy. By actively participating in diplomatic efforts, the diaspora can contribute to fostering positive relations and influencing policies.

7. Global Advocacy for India: Opportunities exist for the diaspora to engage in global advocacy for India. Through participation in international forums, lobbying efforts, and contributions to global discourse, the diaspora can shape narratives and perceptions about India.

In navigating the challenges and seizing opportunities, the Indian diaspora's political engagement evolves as a dynamic force, contributing not only to the host countries' political landscapes but also influencing policies that impact their homeland. The interplay of challenges and opportunities underscores the resilience and potential of the diaspora's political involvement on the global stage.

Technological Connectivity

Technology connectivity for the Indian diaspora represents the transformative influence of technological advancements on communication, community engagement, and cultural preservation within the diaspora. This phenomenon encompasses various dimensions that shape the way individuals connect, collaborate, and contribute to both their host countries and India.

1. Social Media and Virtual Communities

   The widespread use of social media platforms facilitates real-time communication and community building. The Indian diaspora leverages these platforms to create virtual communities, fostering connections, sharing experiences, and organizing events across geographical boundaries.

2. Digital Communication Platforms

   The accessibility of digital communication tools, such as video conferencing and messaging apps, has transformed how the diaspora stays connected with family and friends in India. It serves as a bridge that transcends physical distances, strengthening interpersonal relationships.

3. Cultural Exchange through Online Platforms

   Online platforms provide avenues for cultural exchange within the diaspora. From virtual cultural events and language classes to collaborative artistic projects, technology enables the preservation and celebration of Indian culture among diasporic communities.

4. Political Activism and Advocacy Online

The diaspora actively engages in political activism and advocacy through online channels. Social media platforms serve as powerful tools for raising awareness about political issues, organizing campaigns, and mobilizing support for causes related to India or the diaspora.

5. E-Learning and Skill Development

Technology facilitates e-learning opportunities for the diaspora, allowing individuals to access education and skill development resources. Online courses and virtual workshops empower members of the diaspora to enhance their knowledge and professional skills.

6. Digital Entrepreneurship and Business Networks

The diaspora contributes to the global economy through digital entrepreneurship. Technology enables the establishment of online businesses, and digital platforms connect diasporic entrepreneurs, fostering collaboration and economic growth.

7. Information Access and News Dissemination

Technology ensures timely access to information and news from both host countries and India. Online news portals, social media, and digital publications keep the diaspora informed about current events, fostering a sense of global connectivity.

8. Genealogy and Family History Research

Technology aids the diaspora in exploring genealogy and family history. Online databases, digital archives, and genealogy platforms enable individuals to trace their roots, fostering a deeper connection to their heritage.

9. Virtual Events and Celebrations

The diaspora utilizes technology to organize and participate in virtual events and celebrations. From religious festivals to cultural performances, technology ensures that diasporic communities can come together and celebrate important occasions regardless of physical proximity.

10. Philanthropy and Crowdfunding

Technology plays a role in diasporic philanthropy through online crowdfunding platforms. The diaspora can support charitable causes in India or initiatives within their host countries, contributing to social impact and community development.

In essence, technology connectivity for the Indian diaspora transcends geographic boundaries, fostering a dynamic and interconnected global community. It empowers individuals to maintain cultural ties, engage in political activism, pursue educational opportunities, and contribute to the socio-economic fabric of both their host countries and India.

Impact on Foreign Policy

Foreign policy refers to a government's strategy and approach in dealing with other nations. It encompasses a set of principles, goals, and actions designed to safeguard national interests, promote international cooperation, and maintain peaceful relations on the global stage. Foreign policy extends across various domains, including diplomacy, trade, security, and cultural exchanges.

Impact on Foreign Policy within the Indian Diaspora:

1. Diplomatic Bridge-Building

   a) The Indian diaspora acts as a diplomatic bridge between host countries and India.- Diaspora members engage in cultural diplomacy, fostering positive relations and mutual understanding.

   b) Contributions to foreign policy objectives by enhancing people-to-people ties and promoting India's soft power.

2. Political Representation and Advocacy

   a) Diaspora involvement in host country politics influences foreign policy decisions.Elected diaspora members can advocate for policies aligning with India's interests.

   b) Political lobbying and advocacy contribute to a nuanced understanding of diaspora concerns in foreign policy circles.

3. Economic Contributions and Trade Ties

   a) Economic success of the diaspora enhances India's economic standing globally.Diasporic entrepreneurs and professionals contribute to trade relations and investment.

   b) Economic influence becomes a factor in shaping foreign policy decisions that impact India.

4. Crisis Response and Humanitarian Efforts

   a) Diaspora involvement in crisis response and humanitarian efforts projects a positive image of India.

   b) Mobilization of diaspora resources during global crises contributes to India's foreign policy goals.

   c) Diaspora networks can play a role in fostering international cooperation during emergencies.

5. Cultural Diplomacy and Soft Power

    a) Cultural initiatives by the diaspora enhance India's soft power globally.

    b) Promotion of Indian arts, language, and traditions contributes to positive perceptions.

    c) Soft power influence aids in shaping diplomatic relations and foreign policy narratives.

6. Advocacy for India's Global Role

    a) Diaspora members often advocate for India's rightful place on the global stage.

    b) Contributions to think tanks, policy forums, and international organizations shape narratives.

    c) Diaspora involvement influences perceptions of India's role in global affairs.

7. Diaspora Networks and Track II Diplomacy

    a) Informal diplomacy through diaspora networks contributes to Track II diplomatic efforts.

    b) Diaspora members participate in dialogues, fostering communication between countries.

    c) Track II diplomacy complements official channels, influencing foreign policy discussions.

8. Influence on Immigration Policies

    a) Diaspora engagement influences host countries' immigration policies.

    b) Advocacy for favourable immigration regulations aligns with India's diaspora-centric foreign policy goals.

   c) Immigration policies impact the movement and integration of diaspora members.

9. Leveraging Digital Connectivity

   a) Technology enables the diaspora to influence foreign policy through digital means.

   b) Social media activism and online campaigns raise awareness about diaspora-related issues.

   c) Digital platforms amplify diaspora voices, influencing public opinion and diplomatic considerations.

10. Global Diaspora Networks and Collaboration

   a) Collaboration between different diaspora communities globally fosters a united front.

   b) Joint efforts amplify the diaspora's impact on foreign policy, especially in addressing shared concerns.

   c) Global diaspora networks contribute to a collaborative approach in influencing diplomatic relations.

Case Studies of Successful Political Engagement

Examining case studies of successful political engagement within the Indian diaspora unveils compelling narratives of individuals or groups who have effectively navigated political landscapes, making significant contributions. These cases provide nuanced insights into the strategies, challenges, and achievements of those actively involved in shaping policies and political discourse.

One notable case is that of Indian-American politician Kamala Harris. Her journey from serving as the Attorney General of California to becoming the Vice President of the United States illustrates how a member of the Indian diaspora can attain high political office. Harris's political engagement showcases the importance of strategic career progression, effective communication, and building coalitions to achieve political success.

In the United Kingdom, the case of Priti Patel exemplifies successful political engagement within the Indian diaspora. As the Home Secretary, Patel has played a crucial role in shaping immigration policies and internal security measures. Her ascent in British politics highlights the influence of the Indian diaspora on policy decisions, particularly in areas directly impacting the community.

Beyond individual success stories, the case of the Indian-American political advocacy group, AAPI Victory Fund, demonstrates the collective impact of diaspora organizations. By mobilizing resources and leveraging political networks, the AAPI Victory Fund has actively worked to increase the political representation of Asian Americans and Pacific Islanders, including those of Indian descent. This case underscores the role of diaspora groups in shaping political landscapes and advocating for community interests.

In Canada, the successful political engagement of Harjit Sajjan stands out. As the Minister of National Defence, Sajjan, of Punjabi descent, has exemplified how individuals from the Indian diaspora can attain key positions in government. His case underscores the importance of expertise, leadership, and commitment to public service in achieving political success.

These case studies collectively illustrate the diverse paths to successful political engagement within the Indian diaspora. From elected officials breaking barriers to advocacy groups influencing policies, these narratives offer valuable lessons on the strategies and determination required to navigate and excel in political arenas. They serve as inspirations for the diaspora community, showcasing the potential impact of active political participation on a global scale.

Challenges to Unity

Challenges to Unity within the Indian Diaspora

The concept of unity within the Indian diaspora is inherently complex, marked by a tapestry of regional, cultural, and socio-economic diversities. One significant challenge arises from the diverse cultural backgrounds that members bring from different regions of India. While this diversity is a source of strength, it simultaneously becomes a challenge as individuals navigate varied traditions, languages, and customs. Bridging these cultural gaps to foster a cohesive identity becomes an ongoing struggle, especially as subsequent generations navigate dual cultural influences.

Economic disparities within the diaspora present another formidable challenge. The wide spectrum of socio-economic statuses, ranging from highly successful professionals to those facing economic hardships, contributes to internal divisions. Striking a balance between addressing the diverse needs of this economically heterogeneous community and fostering a sense of collective identity requires careful navigation.

Geographic dispersion further exacerbates challenges to unity. The Indian diaspora is spread across the globe, with distinct communities facing unique local circumstances. This physical distance, coupled with different host-country contexts, hinders seamless communication and collaboration. The challenge lies not only in maintaining connections with the homeland but also in fostering a sense of shared destiny among dispersed individuals.

Political affiliations and divergent views on global and regional politics add another layer of complexity. Influenced by host-country politics and evolving perspectives, the diaspora finds itself navigating differing political landscapes. This challenge is heightened by historical and regional political differences within India itself, leading to internal debates and potential fractures in unity when it comes to political engagement.

Generational shifts pose an ongoing challenge to unity within the Indian diaspora. As subsequent generations grow up in diverse cultural environments, transmitting cultural values and maintaining a diasporic identity become more intricate. Balancing traditional values with the influences of the host culture often leads to intergenerational tensions, impacting the cohesion of the diaspora.

Religious diversity, with members following various faiths, presents both a source of richness and a potential challenge. While religious pluralism is integral to the Indian diaspora's identity, it can also lead to internal divisions. Negotiating differences in religious practices, beliefs, and rituals requires delicate handling to maintain a sense of shared cultural heritage.

In conclusion, the challenges to unity within the Indian diaspora arise from a dynamic interplay of cultural, economic, geographic, political, generational, and religious factors. Addressing these challenges requires a nuanced understanding of the complexities within the diaspora, fostering inclusive dialogues, and developing strategies that celebrate diversity while nurturing a cohesive sense of identity.

Future Trends and Prospects

The future for the Indian diaspora unfolds against a backdrop of evolving global dynamics and shifting socio-cultural landscapes. One notable trend that is expected to shape the diaspora's trajectory is the deepening integration of technology. As digital connectivity becomes even more pervasive, the diaspora will likely harness advanced communication tools to strengthen its bonds, engage in virtual cultural exchanges, and play an increasingly influential role in shaping narratives on global platforms.

Economic prospects for the Indian diaspora are poised for expansion. With a growing number of individuals achieving prominence in diverse fields, from technology to entrepreneurship, the diaspora is likely to continue making significant contributions to the global economy. Investment in innovation, startups, and knowledge-based industries is anticipated to be a key driver, fostering a new era of economic collaboration and entrepreneurship.

The political landscape is likely to witness increased diaspora participation and influence. As more individuals from the Indian diaspora assume political offices globally, there is a growing potential for collaborative efforts to address shared challenges. The diaspora's role in shaping international policies and influencing global perspectives on India is expected to amplify, contributing to a more interconnected and diplomatically engaged global community.

Cultural preservation and revitalization are critical aspects that will define the future of the Indian diaspora. Amidst the challenges of assimilation and generational shifts, there is a growing awareness of the need to preserve cultural heritage. Initiatives leveraging digital platforms, educational programs, and community events are likely to gain momentum, ensuring that future generations maintain a strong connection to their roots.

The concept of a unified diasporic identity is poised for redefinition. While diversity remains a hallmark, there is a palpable push toward fostering a shared sense of identity and purpose within the diaspora. Initiatives that celebrate cultural commonalities, embrace inclusivity, and navigate generational transitions are expected to shape a more cohesive diasporic community.

As environmental consciousness gains prominence globally, sustainability and social responsibility are likely to become integral to the diaspora's endeavours. Initiatives addressing climate change, social justice, and community well-being are anticipated to gain momentum, reflecting a broader commitment to leaving a positive impact on both host countries and India.

In summary, the future trends and prospects for the Indian diaspora encompass a dynamic interplay of technological advancements, economic growth, political engagement, cultural preservation, identity redefinition, and a heightened commitment to global issues. Embracing these trends, the diaspora is poised to play an increasingly influential role, contributing to a more interconnected and vibrant global landscape.

References

- Bauböck, Rainer and Faist, Thomas, editors. *Diaspora and Transnationalism: Concepts, Theories, and Methods*. Amsterdam UP, 2010.

- Ghassem-Fachandi, Parvis. *Indian Diaspora: Historical and Contemporary Contexts*. Routledge, 2017.

- Joshi, Khyati Y. *Indian Diaspora in the United States: Brain Drain or Gain*. Lexington Books, 2017.

Chapter 16

Negotiating Black Identity in England: A Study of Buchi Emecheta's *Second Class Citizen*

Dr. Shradha Gupta

Assistant Professor
Department of English
RMP PG College, Sitapur.
Email Address- shraddhaseemagupta@gmail.com

Abstract

The concept of blackness is socio-political. This collective identityrefers to all the people from Africa and the Caribbean Islands to Europe. In search of better prospects for their lives, the majority of people from colonised nations relocate to England. It has never been easy for them to survive among White people. Individuals from African nations often experience institutional and systemic discrimination based on their race, as well as violations of their fundamental rights. BuchiEmecheta is a prolific writer and cross-culturalfigure from Nigeria who later immigrated to the United Kingdom. Her writings are genuine accounts of black women's experiences in Nigeria and abroad.BuchiEmecheta belongs to the second generation of African women writers. She authentically records the travails of the black diaspora in many of her novels, such as *Second Class Citizen, In the Ditch* and *Kehinde.*This paper is an attempt to explore the experience of a black woman immigrant in England through the analysis of BuchiEmecheta's novel *Second Class Citizen.*

Keywords: Black British diaspora, racism, sexism

Diaspora is simply a displacement of a community into another geographical and cultural origin. The word diaspora is derived from the Greek meaning to scatter or disperse. The word was originally used for Black British Diaspora and is an umbrella term that is used for people of African and Caribbean origin. Stuart Hall, a key figure in Cultural Studies, observed that the formation of the Black diaspora in the period of post-war migration in the fifties and sixties had transformed English social, economic and political life (Hall, 148). Stuart Hall further recalls the history of the construction of Black in England. According to Hall, Black was created as a political category in a certain historical moment. Things were not like this when he was in Jamaica, as the word Black was never uttered. Hall states: "Black is not a question of pigmentation. The black I am talking about is a historical category, a political category; a cultural category". (148)

Thus, the racial identity of the people coming from the African, Caribbean, and Asian sub-continent all were politically constructed. They were different from Europeans, so they were categorized as others. Paul Gilroy, in his essay "The Black Atlantic," questions racial identity as he sees race as intercultural.

Black people constitute almost 10 per cent of the British population now. The people migrating from Afro-Caribbean countries had to face racism in Britain. In the case of black women immigrants, they face plurality of oppression due to their race, gender and class. Any person from a commonwealth nation who belonged to the working class was more likely to encounter oppression as compared to the people who belonged to the high class. As Pramod Kumar Nayar rightly observes,

> The experience of nomadicity is different for migrant labour and the African woman. In these latter cases they cannot escape their racial or ethnic identity because their gender and class mark them different - a difference that cannot be overcome just because they have reached the first world. (Nayar, 180)

> Eminent post-colonial critics such as Rushdie and Bhabha, who had written on in-between identity and obviously belonged to a higher class, did not focus on the experience of working-class women migrants from Asia or Africa in the first-world nations as empowered migrants or as dependent, racially marked minorities. (Nayar, 180)

BuchiEmecheta, the Nigerian-born writer, was one of those migrants who sailed to England to avail better opportunities for education and career following her husband, Sylvester Onwardi. BuchiEmecheta is a prolific cross-cultural writer who has more than 13 books, children's stories, and radio plays to her credit. Her writings are authentic accounts showcasing the lives of black women in and across her country, Nigeria. She has experienced being a black woman immigrant in a country where blackness is marginalized, and in her case, this peripheral position was more serious as she was a woman. Her fiction is structured by her ideological position that moves between her identity as an African woman and as a diaspora writer living in England. In an interview with Jussawala and Reed

Dosenbrock, she speaks of her experience of being black in the United Kingdom:

> Yes and No. There's discrimination here too. When you come here, the Westerner will say, —You are Black. Okay. And that again, is bad. And the West Indian will say —You are African. The Asian will say —You are African. And so when they say black writer, the Asian finds that it suits them to be black when it pays. But when it's not, it suits them to be white. They are black when they know there is something to gain and —white at other times. They are still on that borderline. There are always these fractions I think it's human. And writers explore these themes always because they are there. Many write from the totality of their lived experience. (90)

Emecheta's semi-autobiographical novel *Second Class Citizen* chronicles the experience of a black woman in the United Kingdom by tracing the trials and tribulations of Adah, an alter ego of Emecheta, from her childhood to maturity. Originally published in 1974, this coming-of-age novel addresses the issues of intersectionality or the way the protagonist's race and gender affect her socio-economic marginalization.The journey of Adah's life begins by struggling against the patriarchal system that has dominated the Igbo culture and then against racism being practised in London, where she migrates along with her family. The novel recounts her struggle against the joint forces of colonization and patriarchy. Adah, being born in a traditional Igbo society, is not untouched by the dogmas prevalent in her society as she faces many ordeals in acquiring an education. For instance, Adah's parents, especially her mother, do not support her education, and the death of her father exacerbates the situation and dims the prospects of her advancement.

However, Adah continues her struggle against such hostile societal norms and succeeds in accomplishing her education. While serving the family of her uncle as an unpaid servant, the desire to get an education prompts her, and she experiences the presence of some inner force, a super personal factor – a presence that encourages her constantly to fight against her secondary status for being a female, especially a black female Adah visualizes this presence from early childhood to her maturity which leads her to female empowerment. Emecheta's mouthpiece, Adah, sees education as a weapon to fight against discriminatory practices and to liberate her from the stronghold of racism and sexism.

England attracted the natives of colonized nations like heaven. As was said to her by her father, who voiced it in a hushed tone, wearing such a respectful expression as if he were speaking of God's holiest of holies. Going to the United Kingdom was paying a visit to God. Adah, too, fostered a dream that she would go to the United Kingdom one day that live with her like 'presence' (*Second Class Citizen,* 16). Buchi Emecheta relates this to her own experience of welcoming a lawyer, Nweze, who had returned to his village after paying a visit to God's kingdom. Adah's self-motivating spirit and perseverance made her accomplish her dream of getting a scholarship for further education. As a result of her brilliant performanceon the school leaving examination, she succeeded in procuring the job of librarian at the African consulate in Lagos.

Adah's decision to marry Francis turns out to be imprudent as she thought that Francis would prove to be a pliant husband, but her expectations were not fulfilled. After marriage, Adah consented to the cultural expectations by conforming to the norms set for the ideal wife who produced children, did domestic chores and took care of her husband and his family, and more importantly, she supported them financially,keeping them all going. Even Francis decides to go abroad to continue his studies in England. The first phase of migration (1960s - 1970s) consisted of restrained migration from a few African countries, namely Nigeria and Ghana, and was driven by the desire to acquire education (Domboka, 1). The males were given priority. Adah, though she was not accompanying him, was contented with the fact that she would be there soon as it was her childhood dream to go to the United Kingdom.

Adah's emigration to the United Kingdom is through realising her dreams, but gradually, she learns the truth behind the fantasy. She could deconstruct the meaning of her father's words, 'God's Kingdom.' Her landing on the shore of Liverpool dashed out all her excitement. She, along with all the people of colonized countries, believed and got attracted by England as coming here was compared to paying God a visit. However, she did not receive a warm welcome as she expected rather, she confronted the harsh reality of racial discrimination. She travelled as a first-class citizen, but as she landed in Liverpool, England, she became a second-class citizen.

Emecheta raises the issue of alienation of the West as compared to the warmth of Africa. English education, which she had received after going through many ordeals, made her securea first-class job in her own country, but here in London, she was nothing but a black immigrant only entitled to blue-collar jobs. Her arrival in London makes her reflect on her situation that she has 'run out of the frying pan into the fire' by migrating to London. In Adah's case, things were such that she not only faced gender discrimination but also the grave problem of racial discrimination, something that shattered her dreams of the United Kingdom being an auspicious place just like heaven.

In his essay "Old and New Identities," Stuart Hall recalls his own experience in Jamaica, that people of Jamaica were either black or coloured, but they never referred to themselves as black.

But the word "black" was never uttered. Why? No blacks around? Lots of them, thousands and thousands of them. Black is not a question of pigmentation. The black I am talking about is a historical category, a political category, a cultural category. (Hall,149)

Francis, being a dominating husband, is more offensive towards her and makes her realize about the second-class status in England. Unaffected by his constant failures, he keeps on inflicting all sorts of verbal and sexual brutalities on Adah. Through the depiction of violence between Adah and Francis, Emecheta unleashes the taboo of domestic violence affecting the lives of most African women. The situation is exacerbated in England, where Adah does not find any support.

While living in London, Adah confronts several problems of accommodation and survival due to being a black immigrant. She is astonished to have such a small place for lodging as, according to her husband, who has internalized that second-class status, but Adah finds it quite unacceptable for her as she was qualified for a higher job. This gives a chance to Francis to throw a sarcastic remark:

You must know, my dear young lady, that in Lagos you may be a million publicity officers for the Americans; you may be earning a million pounds a day; you may have hundreds of servants: You may be living like an élite, but the day you land in England, you are a second-class citizen. So you can't discriminate against your own people, because we are all second-class (*Second Class Citizen* 39)

Their neighbours are mostly workers, and Adah, who had been enjoying a first-class status, does not expect to live in the neighbourhood of such people whom she would only hire as her servants in her native country. Francis also expects Adah to work in a garment factory like other women in the neighbourhood.

Adah is shocked that Francis has internalized the inferior status, but Adah is not ready to make any compromise. She knew that his feeling of blackness was firmly housed in his mind. She seeks to challenge this white superiority. Francis informs Adah about the racial discrimination:

You see, accommodation is very short in London, especially for the black people with children. Everybody is coming to London. The West Indians, the Pakistanis, the Indians …We are all blacks, all coloured, and the only houses we can get horrors like these. (*Second Class Citizen* 38)

The English people look at all the brown-coloured foreigners as the same and never wish to have them settled in their own neighbourhood. Avtar Brah observes that each form of racism has a particular history. She compares the Anti-black and anti-Irish racism and finds that, as for the white Europeans, the Irish are placed in a dominant position in comparison to Black people even though they may share a similar class location. (Brah, 436)

Francis is a second-class citizen in London, but as far as Adah is concerned, she is a double second-class citizen as she faces multiple oppression.Emecheta says in an interview that she is a bit of both; first, she is a woman in her society, a second-class citizen and coming here, she becomes a double second-class citizen because she is black as well. (Buchi Emecheta Interview, 00.59-1:04)

Francis keeps on telling Adah that she is nothing but a second-class citizen in Britain as he says, "You keep on forgetting that you are a woman and that you are black. The white man can barely tolerate us men, to say nothing of brainless females like you who could think of nothing except how to breast feed your baby". (*Second Class Citizen*, 167)

Because of their pigmentation, Francis and Adah undergo many troubles such as hiring a babysitter, hunting for accommodation, or getting jobs. Most of black people are not allowed to have their children living with them, so they are asked to send them to foster parents, and the foster mother has to be white as – only first-class citizens live with their children, not the blacks (*Second Class Citizen*, 47). It again proves the racial prejudices and the superiority of whites as they are considered better in everything they do in comparison with black people. As Adah observes:

No one cares whether a woman was suitable or not, no one wanted to know whether the house was clean or not: all they wanted to be sure was that foster mother was white. The concept of whiteness could cover a multitude sins. (*Second Class Citizen*, 44)

Adah's perception of the whites was based on the experience she had lived throughout her life. As she could never think of a white man being a liar before coming into contact with Trudy:

As for Adah, she listened to Trudy destroying forever one of the myths she had been brought up to believe: that the white men never lied. She had grown among the white missionaries who were dedicated to their work, she had then worked among

American diplomats who were working for their country in Nigeria and she came to England she had actually missed with the girls in the library and Janet. (*Second Class Citizen*, 52-53)

The whole incident made her realize the fact that the whites were as fallible as everyone else —There were bad whites and good whites, just as there were bad blacks and good blacks! Why, then, did they claim to be superior? (*Second Class Citizen*, 53) Adah faces racism severely when she finds that her sick son Vicky is taken to Royal Free Hospital, and the doctor who was treating him is biased and advised Adah to do so. The narrator reflects:

> Now an ambulance was speeding her to the royal free? Was it a hospital for the poor people, for second class people? Why did they put the word free in it? Fear started to shroud her? Were they sending her Vicky to second class hospital, a free one because they were blacks? (*Second Class Citizen*, 60)

Francis, whose changed behaviour she had noticed when he had come to receive her. Since all the privileges were for the whites, the outsiders, especially of different races, were to adopt such strategies in order to be like them. Frantz Fanon, in his book *Black Skin White Masks*, argues that language is a powerful tool to rival the —other. To speak a language is to assume a culture and —to support the weight of civilization (17-18). Language is the first way to adapt to that social equilibrium. Francis, who has proved an absolute failure in England, scolds Titi for speaking the Yoruba language and forces her to speak the English language because he thinks that the English language symbolises intelligence. His constant intimidation makes Titi behave strangely.

Adah's realization of her second-class status becomes more apparent when she, along with Francis, starts hunting for accommodation as the place where they were living earlier was not perfect one, but all their expectations offinding a perfect accommodation are shattered when they face the racist notifications by the landlords. The whites were reluctant to allow any black person in their house or locality. Nearly all the offices had — Sorry, no coloureds on them. Her house hunting was made more difficult because she was black, black with two very young children and pregnant with another one. She was beginning to learn that her colour was something she was supposed to be ashamed of (*Second Class Citizen*, 70). While making an appointment with a landlady, Adah mimics the British accent, but she is caught. Homi Bhabha, in *Location of a Culture*, defines mimicry as a tool to come into the cultural ghetto of people showing themselves as superior and powerful. And it has been observed that people mimic the language, accent, and lifestyle to defy their own inferiority among people belonging to superior races. Francis's compulsion to learn how to speak English like the British is an example of such practice.

> Adah and Francis were ready to pay double rent but they face disappointment in getting suitable accommodation. Adah keeps on reflecting about the myths she had believed about the whites and the reality she faces in England. She wishes even they could paint their faces until the first rent (*Second Class Citizen* 64)

The novel questions the traditional gender roles where the males are assigned to provide for the family, and women are confined to household management. Francis, who could not succeed in his previous exams, does not think about earning money and providing for the family instead, he squanders the hard-earned money of Adah. He does not wish to shoulder the responsibility of looking after his children and pours out his frustration. He blames his children as the cause of his failure. He becomes more aggressive and demanding and expects total subservience from his wife, Adah. He sometimes looks at Adah with new eyes as the narrator observes:

> Somebody had warned him that the greatest mistake an African could make was to bring an educated girl to London and let her mix with the middle-class English women. They soon know their rights. What was happening to them? he wondered. (*Second Class Citizen,* 64)

Education and self-reliance have somewhat brought a transformation in Adah. She argues with Francis equally for her rights. When she discovers Francis with Trudy, she reacts like a tigress threatening them to kill: Adah, though being a much educated and financially self-dependent woman, cannot escape from this. Adah compares and contrasts the life she spent in Lagos and here in London, and she feels that in Lagos, it was quite possible to share one's personal problems, frustration, and anger with the neighbours, but in England, everyone was too preoccupied to take an interest in other's affairs. Francis' failure as a student brings more trouble to Adah as he pours out his frustration on Adah, accusing her of being the reason for his constant failure.

Not only Adah and Francis but all the migrants depicted in the novels have been the target of racism. Mr Noble was one of the African migrants who had come to England with an aspiration to become a cultural elite, but he could not accomplish his dream and became a lift operator. He is teased by his co-workers, who would ask him to perform African tricks just for their amusement, and he would readily perform. Those mates working with him asked him to remove his trousers in order to show them the tails of the Africans they had heard in the stories. This incident made him popular, and he got an English name Mr Noble for his clownish activities (*Second Class Citizen,* 82)

Despite these travails, Adah does not yield to the adverse circumstances surrounding her life. Adah never acceptedsecond-class status, and she continued to make adjustments by confronting the laws the black people lived by, she worked with first-class people and did everything to ensure a better living for her family. Francis is a failure in his studies, and he is a failure in personal development, he chooses to be a corrupt second-class citizen, whereas Adah moves forward, and in Homi Bhabha's term in the third space, she constructs an existence where she benefits from the opportunities and legal systems and rights of the United Kingdom (B.Erol, 593). Her colleagues encourage her to write. Her first novel, which her husband finally burned, was the height of her suffering. When Adah pleads with Francis to read the manuscript of her first novel, he snubs at her, —You keep forgetting that you are a woman and that you are black (*Second Class Citizen*, 167). His sexist remarks were to demoralize her as it was quite unbearable for him to see —a woman writer in his own house, in a white man's country. (*Second Class Citizen*,167)

The novel ends in the court with Francis disowning Adah. He takes away the documents, including the marriage certificate, and Adah and her children are left alone. Adah is hailed as —Nnenna (*Second Class Citizen*, 174).

A single mother with five children in England is left alone with new challenges, which Emecheta has recorded in her other novel, *In the Ditch.*

The study of her novel offers a new perspective to explore the life of a black woman immigrant who not only faces alienation and deprivation but also multiple forms of oppression.

Conclusion

BuchiEmecheta's semi-autobiographical novel *Second Class Citizen* projects the nuances of the experience of a black. The novel traces the journey of a black woman immigrant, her romanticization with England, and then her encounter with reality and her emancipation. She adapts to the foreign land without shedding her own cultural identity. She protests against social injustice and eventually succeeds in carving her own identity. There has always been a huge demand for the inclusion of black history in British history, and schemes for their welfare are being implemented, but still, the issues of xenophobic attacks are of global concern. The experiences of immigrants, especially black women immigrants, provide a new dimension to diaspora studies and help understand the multiple folds of oppression women from Afro-Caribbean countries face in first-world countries.

References

- Brah, Avtar. "Difference, Diversity, Differentiation: Process of Racialisation and Gender." *Theories of Race and Racism: A Reader*, edited by Les Back and John Solomos, Routledge, 1999.

- "Buchi Emecheta Interview | Civil Rights | woman's rights" Youtube, uploaded by Thames TV.13th July 2018 http://youtu. be/KJPIJ8JpOFk

- Domboka, Thomas. "The Migration History of Black Africans to Britain." *IGI Global eBooks*, 2019, pp. 1–18. https://doi. org/10.4018/978-1-5225-6918-3.ch001.

- Emecheta, Buchi. *Second Class Citizen*. George Brazilier, 1975.

- Erol, Burçin. "Destination England: Buchi Emecheta's *Second Class Citizen* and Caryl Phillips's *The Final Passage*." Neohelicon, vol. 46, no. 2, 2019, pp. 591-99. doi:10.1007/s11059-019-00492-

- Fanon, Frantz. *Black Skin White Masks*. Translated by Charles Lam Markman. Grove P, 1967.

- Gilroy, Paul. "The Black Atlantic: Modernity and Double Consciousness." *African American Review*, vol.31, no.3, Jan.1997, p.506. doi.org/10.2307/3042577.

- Hall, Stuart. "Old and New Identities, Old and New Ethnicities." *Theories of Race and Racism: A Reader*, edited by Les Back and John Solomos, Routledge, 1999, pp. 144-53.

- Jussawala, Feroza, and Reed Way Dasenbrock, editors. "BuchiEmecheta." *Interviews with Writers of the Post-Colonial World*, UPof Mississippi, 1992, pp. 82-99.

- Nayar, P. K. *Postcolonial Literature: An Introduction*. Pearson Longman, 2008.

Chapter 17

Harnessing the Potential of the Indian Diaspora: Opportunities for Collaboration in Zoological Research and Education

Dr. Sunita Rawat

Assistant Professor
Department of Zoology
Government Degree College, Gosaikheda, Unnao, U.P.
E-mail address- sunitamahi4@gmail.com

Abstract

This research paper delves into the potential of the Indian diaspora for advancing zoological research and education in India. It begins with an overview of the Indian diaspora, highlighting their significant role in scientific collaboration globally. The paper then examines the current state of zoological research and education in India, emphasizing the potential for growth and development.

The core of the paper profiles the Indian diaspora involved in scientific fields, assessing their contributions to zoological research and identifying opportunities for collaboration. It presents case studies of successful collaborations between the Indian diaspora and institutions in India, demonstrating the positive impact on zoological research and education.

However, the paper also acknowledges challenges and barriers to these collaborations, including cultural differences, legal hurdles, and resource limitations. To address these challenges, it proposes strategies such as cross-cultural training, policy advocacy, strengthening institutional support, and leveraging international networks.

The paper concludes by discussing future directions in harnessing the potential of the Indian diaspora for zoological research and education. It underscores the role of stakeholders, including researchers, educators, policymakers, and members of the Indian diaspora, in realizing this potential.

Keywords: Indian Diaspora, Zoological Research, Education, Collaboration, Challenges, Opportunities, Case Studies, Future Directions.

Introduction

The Indian diaspora, one of the world's largest, can significantly impact zoological research and education in India through collaborations, research involvement, and educational programs. Highly skilled members of this diaspora have played essential roles in academia, politics, and the corporate sector worldwide, enhancing India's global reputation. However, the complex relationship between diasporas and their home countries remains inadequately addressed. Understanding their potential in zoological research and education is crucial for identifying collaboration opportunities and addressing challenges. The paper's primary objective is to explore this potential, covering historical contexts, the role of the diaspora in fostering scientific collaboration, past initiatives, challenges associated with international cooperation, and contributions to zoological research and education. It also presents case studies of successful collaborations and strategic approaches to overcome obstacles and envisions potential future directions. The research aims to elevate the standards of zoological research and education in India through the pivotal role of the Indian diaspora, guided by specific research questions and objectives.

Historical Perspective of the Indian Diaspora

The historical trajectory of the Indian diaspora is multifaceted and influenced by socio-economic factors over different time periods. It began with Imperialism-Induced Migration during the British Empire's influence, where Indians migrated within the empire as traders, labourers, and colonial administrators (Civils Daily, 2022). The migration of Indian indentured labourers in the nineteenth century led to Indian communities in places like Africa, the Caribbean, and Fiji (Civils Daily, 2022).

Post-independence migration was driven by political and economic reasons, involving professionals and students seeking opportunities in developed countries (Kapuria, 2017; Pandey A., 2017). Contemporary migration, shaped by globalization, includes the influx of highly skilled IT professionals from India into countries like the USA and the UK (Pandey A., 2017; Kapuria, 2017).

Understanding this historical context is crucial for exploring the diverse experiences and identities within the Indian Diaspora and for recognizing their potential contributions to zoological research and education (Pandey A., 2017; Kapuria, 2017).

Role of Diaspora in Scientific Collaboration

Countries have recognized the potential of their scientific Diaspora in contributing to national development and Science, Technology, and Innovation (STI) through Science Diplomacy (Pandey,Srinivas, & Deepthi,2022). While Science Diplomacy is often associated with international science collaboration, engaging the Diaspora requires tailored strategies (Pandey, Srinivas, & Deepthi, 2022). India, a prominent developing nation, has emphasized involving its scientific Diaspora and has established itself in global Science Diplomacy (Pandey, Srinivas, & Deepthi, 2022).

Diaspora organizations from Latin America and the Caribbean actively engage with governmental and non-state entities in science diplomacy, promoting their home countries' scientific progress and facilitating research collaborations (Echeverría-King, et al., 2022). Understanding the role of Diasporas in scientific collaboration is crucial, providing insights into how they can contribute to scientific advancements. This understanding serves as a foundation for exploring their potential roles in zoological research and education (Echeverría-King, et al., 2022; Pandey, Srinivas, & Deepthi, 2022).

Zoological Research and Education in India

The Zoological Survey of India (ZSI), founded in 1916, is a crucial institution dedicated to taxonomic research, providing extensive information on animal taxa from Protozoa to Mammalia. The Records of the ZSI serve as a platform for sharing zoological insights on taxonomy, faunistic, biology, ecology, and populations (Zoological Survey of India, 2015). A study in Kanpur, India, found that students are aware of climate change, perceive it as a significant threat, associate it with rising temperatures, and are eager to expand their knowledge and take action. Understanding the state of zoological research and education in India is vital for potential collaboration with the Indian Diaspora (Goel, et al., 2023).

Previous Initiatives and Collaborations

The Indian diaspora has a history of contributing to various fields, including zoology. The Zoological Survey of India (ZSI) has been instrumental in promoting research and exploration to understand India's diverse animal life. ZSI provides a wealth of information across all animal taxa, benefiting researchers, students, conservation managers, and naturalists (Fernandez & Martin, 2021).

Efforts to enhance animal welfare in zoos include the use of training methods and environmental enrichment based on operant conditioning and reward-based approaches to behavioural psychology (Fernandez & Martin, 2021).

The Sofia Zoo has established an Environmental Education and Research Centre, focusing on formal and informal education, especially for children. It supports university student research and actively participates in conservation projects (Zareva-Simeonova, Zlatanova, Racheva, Angelov, & Asenova, 2009). These initiatives and collaborations within the diaspora offer valuable insights into the potential for zoological research and education.

Challenges in International Collaboration

International collaborations offer numerous benefits but come with unique challenges, such as scheduling conflicts due to different time zones, cultural and linguistic differences affecting communication, technological disruptions, geographical separation hindering coordination, and disparities in collaborators' career stages affecting perspectives and priorities. Overcoming these challenges requires careful planning, strong relationships, adaptability, and recognition of career stage disparities (See, 2018) (Dusdal & Powell, 2021). Effective communication and coordination are essential in navigating these obstacles within international collaborative projects.

The Indian Diaspora in Zoological Research and Education

The Indian diaspora is extensive and influential, particularly in scientific fields like zoology. Many individuals of Indian origin are actively engaged in science globally, with 73% of H-1B visas in the US going to them in 2022 (The Economist, 2023). They have made significant contributions, with some achieving Nobel laureate status, and have been involved in various initiatives, advancing scientific knowledge and innovation. India has programs like the Vaishvik Bhartiya Vaigyanik to engage with its scientific Diaspora, encouraging collaboration with Indian institutions (Dajani, 2023).

In zoological research, diaspora members have left a lasting impact, from research publications and leadership positions in academia to participation in collaborative endeavours. They have played a pivotal role in advancing scientific knowledge and fostering innovation (Dubey, 2016).

Furthermore, diaspora members actively engage in education and mentorship in scientific fields. They lecture at universities, guide students and researchers, and contribute to educational curricula. Programs like the Vaishvik Bhartiya Vaigyanik promote research collaboration and knowledge exchange between Diaspora members and Indian institutions (Department of Science & Technology, 2023).

Opportunities for Collaboration

Bilateral and multilateral partnerships play a crucial role in advancing zoological research and education. Bilateral collaborations involve two parties, often from different countries, facilitating the exchange of knowledge and resources. Multilateral partnerships are effective for addressing global challenges and can drive large-scale research projects, promote international standards, and support capacity-building efforts (Akpabio, 2021; Lazarou, 2020).

Funding for zoological research and education comes from various sources, including government agencies, non-profit organizations, and private foundations. For instance, the American Association of Zoo Veterinarians and the European Association of Zoo and Wildlife Veterinarians offer grants to support research and education(European Association of Zoo and Wildlife Veterinarians, 2020).

Capacity-building involves strengthening human competencies and institutional capabilities through training programs and fellowships, while knowledge exchange involves sharing information and insights through research collaborations, conferences, and publications (Danaher, et al., 2014; Greenwell, et al., 2023).

Utilizing technology and digital platforms has transformed zoological research and education, with online learning platforms enhancing students' academic performance and satisfaction. Digital technologies, online games, multimedia resources, and scientific digital platforms facilitate collaboration, resource access, and research sharing (da Silva Neto & Chiarini, 2023; Kumi-Yeboah, Sallar, Kiramba, & Kim., 2020). These mechanisms provide significant opportunities for collaboration between the Indian Diaspora and Indian institutions, fostering knowledge exchange, strengthening capacity-building, and improving academic achievements and satisfaction (Danaher, et al., 2014).

Case Studies

Successful collaborations between the Indian diaspora and institutions in India:

Successful partnerships between the Indian diaspora and Indian institutions showcase their substantial potential in contributing to scientific progress. Notable examples include the India-US Civil Nuclear Deal, where the diaspora in the United States played a vital role in its advocacy, demonstrating their influence in bolstering bilateral relations. The diaspora's involvement in technology start-ups has accelerated international expansion for domestic firms. Moreover, scholars have cultivated personal and institutional collaborations with Indian researchers, resulting in significant contributions to research advancement and global research networks.

Impact of such collaborations on zoological research and education:

Partnerships between the Indian diaspora and Indian institutions have significantly impacted zoological research and education. They have led to advancements in research, resulting in numerous publications, patents, and innovations. Collaborations have also influenced zoological education, introducing innovative curricula, teaching methods and enriching learning resources. Students benefit from international exposure through exchange programs. Moreover, capacity building in zoological research and education has been strengthened, enhancing the skills and competencies of researchers and educators. These collaborations have left a profound mark on zoological research, education, and capacity building in India.

Challenges and Barriers

Collaboration between the Indian diaspora and Indian institutions in zoological research and education presents both opportunities and challenges. Cultural and communication differences, legal and regulatory complexities, limited funding and resources, and institutional administrative constraints can hinder international collaborations. Recognizing and addressing these challenges is essential to develop effective strategies that enable the Indian diaspora to contribute fully to the advancement of zoological research and education in India.

Strategies for Overcoming Challenges

To ensure effective collaboration between the Indian diaspora and institutions in India for zoological research and education, several key elements are essential:

- Cross-Cultural Training and Sensitivity: To address the challenges of cultural differences, tailored cross-cultural workshops, mentorship programs, inclusive communication platforms, and regular cultural exchange sessions can be implemented (Walden University, 2022). These measures foster understanding and harmonious working environments.

- Advocacy and Policy Recommendations: Collaboration among collaborators and institutions, policy think tanks, workshops, and regular engagement with government agencies are vital to navigate legal and regulatory challenges. These efforts help promote policy changes that support international collaborations in zoological research and education.

- Strengthening Institutional Support: To enhance institutional backing for international collaborations, it is crucial to advocate for dedicated resources, develop supportive policies, establish research collaboration centres, and provide faculty and staff training (Walden University, 2022). These initiatives encourage a culture of collaboration and facilitate research projects.

- Leveraging International Networks: Forming strategic partnerships with international organizations, sharing resources, collaborating on funding proposals, and utilizing online collaboration platforms are vital to overcoming resource limitations in zoological research and education (Rose & Riley, 2022). These strategies help bridge cultural, legal, and administrative barriers, enhancing collaboration and advancing the field.

Collectively, these elements ensure effective collaboration and address the multifaceted challenges associated with harnessing the potential of the Indian diaspora for zoological research and education.

Future Directions

The future of collaboration in zoological research and education with the Indian diaspora is promising. Advancements in technology, increased funding opportunities, and global recognition of diaspora achievements will drive this progress. The Indian government and international organizations will play vital roles by introducing funding initiatives, establishing policy frameworks, and creating collaboration platforms. Emerging trends in zoological research involve conservation, technological integration, and interdisciplinary approaches, benefiting from diaspora expertise. These factors converge to create an environment conducive to innovation, knowledge exchange, and the advancement of zoological science and education.

Conclusion

This research paper offers a comprehensive understanding of how the Indian diaspora can significantly impact zoological research and education in India. It emphasizes the myriad opportunities for collaboration while also recognizing and addressing the challenges that may arise. By providing recommendations and a call to action, the paper encourages active involvement from stakeholders, including researchers, educators, policymakers, and the Indian diaspora. In essence, it underscores the pivotal role the diaspora can play and urges collective efforts to harness their full potential in advancing zoological research and education within the country.

References

- Akpabio, E. "Attaining SDGs in Africa Through Bilateral and Multilateral Partnerships." In F. W. Leal, A. A. Marisa, L. Brandli, S. A. Lange, & T. Wall, *Partnerships for the Goals. Encyclopedia of the UN Sustainable Development Goals.* 2021, pp. 37-47, Springer, Cham. doi:10.1007/978-3-319-95963-4_56

- Civils Daily. (2022, January 17). *[Sansad TV] Perspective: Contribution of Indian Diaspora.* Retrieved from CivilsDaily: https://www.civilsdaily.com/sansad-tv-perspective-contribution-of-indian-diaspora/

- da Silva Neto, V., & Chiarini, T. "The Platformization of Science: Towards a Scientific Digital Platform Taxonomy." *Minerva*, 2023, 1-29.

- Dajani, R. (2023, October 24). *Scientists in diaspora are a powerful resource for their home countries.* Retrieved from Nature: https://www.nature.com/articles/d41586-023-03300-2

- Danaher, P. A., Davies, A., De George-Walker, L., Jones, J. K., Matthews, K. J., Midgley, W.,... Baguley, M. "Knowledge Sharing Practices and Capacity-Building." In P. e. Danaher, *Contemporary Capacity-Building in Educational Contexts.* Palgrave Macmillan, 2014, pp. 87-98..

- Department of Science & Technology. (2023, June 15). *VAIBHAV Fellowship Programme announced to connect Indian STEMM diaspora with Indian Higher Educational Institutions.* Retrieved from Department of Science & Technology: https://dst.gov.in/vaibhav-fellowship-progrsamme-announced-connect-indian-stemm-diaspora-indian-higher-educational

- Dubey, A. "The Indian Diaspora as a Heritage Resource in Indo–African Relations." In A. Dubey, & A. Biswas, *India and Africa's Partnership: A Vision for a New Future* 2016, pp. 115-136. Springer India. doi:10.1007/978-81-322-2619-2_7

- Dusdal, J., & Powell, J. J. (2021, April). Benefits, Motivations, and Challenges of International Collaborative Research: A Sociology of Science Case Study. *Science and Public Policy, 48*(2), 235-245. doi:10.1093/scipol/scab010

- Echeverría-King, L. F., Camacho, T. R., Figueroa, P., Galvis, L. A., González, A., Suárez, V. R.,... Widmaier, M. C. (2022). Organized Scientific Diaspora and Its Contributions to Science Diplomacy in Emerging Economies: The Case of Latin America and the Caribbean. *Frontiers in Research Metrics and Analytics, 7*(22). doi:10.3389/frma.2022.893593

- European Association of Zoo and Wildlife Veterinarians. (2020). *Conservation Research Grants: EAZWV provides Grant Funding via the Zebra Foundation for Veterinary Zoological Education.* Retrieved from EAZWV: www.eazwv.org/page/grants

- Fernandez, E., & Martin, A. (2021). Animal Training, Environmental Enrichment, and Animal Welfare: A History of Behavior Analysis in Zoos. *Journal of Zoological and Botanical Gardens, 2*(4), 531-543. doi:10.3390/jzbg2040038

- Goel, A., Iyer-Raniga, U., Jain, S., Addya, A., Srivastava, S., Pandey, R., & Rathi, S. (2023). Student Perceptions of Environmental Education in India. *Sustainability, 15*(21). doi.org/10.3390/su152115346

- Greenwell, P., Riley, L., Lemos de Figueiredo, R., Brereton, J., Mooney, A., & Rose, P. (2023). The Societal Value of the Modern Zoo: A Commentary on How Zoos Can Positively Impact on Human Populations Locally and Globally. *Journal of Zoological and Botanical Gardens, 4*(1), 53-69. doi:10.3390/jzbg4010006

- Kapuria, S. (2017). Perspectives on the Indian Diaspora. In A. D. Singh, & S. I. Rajan, *Review of Politics of Migration: Indian Emigration in a Globalized World* (Vol. 52, pp. 31-33). Economic and Political Weekly. Retrieved from www.jstor.org/stable/26695932

- Kumi-Yeboah, A., Sallar, A., Kiramba, L., & Kim., Y. (2020, December). Exploring the use of digital technologies from the perspective of diverse learners in online learning environments. *Online Learning, 24*(4), 42-63.

- Lazarou, E. "The future of multilateralism and strategic partnerships." *European Parliamentary Research Service* 2020, pp. 1-12. European Parliamentary Research Service.

- Pandey, A. "Women in Indian Diaspora: Redefining Self Between Dislocation and Relocation." In A. Pandey, *Women in the Indian Diaspora* 2017, pp. 1-12. Singapore: Springer Nature Singapore Pte Ltd.

- Pandey, N., Srinivas, K. R., & Deepthi, T. R. (2022, June 22). Emerging Technologies, STI Diaspora and Science Diplomacy in India: Towards a New Approach. *Frontiers in Research Metrics and Analytics, 7.* doi:10.3389/frma.2022.904100

- Rose, P. E., & Riley, L. M. (2022). Expanding the role of the future zoo: Wellbeing should become the fifth aim for modern zoos. *Frontiers in Psychology, 13.* doi:10.3389/fpsyg.2022.1018722

- See, M. (2018). 18 International collaboration: Are the challenges worth the benefits? *Journal of Animal Science, 96*(suppl_3). doi:10.1093/jas/sky404.003

- The Economist. (2023, June 12). *India's diaspora is bigger and more influential than any in history.* Retrieved from The Economist: www.economist.com/international/2023/06/12/indias-diaspora-is-bigger-and-more-influential-than-any-in-history

- Walden University. (2022, 11 8). *7 Research Challenges (And how to overcome them).* Retrieved from Walden University: www.waldenu.edu/news-and-events/publications/articles/2010/01-research-challenges

- Zareva-Simeonova, K., Zlatanova, D., Racheva, V., Angelov, V., & Asenova, I. (2009). The Zoos and their Role in the Formal and Informal Environmental Education. *Biotechnology & Biotechnological Equipment*, 19-23. doi:10.1080/13102818.2009.10818355

- Zoological Survey of India. (2015). Zoological Survey of India| Digital Archives of their Publications. Retrieved from Fauna of India: faunaofindia.nic.in/

Chapter 18

The Importance of the Indian Diaspora with Global Connections

Dr. Brajesh Kumar Gupta 'Mewadev'

Principal, S. K. Mahavidyalaya,
Jaitpur, Mahoba (U.P.)
Email Address- dr.mewadevrain@gmail.com

Abstract

The Indian diaspora is one of the largest and most influential diaspora communities in the world. It comprises people of Indian origin living in various countries around the globe. The impact of the Indian diaspora on both the host countries and India itself is a subject of extensive research. The transnational impact of the Indian diaspora encompasses economic, cultural, social, and political dimensions. The Indian diaspora's transnational impact is a testament to the power of migration and globalization. It underscores the interwoven destinies of nations, the fluidity of identities, and the capacity of individuals and communities to transcend borders, forging connections that resonate across the globe. The Indian diaspora's impact stands as a powerful example of how diversity, multiculturalism, and global interconnectedness can be forces for positive change and progress in an increasingly interconnected world. Overall, the Indian diaspora's influence on host countries is diverse and multifaceted, and it varies based on the size and composition of the diaspora community, the host country's policies, and the opportunities available. Their contributions are often recognized and valued for the positive impact they bring to the social, economic, and cultural fabric of their host nations.

Keywords: culture and Indian diaspora, literary development, political connection, women and patriarchy, global connections.

Introduction

The Indian diaspora, one of the most extensive and influential in the world, extends its roots across the globe, bridging continents, cultures, and economies. With a history marked by waves of migration, Indian communities have established deep and enduring connections with their host countries while maintaining strong ties with their homeland. This dynamic and diverse diaspora has not only redefined the contours of cultural diversity but also yielded a profound transnational impact, impacting both their adopted nations and India.

This narrative unfolds the story of the Indian diaspora and the global connections that weave through its presence in countries far and wide. It is a tale of economic contributions that strengthen the financial bonds between nations, a story of cultural exchange that enriches societies with traditions and heritage, and an exploration of political engagement that influences policies and international relations. The Indian diaspora's imprint transcends borders and reaches into the realms of education, innovation, and advocacy for global issues.

As we embark on this journey through the myriad facets of the Indian diaspora's global connections, we will uncover the multifaceted ways in which this community has become a cornerstone of transnational relations. From remittances that fuel economic growth to the vibrant cultural festivals that bridge cultural gaps, from influential political voices that resonate in foreign capitals to the academic collaborations that enrich the world's collective knowledge, the Indian diaspora's transnational impact is a testament to the power of migration, multiculturalism, and globalization in an ever-connected world.

The Indian diaspora has had a notable influence on their host countries in several ways:

Economic Contributions: Members of the Indian diaspora have made significant economic contributions to their host countries. Indian entrepreneurs and professionals have created businesses, generated employment, and contributed to economic growth. In the United States, for example, Indian immigrants have founded and led many successful companies in the technology and healthcare sectors.

Cultural Diversity: The Indian diaspora has enriched the cultural diversity of their host countries. They have introduced Indian cuisine, art, music, and traditions, contributing to a more diverse and multicultural society. Indian cultural events and festivals are celebrated worldwide.

Academic and Scientific Achievements: Indian diaspora members are often highly educated and have made significant contributions to academia and scientific research in their host countries. Many Indian scientists, scholars, and researchers have excelled in various fields, enhancing the intellectual capital of their adopted nations.

Social and Community Engagement: The Indian diaspora actively engages in social and community activities, contributing to philanthropy and social initiatives in their host countries. They often establish cultural and religious organizations that provide support and promote cross-cultural understanding.

Political Participation: Some members of the Indian diaspora have become politically active in their host countries. They have been elected to public office and played roles in local and national governance, advocating for the interests of their communities and contributing to diverse representation.

Diaspora Networking: The Indian diaspora often forms strong networks and associations that facilitate economic, political, and social cooperation with their host countries. These networks can promote bilateral trade, investments, and cultural exchanges.

Diplomacy and International Relations: Prominent members of the Indian diaspora have been influential in international diplomacy. They have served as ambassadors, contributed to foreign policy discussions, and fostered closer ties between their host countries and India.

Social Integration: The Indian diaspora has promoted social integration and multiculturalism in their host countries. Their contributions to society help build bridges and promote understanding among diverse communities.

Scientific and Technological Advancements: Indian diaspora professionals, particularly in fields like information technology and medicine, have played a significant role in driving technological and medical advancements in their host countries. They contribute to research, innovation, and technological progress.

Culture and Indian Diaspora

Cultural exchange is a significant aspect of the Indian diaspora's influence both within their host countries and with India. The Indian diaspora has played a crucial role in promoting cultural exchange in various ways:

Promotion of Indian Culture: Members of the Indian diaspora actively promote Indian culture in their host countries. This includes celebrating traditional festivals like Diwali, Holi, and Navratri, organizing cultural events, and sharing aspects of Indian art, music, dance, and cuisine with their local communities.

Cultural Festivals and Events: Indian diaspora communities frequently organize cultural festivals and events that showcase Indian traditions and customs. These events provide an opportunity for people from different backgrounds to experience and learn about Indian culture.

Yoga and Meditation: The Indian diaspora has played a significant role in popularizing practices like yoga and meditation in their host countries. Many yoga studios and meditation centres are run by individuals of Indian origin, and these practices have become mainstream and widely adopted.

Language and Literature: Indian languages, particularly Hindi and English, are taught and spoken within the diaspora communities. Indian literature and philosophy, including the works of writers like Rabindranath Tagore and Mahatma Gandhi, are actively shared and studied.

Cultural Centres and Institutions: Many Indian diaspora communities have established cultural centres and institutions that serve as hubs for promoting Indian culture. These centres often offer language classes, dance and music lessons, and host cultural events and exhibitions.

Art and Entertainment: The Indian diaspora has made significant contributions to the entertainment industry, both in India and globally. Indian filmmakers, actors, and musicians have gained international recognition, helping to spread Indian culture through films, music, and the performing arts.

Cuisine: Indian cuisine has become increasingly popular worldwide, with Indian restaurants and food outlets present in most major cities. The Indian diaspora has played a crucial role in introducing and popularizing Indian dishes and flavours.

Religious and Spiritual Traditions: The Indian diaspora often maintains religious and spiritual traditions, including the construction and maintenance of temples, gurdwaras, and mosques. These places of worship become centres for cultural exchange and community activities.

Cross-Cultural Collaborations: Indian diaspora members often collaborate with artists, musicians, and cultural institutions in their host countries, leading to fusion and cross-cultural projects that blend Indian and local cultural elements.

Cultural Diplomacy: The Indian government often utilizes the Indian diaspora as cultural ambassadors. Cultural events and initiatives are organized to enhance India's soft power and cultural diplomacy efforts.

The Indian diaspora's commitment to preserving and promoting their cultural heritage and traditions has contributed to a greater understanding and appreciation of India's rich and diverse culture across the world. This cultural exchange benefits both the diaspora communities and their host countries, fostering greater cross-cultural awareness and appreciation.

Indian Diaspora in Literature Development

The Indian diaspora has made substantial contributions to English literature through the exploration of themes, identities, and experiences that reflect the complexities of being part of a transnational and multicultural community. Here are some of the key contributions of the Indian diaspora to English literature:

Multicultural Perspectives: Many authors from the Indian diaspora have enriched English literature by bringing diverse cultural perspectives into their works. They often incorporate elements of Indian culture, traditions, and languages into their writing, providing readers with a richer and more inclusive literary experience.

Identity and Diaspora Literature: Indian diaspora authors frequently explore themes related to identity, belonging, and displacement. They examine the challenges of straddling multiple cultural worlds and often highlight the tension between the homeland and the adopted country. Works by authors like Salman Rushdie and Jhumpa Lahiri are prime examples of this.

Hybrid Identities: Diaspora literature often delves into the idea of hybrid identities, where characters grapple with multiple cultural, racial, and national affiliations. This exploration of hybridity is a significant contribution of the Indian diaspora to the broader discourse on multiculturalism and post-colonial identities.

Cultural Syncretism: Authors from the Indian diaspora explore cultural syncretism, showcasing how various cultures blend and influence each other. This is evident in the way they incorporate elements of Indian mythology, folklore, and religious practices into English-language narratives.

Language and Linguistic Innovation: Many Indian diaspora authors experiment with language and linguistic styles to reflect the multilingual and multicultural nature of their experiences. They may incorporate multiple languages and dialects into their writing to capture the nuances of communication within diaspora communities.

Globalization and Transnational Themes: Indian diaspora literature often engages with themes related to globalization, transnationalism, and the interconnectedness of the modern world. These authors explore how diaspora communities navigate these global forces while maintaining ties to their cultural roots.

Social and Political Commentary: Indian diaspora authors often use their works to comment on social and political issues, including immigration, racism, xenophobia, and the challenges faced by immigrant communities. Their literature serves as a platform for social critique and awareness.

Representation and Inclusivity: Indian diaspora literature contributes to greater representation and inclusivity in English literature. It showcases stories and voices that have historically been underrepresented in mainstream literature.

Notable authors from the Indian diaspora who have made significant contributions to English literature include Salman Rushdie, Jhumpa Lahiri, Arundhati Roy, V.S. Naipaul, Chitra Banerjee Divakaruni, and many others. Their works have not only enriched the literary world but have also helped bridge cultural gaps and promote a more inclusive and diverse literary landscape.

Indian Diaspora and Political Connection

The Indian diaspora has been politically engaged in their host countries and, to some extent, in India itself. Their political engagement can take various forms and has had notable impacts in several countries. Here are some aspects of Indian diaspora political engagement:

Voting and Civic Participation: Indian diaspora members who have acquired citizenship in their host countries often participate in local, state, and national elections. They exercise their right to vote and engage in civic activities like volunteering and advocacy.

Political Representation: Some members of the Indian diaspora have successfully run for and held political office in their host countries. They have been elected as local councillors, mayors, members of parliament, or members of Congress and have contributed to legislative and policy-making processes.

Advocacy for Indian Interests: Indian diaspora organizations and individuals often advocate for issues and policies that are important to India. They may lobby their host country's government on matters such as trade relations, immigration policies, and bilateral agreements.

Support for Human Rights and Democracy: Many members of the Indian diaspora are engaged in promoting human rights, democracy, and social justice, both within their host countries and in India. They may support causes related to religious freedom, environmental protection, and social equality.

Diaspora Organizations: Various Indian diaspora organizations and associations are dedicated to political engagement. They organize events, campaigns, and lobbying efforts to influence policy decisions and support Indian interests.

Political Donations: Some individuals from the Indian diaspora contribute financially to political campaigns and parties in their host countries, particularly if they align with their views or if the candidates express support for India.

Community Activism: Diaspora members often engage in community activism and awareness campaigns. They work on issues such as anti-discrimination, multiculturalism, and the promotion of Indian culture and heritage.

Cultural and Diplomatic Exchange: Cultural and diplomatic events organized by the Indian government often involve the participation of the diaspora, fostering cultural exchange and reinforcing diplomatic ties.

Engagement with Indian Politics: While living in their host countries, members of the Indian diaspora may remain politically engaged with events and developments in India. They follow Indian elections, express their opinions, and may contribute to political discourse through social media, discussions, and blogs.

Diaspora's Role in Global Politics: The Indian diaspora's political engagement can extend beyond their host countries and have implications for global politics. They may be involved in international advocacy for various causes, thereby impacting international relations.

The Indian government has recognized the importance of the Indian diaspora in shaping global perceptions of India and has implemented programs like the Pravasi Bharatiya Divas to engage with and harness their political and economic contributions.

Overall, the Indian diaspora's political engagement plays a significant role in shaping both domestic and international policies and relations.

Women and Patriarchy

The role of Indian diaspora women in the context of patriarchy is complex and multifaceted. Patriarchy, a social system where men hold primary power and authority, continues to influence the lives of Indian diaspora women to varying degrees. The experiences and challenges faced by these women can be influenced by a combination of cultural, generational, and individual factors. Here are some key points to consider:

Cultural Background and Generational Differences: The extent to which Indian diaspora women are influenced by patriarchy can vary significantly based on their cultural background and generational differences. First-generation immigrants may be more traditional in their beliefs and practices, while subsequent generations may adopt more progressive attitudes.

Traditional Gender Roles: Indian diaspora women often grapple with traditional gender roles and expectations that can be associated with patriarchy. These roles may include responsibilities related to family, household, and caregiving.

Cultural Values and Norms: Cultural values and norms from India can continue to shape the lives of women in the Indian diaspora. This may manifest in conservative dress, adherence to traditional customs, and expectations regarding marriage and family life.

Educational Attainment: Education plays a crucial role in empowering women in the Indian diaspora and challenging patriarchal norms. Many women in the diaspora pursue higher education and careers, enabling them to have greater independence and agency in their lives.

Career and Economic Independence: Economic independence and participation in the workforce can provide Indian diaspora women with greater autonomy and the ability to challenge traditional gender roles and expectations.

Intersectionality: The experiences of Indian diaspora women are influenced by multiple intersecting factors, including religion, caste, race, ethnicity, and sexual orientation. These factors can intersect with patriarchal norms in complex ways.

Community and Peer Support: Indian diaspora women often find support and solidarity within their communities, where they can discuss issues related to patriarchy and gender roles. Support from peers can be empowering and help challenge patriarchal norms.

Transnational Experiences: Indian diaspora women may navigate transnational identities, which can involve reconciling the cultural norms of their host country with those of their heritage. This experience can both challenge and reinforce patriarchal ideals.

Advocacy and Activism: Some Indian diaspora women are actively engaged in advocacy and activism to address gender-based inequalities and patriarchy. They may support women's rights and social justice causes in their host countries and India.

Changing Norms: Over time, many Indian diaspora communities have seen shifts in traditional gender norms, with increasing acceptance of diverse gender roles and relationships. These changes can be attributed to generational differences and evolving cultural attitudes.

Global Connections

The Indian diaspora, one of the world's largest and most widespread, has established significant global connections, both within their host countries and with India. These connections encompass various aspects, including cultural, economic, social, and political ties. Here are some of the key dimensions of the Indian diaspora's global connections:

Economic Connections

Remittances: Indian diaspora members send billions of dollars in remittances back to India, providing a vital source of foreign exchange and financial support to families and communities.

Investments: The diaspora contributes to investment in India through businesses, startups, real estate, and financial institutions.

Cultural Connections: Promotion of Indian Culture: The diaspora actively promotes Indian culture through cultural events, festivals, art exhibitions, and the dissemination of Indian music, dance, and cuisine.

Multilingualism: Indian languages, literature, and linguistic diversity are preserved and promoted, fostering connections between languages and cultures.

Social Connections

Community Associations: The Indian diaspora often forms strong community and cultural associations that facilitate social connections, support networks, and community activities.

Philanthropy: Many diaspora members are involved in philanthropic activities, contributing to various social causes, including healthcare, education, and poverty alleviation, both in their host countries and in India.

Political Connections

Political Engagement: Members of the diaspora are politically engaged in their host countries, advocating for issues relevant to India and participating in local, state, and national politics.

Diaspora Organizations: Various organizations and associations are dedicated to political engagement, lobbying for policies that align with Indian interests.

Diplomatic Connections

Diaspora in Diplomacy: The Indian government often utilizes the Indian diaspora as a valuable diplomatic resource, involving them in diplomatic missions and events to foster international relations and diplomacy.

Educational and Knowledge Connections

Academic and Research Collaborations: The diaspora plays a role in fostering academic collaborations between universities, research institutions, and individuals, promoting knowledge exchange and research partnerships.

Knowledge Transfer: Highly skilled diaspora members contribute to knowledge transfer by participating in academic conferences, workshops and sharing their expertise.

Business and Trade Connections

Trade and Business Networks: The diaspora forms business and trade networks, facilitating international commerce and economic relations between their host countries and India.

Cultural Diplomacy and Soft Power

Cultural Exchange: The Indian diaspora's promotion of Indian culture enhances India's soft power and cultural diplomacy efforts globally.

Influence on Global Perception: The diaspora's achievements and contributions shape the global perception of India, influencing international relations and foreign policy decisions.

Technology and Innovation

Tech and Innovation Networks: Highly skilled diaspora members have established networks in the fields of technology and innovation, fostering collaboration and partnerships in these sectors.

Advocacy for Global Causes

Advocacy for Global Issues: Indian diaspora members often advocate for global causes, such as human rights, environmental conservation, and social justice, fostering connections with international organizations and institutions.

The Indian diaspora's global connections are integral to India's economic growth, cultural influence, diplomatic efforts, and international relations. They contribute to India's standing in the global community and support the development of strong bonds between India and the rest of the world.

The contributions of the Indian diaspora to India's development have been significant in various ways. Here are some key aspects in which the diaspora has made contributions to India's development:

Remittances: One of the most direct and substantial contributions is through remittances sent back to India by members of the Indian diaspora. These remittances provide a vital source of foreign exchange, support families, and contribute to the country's economic stability.

Investment: Many members of the Indian diaspora have invested in India through businesses, startups, and real estate ventures. Their investments help create jobs, stimulate economic growth, and promote entrepreneurship.

Technology and Innovation: Highly skilled members of the Indian diaspora, particularly in the fields of technology and innovation, have played a significant role in driving India's IT and software industry. They have also contributed to research and development.

Education: The Indian diaspora has been involved in educational initiatives, from setting up scholarships to establishing educational institutions. These contributions help improve access to quality education in India.

Philanthropy and Social Initiatives: Many members of the Indian diaspora are actively involved in philanthropic activities, supporting various social causes and initiatives, such as healthcare, sanitation, and rural development.

Cultural Exchange: The Indian diaspora also plays a crucial role in promoting Indian culture, arts, and traditions globally. This fosters cultural exchange, tourism, and soft power.

Networking and Advocacy: Indian diaspora organizations and individuals often advocate for India's interests, and they help create connections and opportunities for trade, diplomacy, and collaborations with their host countries.

Knowledge Transfer: Highly skilled diaspora members contribute to knowledge transfer by participating in academic collaborations, workshops, and conferences, enhancing India's access to international expertise.

Political Engagement: Some members of the Indian diaspora are involved in politics and diplomacy in their host countries, which can influence international relations and policies beneficial to India.

These contributions have a far-reaching impact on India's economic, social, and cultural development. The Indian government has recognized the importance of the Indian diaspora and has established mechanisms, such as the PravasiBharatiya Divas, to engage with and harness their contributions to the nation's growth and development.

The experiences of Indian diaspora women in relation to patriarchy are influenced by a range of factors, including cultural background, generational differences, education, economic independence, and the presence of support networks. While many women continue to navigate traditional gender roles and patriarchal norms, others actively challenge and reshape these norms through their actions and advocacy efforts. The experience of Indian diaspora women is not monolithic, and it reflects the complex interplay of cultural, social, and individual factors.

Conclusion

In conclusion, the global connections of the Indian diaspora unveil a rich tapestry of transnational impact that extends across diverse domains of society, culture, economy, and politics. These connections are a testament to the diaspora's dynamism and the enduring significance of its presence in countries around the world. The Indian diaspora's transnational impact is characterized by its ability to bridge cultures, foster economic growth, contribute to the global exchange of ideas, and influence political landscapes.

Economically, the Indian diaspora has played a pivotal role through remittances, investments, and business networks, contributing not only to India's prosperity but also to the economies of their host countries. This financial exchange reinforces the interdependence of nations in today's globalized world.

Culturally, the diaspora has served as a vibrant cultural ambassador, sharing India's traditions, languages, and heritage with their host communities. This cultural exchange enriches the tapestry of multiculturalism and contributes to cross-cultural understanding and appreciation.

In politics, the diaspora's engagement ranges from local activism to global diplomacy. Members of the diaspora participate in political processes, advocate for Indian interests, and often occupy positions of power and influence in their host countries, thereby shaping policies and international relations.

The educational and knowledge connections facilitated by the Indian diaspora contribute to global knowledge sharing and research collaboration. Their participation in academic institutions and knowledge transfer bolsters the intellectual capital of both their host countries and India.

Furthermore, the Indian diaspora's global connections are underpinned by its role in business and trade, advocacy for global issues, and promotion of Indian culture as a tool of soft power and cultural diplomacy.

While acknowledging the myriad contributions of the Indian diaspora to their host countries and India, it is important to recognize that their experiences, challenges, and impact vary widely based on individual circumstances, generational differences, and cultural backgrounds.

References

- Cohen, R. *Global Diaspora: An Introduction.* Uof Washington P, 1997.

- Friedman, J. "The Past in the Future: History and the Politics of Identity". *American Anthropologist.* Vol. 94 no. 4, 1992, pp. 837-59.

- Kapur, Devesh. "Bibliography." *Diaspora, Development, and Democracy: The Domestic Impact of International Migration from India.* Princeton UP, 2010, pp. 297-314.

- Lie, J. "From international migration to transnational Diaspora". *Contemporary Sociology,*Vol. 24, no. 4,1995, pp. 303-06,.

- Shukla, Sandhya. "Locations for South Asian diasporas". *Annual Review of Anthropology.* Vol.30, 2001, pp. 551-72.

- Varma, Sushma J.,and Radhika Seshan, editors.*Fractured Identity: The Indian Diaspora in Canada.* Rawat Publication, 2003.

Chapter 19

Voices Beyond Borders: Transnational Narratives by Women Writers

Ms. Varsha Sahebrao Aher

Assistant Professor
Department of English
K.J. Somaiya College of Arts, Commerce and Science,
Kopargaon
Email Address- varshasaher@gmail.com

Abstract

Recent South Asian literature has seen a proliferation of significant women's writings. Researchers worldwide are exploring and amplifying new dimensions and aspects of immigrant narratives. Migration Studies encompass various fields, including Spatial Studies, Geocritical Studies, Gender Studies, Culture Studies, Trauma and Rehabilitation Studies, and Psychoanalytical Studies. Women's writing reflects a mosaic of themes, given the diversity of communities, religions, and linguistic groups in India, nurturing their transnational identities. Immigrant writers use their works to share their psychopathology with readers, providing insights into their experiences in the host land. Women writers grapple with issues of dislocation while negotiating their identities and shifting territories. The study examines transnational feminism as a means of narrating the multicultural aspects of postcolonialism, mass migration, and contemporary women's identities. Transnational narratives explore issues related to identity, cultural assimilation, family relationships, and transnational spaces within nation-states.

Keywords: transnational narratives, gender studies, culture studies.

The spectrum of literature reflects the dynamics of socio-cultural perspectives, contributing to the stimulation of human consciousness. While literature and society do not have a direct one-to-one correspondence, over the centuries, literature has served as a public forum for the expression of torture, anguish, and discrimination.In the context of Indian writing in English, this tradition has become a powerful voice for Indian culture and civilization on a global scale. Although it began with the poetic works of Sir Aurobindo Ghosh, Toru Dutt, Rabindranath Tagore, Sarojini Naidu, and other notable writers, its true strength emerged in the post-independence era.

Throughout Indian literary history, we have witnessed the idealized, silenced image of Indian womanhood, rooted in the publication of Bankim Chandra Chatterji's *Rajmohan's Wife* in 1864. This silence symbolizes both conformity and resistance, reflecting the influence of the Hindu moral code known as The Laws of Manu, which denied women independent existence apart from their husbands or their families. Traditional depictions of suppressed women have persisted in a culture permeated by religious images of virtuous goddesses like Sita, Savitri, Draupadi, and Gandhari, reinforcing the archetype of the patient, chaste, and self-denying wife. The rich heritage of folk tales, myths, epics, sagas, and Indian tradition has often depicted silence and endurance as virtues, though it can also be seen as a symbol of suffocation and subjugation, with speech representing self-articulation.

The tradition of Indian women writers began in the late 19th century with authors like Toru Dutt, Mrs. Ghoshal, Krupabai Sathianathan, Sorabji Cornelia, Shevantibai Nikambe, and Raj Lakshmi Debi. These early writings often portrayed women as silent sufferers, embodiments of patience and endurance, and custodians of Indian culture. However, this image of uncomplaining silence gradually evolved into the defiant silence of The New Woman in India.

Interdisciplinary Relevance

This study delves into the theoretical frameworks of feminism, transnational feminism, post-colonialism, transnational acculturation, and trans-cultural globalization. It analyzes specific texts authored by South Asian women from the diaspora in the late twentieth century to explore how multiculturalism shapes contemporary narratives and identities.

Transnationalism is a complex concept with relevance in various academic disciplines, including Political Science, Public Administration, International Politics, Geography, Migration Studies, Human Geographies, Trauma Studies, Gender Studies, and Culture Studies. It revolves around the movement of people and policies across national boundaries and offers multiple perspectives on its facets.

Human migration has historical roots in the search for comfort, safety, education, and health, often driven by factors like warfare, political ideologies, religious segregation, and natural disasters. The study of transnationalism sheds light on the intricate issues associated with human mobility, making it significant for both readers and researchers.

Transnationalism: Shifting Paradigms in the Age of Globalization

Transnationalism plays a crucial role in exploring the dimensions of postcolonialism, mass migration, and evolving identities within South Asian women's narratives. These writings highlight themes such as identity formation, cultural assimilation, familial ties, and the notion of transnational spaces within and beyond nation-states.

Transnationalism is a dynamic process that goes beyond permanent relocation or complete cultural assimilation. It involves establishing and maintaining multifaceted social connections between societies of origin and settlement. These connections encompass information exchange, financial transactions, and influence on local and national events in both the home and host countries.

This research aims to understand the theme of displacement in the early stages of migration and how it transforms into the process of assimilating host cultures to attain transnationality. It argues that transnationalism empowers South Asian immigrant women to envision their own spaces and instigate social changes within their socio-cultural environments.

To support these arguments, the study draws upon Steven Vertovec's concept of transnationalism and Robin Cohen's ideas on diaspora. Transnationalism, in this context, refers to ongoing exchanges of information, money, resources, travel, and communication between diaspora members and their homeland or the globalized ethnic community. It fosters a strong diaspora consciousness, leading to the fluidity of ethnic identities and the development of collective identities.

Contemporary transnational communities bridge the homeland, hostland, and global and local spheres. This research emphasizes that transnationalism is not limited to permanent relocation but involves maintaining diverse social connections that link societies of origin and settlement. It serves as a pivotal lens to explore the multifaceted dimensions of postcolonialism, mass migration, and evolving identities within South Asian women's narratives.

Transnational Identities

Homi K. Bhabha's insights, as presented in *The Location of Culture*, offer a profound and thought-provoking definition of the intricate concept of transnational experiences, shedding light on the complex interplay of contemporary global dynamics and their profound impact on identity formation.

The modern era, marked by factors like modernity, cosmopolitanism, ethnicity, and transmigration, introduces new dimensions to the concept of diasporic identity. These dimensions are vividly reflected in the narratives of diasporic communities. Steven Vertovec further delves into the complexities of diaspora, drawing distinctions between various aspects, such as the process of dispersal, the diasporic communities residing in foreign lands, and the geographic spaces where these dispersed groups settle. This differentiation is crucial for a nuanced understanding of the multifaceted meanings of diaspora.

Robin Cohen extends the notion of the diaspora in his work, *Global Diasporas: An Introduction*, categorizing it into different types, including 'victim,' 'labour,' 'trade,' 'imperial,' and 'cultural' diasporas. This categorization helps us better comprehend the politics and dynamics of diaspora. Over time, as contemporary technologies and communication methods reshape the diasporic experiences, he introduces the term 'deterritorialized diasporas' to replace 'cultural diasporas.' These evolving definitions reflect the changing landscape of diasporic communities in our interconnected world.

In the context of modern migration trends and the global flow of cultures, Arjun Appadurai's work in *Modernity at Large* offers valuable insights into how mass-mediated communication, including radio, television, cassettes, videos, and newsprint, transcends national boundaries and exerts a significant influence on how individuals adapt to new environments. These mediums bridge gaps and enable the creation of transnational spaces where cultural identities intermingle.

Identity is a multifaceted and contextual concept, often tied to a shared territory, language, culture, and ethnicity. However, the complexity of transnational identity emerges from the assimilation of diverse cultural identities beyond the confines of one's specific homeland or ethnicity. Transnationalism can be defined as activities that necessitate sustained social interactions across national borders over time, contributing to the tension between notions of 'self' and 'other' as well as 'home' and 'host' lands. This tension is a defining characteristic of transnational identities.

Transnationalism, while often associated with diaspora, multiculturalism, and the blending of global and local experiences ('glocal'), possesses a distinct character. It involves the creation of imagined communities and spaces through migration, further complicating the notion of identity by emphasizing the fluid and dynamic nature of transnational identities in our increasingly interconnected world.

Transnationalism and Postcolonial Women's Writing

In recent South Asian literature, women writers have emerged as significant contributors, offering diverse perspectives rooted in their multiple identities and exposure to different cultures. While they explore a wide range of issues from a liberated standpoint, the question of identity remains central in their narratives, particularly within the context of postcolonialism, displacement, and deterritorialization.

These women writers redefine the concept of 'home', which may no longer exclusively refer to their homelands but can encompass any place where they feel a sense of belonging. Globalization blurs national borders, fostering cultural negotiations and giving rise to transnationalism as a profound cultural phenomenon.

The core objective of this study is to examine whether the tensions and complexities surrounding identity, as well as the experiences of dislocation and deterritorialization, find expression in the diasporic writings of South Asian women writers. These writers navigate shifting paradigms of female subjectivity, identity, and territoriality, offering unique perspectives on the interconnectedness of cultures and identities in today's globalized world.

In summary, South Asian women writers are making significant contributions to world literature. They bring a distinct lens to social, political, and geographical aspects, shedding light on issues such as East-West conflicts, subjugation, and freedom of expression. Their works encapsulate the intricate interplay of cultures and identities in our contemporary globalized landscape.

The postcolonial South Asian writings delve into themes of decolonization and the subjugation of gendered spaces. These texts also engage with postcolonial issues and concerns, making it imperative to discuss postcoloniality in the context of transnationalism and feminism. Transnational identity provides insights into the in-between lives of "Others" in their host countries. Being cast as the "Other" has often projected a subordinate image of migrants in Western countries. The process of colonization scattered South Asians beyond the geographical limits of their homeland. As they write back, their colonial past resonates in their present experiences in the West. Postcoloniality in their works intersects with themes of hybridity and identity as they navigate their lives on the border. Postcolonial women's writing allows the authors to carve out a unique space for representing the lives of South Asian women and claim a position in the realm of feminist studies. Immigrant writing that grapples with postcoloniality demonstrates the process of adapting to different cultures and the complex relationship between the native land and the host land.

Hélène Cixous, in her essay 'The Laugh of The Medusa,' questions male dominance in literary spaces and encourages women to step forward and express themselves. She emphasizes the need for women to write about their experiences and their own voices.

Susan Lanser, in her essay 'Toward a Feminist Narratology,' explores the relationship between feminism and narratology. She highlights the differences between the two, with feminism being evaluative and political while narratology is scientific and descriptive. Lanser seeks to understand whether the two can complement each other and enrich the field of literary criticism.

Postcolonial literature responds to colonization, with the new writers attempting to reclaim their voices and 'write back to the empire.' This literature often involves deconstruction and reconstruction, reinterpreting established narratives. For example, Jean Rhys's novella, *Wide Sargasso Sea*, challenges the portrayal of the non-white woman in Charlotte Bronte's *Jane Eyre*. South Asian literature negotiates the female identity within established narrative spaces.

Despite various challenges, South Asian literature thrives when writers respond to the language of the colonizer. As Salman Rushdie notes, "English has become an Indian language." The question of representing diasporic and transnational experiences in a foreign language becomes crucial. South Asian women writers have chosen English as their medium of expression for various reasons, including personal preference, comfort, familiarity, and the ability to address taboo topics without constraints imposed by their native tongue.

Conclusion

The term 'Diaspora' pertains to belonging to imagined communities and emerges as a consequence of border-crossing. These boundaries involve complex negotiations that result in a glocal space, where people are aware of multiple cultures and settings, giving rise to a contrapuntal awareness of simultaneous dimensions.

The transnational feminist study encompasses key terms such as 'home', 'hybridity', 'borders', 'identity', 'culture', 'resistance', 'survival', 'boundaries', the theories of Third World transnational writing, transcultural studies, and migration studies. South Asian women writers construct a unique literary space to address social issues, grapple with identity, and explore the clash of cultures. They use cultural clashes as tools to create transnational identities and empower themselves. Their writing reflects the complexities and resilience of 'third-space' identities in the face of cultural challenges.

References

- Appadurai, Arjun. *Modernity at Large: Cultural Dimensions of Globalization.*U of Minnesota P, 1996.

- Ashcroft, Bill, Gareth Griffiths, and Helen Tiffin. *The Empire Writes Back: Theory and Practice in Post-colonial Literatures.* Routledge, 1989.

- Bhabha, Homi K. *The Location of Culture.* Routledge, 1994.

- Brah, Avtar. *Cartographies of Diaspora: Contesting Identities.* Routledge, 1997.

- Cixous, Helene. *The Laugh of Medusa. Critical Theory Since 1995.*1989.

- Cohen, Robin. *Global Diasporas: An Introduction.* Washington P, 1997.

- Lanser, Susan S. *Toward A Feminist Narratology.* 1986, pp. 674-93.

- Rushdie, Salman, and Elisabeth West,editors. *The Vintage Book of Indian Writing 1947-1997.* Vintage, 1997.

- Vertovec, Steven. *Transnationalism.* Routledge, 2009.

Chapter 20

Diasporic Elements in the Novels of Anita Desai

Mrs. Afroz Jahan

Assistant Professor,
Department of English,
Sahu Ram Swaroop Girls P. G. College, Bareilly, Uttar Pradesh.
Email address- afrozjahan811@gmail.com

Abstract

Diasporic literature is an umbrella term that includes all types of literary works written by authors outside their native country, and these works are closely related to native culture and tradition. Therefore, all those writers who write outside their own country but remain related to their homeland through their works can be regarded as writers of Diasporic literature. Diasporic literature has its roots in the apparent loss of identity and alienation, which came into view as a result of migration and deportation. Generally, it is shared with alienation, displacement, existential rootlessness and a quest for identity.

In Anita Desai's fiction, women protagonists methodize the novelist's quest for psychological insight, perception, and cooperation. They are the focus point between the writer's consciousness and the world from which they are disunited. Therefore, her fictional women have to face contests, make an effort to break away to maintain their individuality and ponder over whether their resolution to do so is the accurate one, how to resolve the identity crisis, and how to appear triumphant from the trauma. Through these questions, Desai seems to examine her female characters. Her plots surely reach the raw nerves of human experience.

Keywords: Anita Desai, diasporic literature, rootlessness, migration, deportation, alienation, displacement

Anita Desai and Diaspora

Anita Desai was born on 24 June 1937. She is an Indian novelist and the Emerita John E. Burchard Professor of Humanities at the Massachusetts Institute of Technology. As a writer, she has been shortlisted for the Booker Prize three times. She received a Sahitya Akademi Award in 1978 for her novel *Fire on the Mountain* and 'The British Guardian Prize' for *The Village by the Sea.*

Anita Desai admits she feels about India as an Indian but thinks about it as an outsider. This point of view is derived from her German mother, whom she described as carrying a European core in her, which did not mingle with many of the Indian ways and became a cause for a kind of separateness. The lives of outsiders have been explored within Indian society and also within the West. Her fiction works have themes such as women's oppressional pursuit of a fulfilling identity, family bonding and contrasts, the disintegrating of traditions, and anti-Semitism. In her fiction, Eurocentric and social biases are often detected; therefore, it could be read as the result of the author's concentration on pulled-up and diminished identities. Desai's novels arouse characters, events, and contemporary themes with recourse to accurate use of visual imagery and details, and it led to juxtapositions with the modernist sensibilities of T. S. Eliot, William Faulkner and many others. For three decades of the last century, she has been an extended name in English literature, fascinating her readers and astonishing her contemporaries with her flawless writing.Anita Desai's novels have one of the themes of an individual's yearning to treat family relations.The central figures of the novels try to find their own identitiesand individualities consciously, and try to break away from the kind of life they are regretful for. It shows the way to expose the conflict between two sets of values–one standing for the supremacy of social ranking and the other for that of the individual.

Anita Desai is more interested in the interior landscape of mind and heart of her characters, in contrast with other Indian women novelists in English like Nayantara Sahgal, Ruth Prawar Jhabvala, Kamala Markandaya, and Shashi Deshpande. She is highly concerned with the inner spirit of human beings. She also concentrated on the man in a contest with his mind.She tries to explore the human psyche. Desai loves to focus her attention both on the journey fromothers and the inner part of human existence. Her novels have persistent themes such as human relationships, alienation, loneliness, East and West encounters, violence, and death.

Anita Desai, hence, attempts to present a modern psychological control and projects a sensibility generally not engaged in other Indo-Anglican writers of fiction. As a novelist, her distinguishing qualities are the subordination of the background to the characters and the deft handling of the language, imagery and syntax in order to transport an intimate expression of the inner world of her characters. Her works are consummated so completely that her treatment gets the look of a philosophical system- a system that has been familiar to the world in the form of 'existentialism'. Presentations of existentialism are testimony in the whole framework of her stories. Existentialism means – "the one alone", the man who has no record, seems to be a cherished subject of Anita Desai. Not being something unique, loneliness is still a characteristic of the society of our time. Today, a lot of people also feel alone, unconnected to society, and unable to communicate with those around them. The theme of her works is the problems of an individual who feels emotionally and spiritually alone. Most of the critical writing of her novels focuses on her preoccupation with her urban sensibility and a style of what she calls 'The Language of the Interior'.

She is immanently a candid writer engaged in probing the reality of society and Indian families. As a woman, she is capable enough of understanding women's psyche and mental position better than the male writers. We can see this in her portrayal of women characters in her novels with a special insight and superbness of sentiment. Her novels have tragic characters forever; as they admit their destiny, they refuse to surrender. Apart from their temperamental indifference, the outside forces, such as the city, nature, and family, play major roles in making them tragic and awkward. The moral, physical, and spiritual heartache of urban life results in a lot of difficulty, alienation, loneliness, and a desire for human values, and the protagonists fall prey to them. It ultimately results in an attitude of frustration and disillusionment, leading to a preoccupation with the idea of death and dying. She is the novelist of the inner weather of the mind and has a remarkable ability to probe into the recesses of the heart, which is her forte.

Diaspora means scattered identity. Diasporic literature is written by authors who feel rootlessness abroad. There are various types of diaspora. It can be graded as victim diaspora, trading diaspora, labour diaspora, and imperial diaspora. Different critics and authors have different notions regarding the concept of diaspora. Anita Desai is one of the authors who have mixed parentage. This is the reason that she is considered both an insider and an outsider.

Her Works

Her first novel, *Cry, the Peacock,* is chiefly concerned with the theme of a marital relationship between Gautama and Maya. This novel is a story about the spiritual prayers of the female protagonist, Maya, the half-child, half-woman romantic heroine. She analyzes herself as a peacock in the torture of rapture of his deadly love experience. We can learn an impression of the marital disruption and encountered matrimonial life through this novel. Maya is married to Gautama, who is shrewd, calculating, and extremely matter-of-fact about the gravest matters, while Maya seems innocent and highly sensitive. She is embedded within her own psyche space. She has no ability to place her own self in defiance of the heterosexual space given to her by her husband.

Maya's husband, Gautama, wants his wife to be traditional, docile, permissive, and compromising, but she perceives that no one attends to her physical and emotional needs, and she is called a neurotic. Her authentic self is suppressed, and the false self generates an unhealthy mental state, which results in her personality becoming disintegrated. She is mentioned with her two selves – real and pseudo. An incident that proves traumatic to her means nothing to her husband. There is a very vast difference in the attitude and nature of both that one cannot but expect a painful incompatibility between them.

For Maya, the ideal love was offered by her father. She was never reprimanded by her father; therefore, she could not finish her innocence for being a mature and practical woman. In pain, she fondly remembers how everything has grace and dignity with him. Maya studies the root cause of their inconsistency. We get to know her past life and her engagement with the Albino astrologer who had once told her that from both, one would die within four years of her marriage. The diffidence caused by this prophecy had become destroyed with the journey of time, but with the death of their dog, Totto, all these past memories woke up and began to plague her again. With the burden of the past, the memories of her childhood, the constant fear of death and her retrogression, she is closely connected with her recollection of the words of the astrologer.

In this novel, there are hardly any elements of diaspora but the pain and agony caused due to identity crisis and seclusion give us a glimpse of detachment and firm connection to their homeland and people.

Her second novel, *Voices in the City*, is a powerful attempt by Anita Desai at the research and analysis of the dark recesses of the consciousness of its three characters- Nirode and his two sisters, Monisha and Amla. Each of these characters in the novel is distressed by the senseless and meaningless being in Calcutta. Every person is highly influenced by it and tries to find themselves confined in the prison of isolation without any hope of escape from it. Here, Anita Desai portrays the feminine psyche chiefly with the character of Monisha, though there are other women characters also in the novel. Monisha is similar enough to Maya in the sense that she has no children, and she is sensitive and a victim of ill-matched marriage.The novel's protagonist is Nirode, a proven sensitive and talented young man with some qualities that subdue others. However, he is negligent of himself and of his target in life and suffers from aninferiority complex.His father had set apart a certain amount of money for the education abroad of one of the two sons, who would be able to come through in studies. Nirode's younger brother makes a praiseworthy effort in his studies andgames.When he succeeds the amount of money loaded separately for him by his father, Nirode reflectsthat his father might have known that he could not be successful.This inferiority complex haunts him badly.

We can see the impressive contrast between the two brothers. Arun stands on success, the other on failure. In real life, Nirode is not able to be a part of academic acquirements for extra-curricular activities, but Aruna has joined all the activities.This also intensifies his sense of inferiority. He has feelings of humiliation, isolation, and belittleness. Sometimes, he assumes that the adventures of his boyhood have been a dream, not a real journey because he has never been able to make a start. He is unable to start a journey, which is indicative of the basic uncertainties in his temperament.It is imputable to his lack of preference that he is helpless to do anything and set out on his journey. Here, we see a variety of characters with a variety of detached emotions.

Bye-Bye, Blackbird, the third novel by Anita Desai, deals with the theme of coloured immigrants in England. It bestrews Adit and Sarah's difficulties of modification and explores their fragmented psyche. Here, Desai employs the flashback technique and narrates the situation bringing about the marriage of Adit and Sarah. This novel is divided into three parts- Departure, Discovery and Recognition.This division has helped Desai to portray this novel's themeand their relationship with each other and execute her notions methodically and effectively. This novel also has nostalgia, which is used as a narrative technique. It is represented differently; Adit's nostalgia for the *hilsa* fish and for the Bengal surroundings is a deep expression of a necessity to pertain and to bring the gulf between London and Calcutta. The female protagonist, Sarah, is a working woman. She is not an Indian; still, she is one who endeavours to be Indian, despising her identity and existence as a white woman. She is a woman with self-control and a sense of sacrifice. She is in the habit of attempting compromises according to a situation. Sarah suffers from alienation and isolation, yet she stands with courage and stoicism. Sometimes she wonders about her real identity being in confusion. She thinks about who she is – is an English lady or the Head's secretary in the school for English children in England or just Mrs. Sen for Adit Sen, a Bengali.

The percolation of maladjusted marriage continues in this novel, and it also deals with social issues. Four characters, Adit and Sarah, Sama and Bella, are the sacrifices of alien culture and tradition, as this novel is based on immigrants' problems. There is a consummate turbulence and escapism in their marriage. Adit marries an English girl, Sarah, and arouses the excitement of the white society of London. They both suffer from this situation. Sarah has broken the social cryptography of England by marrying a brown Asian and is wreaked by taunts not only of her colleagues but also of the young pupils of the school where she works as a clerk. She was taunted and ignored by her pupils.

Sarah had a deep love for India. She is eager to know more about India, and she expressed her interest in India through stamps. However, she does not like to confess this part of her character to everyone. She also bears an identity crisis for this reason. Both Adit and Sarah have to pretend to be the frontage of happily married life. She faces the tension between hypocrisy and actuality, apparition and reality, resulting in schizophrenia. She is also affected by tortures of anxiety and insecurity.

In *Bye-Bye, Blackbird,* the novelist Anita Desai tries to show us the conditions of Indian immigrants living in foreign countries.

In her next novel, *Where Shall We Go This Summer?*Anita Desai leads to the theme of alienation and the desire for proper communication in the protagonist's life.This can represent the conditions of the whole society as here the treatment is more restrained, and the wife's loneliness is the loneliness of the woman, wife, and mother loneliness modified by the society and family: Sita suffers from domestic and temporal aches.

The female protagonist, Sita, a middle-aged woman, is sick of the temporal routine of insignificant existence. She suffers from suffocation in her well-ordered, posh flat in Bombay and strives to get rid of it all. Here, we see her trip to Manori Island, her maiden home. She wants to recall all the pleasant memories of her past. She flees to the island in order not to give birth to her fifth child, as four children are already there. Sita is also haunted by her loveless marriage with Raman, like "Maya and Monisha" in other novels. She finds it difficult to understand that though they lived so intimate with each other, Raman could not know the basic point about his wife, that she was fed up with life. She was in the habit of realizing the emptiness and loneliness of her marriage.The maladjustment between Raman and Sita is focused on values, doctrines of faith, and their standard.

This novel shows a woman's urge for sovereignty. Here, Sita repays to the feminine-semiotic landscape in backtracking to

Manori Island. This novel is about the secret selves of the characters but remains quashed and undistinguished in most feminine lives. The event, in retrospection, is brought about by her fifth pregnancy. Sita's uncommon childhood plays an important role in moulding her feminine sensibility. It is probation for Sita when she becomes pregnant for the fifth time, but she does not want to deliver the child. She begins to think of the enchanted island of miracles, Manori Island and decides to go there along with her two children, Maneka and Karan, during her initial period of pregnancy without her husband's suggestion. There, she awaits a mysterious miracle, but nothing happens. She begins to revive her connection with the past, but all is in vain, and her children get vexed and fed up with their primitive lives. She has to return to her normal life with her children.

Her novel, *Fire on the Mountain*, is a story of the bewailing cry of an old woman, Nanda Kaul who has got too much of this society and yearns for a quiet and secluded life. Her life is an instance of marital dissonance. Her husband, Prof. Kaul, was the Vice Chancellor who carries on a lifelong attachment with Miss David, the Math teacher. However, she was a Christian, so he could not defend marrying her in that society. Nanda and Prof. Kaul's marriage is only based on physical desire and circumstantial convenience for the husband, who lives a dual life. Apparently, they were an ideal couple to the general community, but from inside, their relationships were all devoid, and the whole social role and socializing was an illusion. Nanda knows and bears her husband's affair with a frigid smile on her face. She nourishes the whole family, his house, and his children, supervising the cooks and the servants, fascinating the guests with efficiency and a maintained poise. However, with all these things, she begins to lose her individuality and identity in the process. She was unhappy in this house, enduring with the large family and stream of quests that come to their house repeatedly. Their relationship was nothing beyond the duties and covenants they had for each other.

Clear Light of Day is the sixth novel by Anita Desai, who elaborates here on the relationship of two brothers and two sisters. The elder brother, Raja, is a poet married to a Muslim girl.He lives in Hyderabadand maintains a nebulous connection with his siblings, who live in Delhi.This novel also deals with the theme of derangement in marriage. All the marriages depicted in the novel are not satisfactory.The parents do not utilize their time with their children.They were engaged in playing bridge at home or the club only for their enjoyment.The mother had to face severe diabetes and be attended to by the husband, as it was his duty to care for his wife. Soon, she is hospitalized. Then,the father visits her every evening.Her marriage and her life were equal to a card house.Tara is married to Bakul and their marriage is also a convenience. She wants to escape from the dark, shadow, and proscribe house to a life of laughter and gladness, that is why she marries Bakul. He also was in need of a wife who would adjust according to his needs.Tara felt something mysterious to be ill and that anyone living in that house was bound to be ill. She also wanted to escapefromcollege. Bakul has engraved Tara according to his choices.One thing thatdisturbs him is that she becomes the old Tara of her youth as she invades her old house. She has reversed into the pointless person she was before their marriage. She doesnot experience enough love in her marriage institution, and they both admit it as a form of biological necessity. Bakul, being employed in a foreign country, looked for a wife. He does not consider his wife a companion but treats her as a thing to take pride in, like a showpiece. Soon, Tara realized that she had pursued him enough.

Baumgartner's Bombay deals with the modern circumstances of immigrated persons. This novel is an inspiring account of a nameless, nationless man. He is unable to go anywhere to recover his lost identity. It narrates the life story of Hugo, from his prosperous early days in Germany to the horror of his murder in India by another German. The series of disasters- losing his home, business, and mother- makes him silent and acquiring.

This novel focuses on the life of two persons separated from Germany, without their family and country. Hugo Baumgartner and Lotte, a female cabaret dancer, are alone foreigners in India and overturned from their own culture. Baumgartner, a German Jew, lives his lost life in alienation in a duty flat in Bombay. He lives alone, and Lotte is an old lady losing her youth and beauty. She had a false marriage with one of her admirers, KantilalSethia, and is left alone after his death. Kantilal's sons do not like her. Baumgartner and Lotte are alone and choose each other as companions, getting rid of their frustration and agony because of loneliness. They are in a soft relationship with each other. Lotte can go nowhere except Baumgartner. Baumgartner feels seduced, isolated, and deceived, and he lives on with a fear of loneliness. Lotte, with brotherly inclination, distributes his loneliness with her. She is also in regular search for identity to live perfectly in Indian society. She marries Kanti Sethia in order to get Indian citizenship but is shocked when he leaves her in Bombay like a widow and lives in Calcutta himself. After the death of Kanti, Lotte leans upon Baumgartner for companionship. As Hugo is profane in his heart and soul, he develops a spiritual insight. The novel ends abruptly and we find the shattered life of Baumgartner is full of pathos and irony. We find that he keeps himself busy most of the time by remembering his family and relatives in Berlin. The concept of diaspora in the novels of Anita Desai is unique because the novelist has tried to analyze her characters from different angles.

Conclusion

Indian immigrants are spread around the world and shape an essential part of the global diaspora. There have been social and cultural exchanges in the job market. In this context, the literature coming out from the diasporic people assumes significance. The literature of Indian diaspora is a frame of works of people who identify themselves as being of Indian origin but also belonging to foreign lands. Therefore, diaspora is a scattering of the seeds in the wind. History has significant diasporic movements, as they carry within themselves the kernel of the nation's history. Diaspora is a journey towards self-realization, self-recognition, and self-definition. The diasporic writings present an element of productivity, which helps reimburseany losses suffered.

References

- ashvamegh.net/elements-of-diaspora-anita-desais-bye-bye-black-bird/

- Desai, Anita. *Baumgartner's Bombay*, New Delhi, Vintage Publishers, 2001.

- Desai, Anita. *Bye-Bye, Blackbird*, New Delhi, Orient Paperbacks, 2019.

- Desai, Anita. *Clear Light of Day*, New Delhi, RHI Publishers, 2021(New Print).

- Desai, Anita. *Cry, the Peacock*, New Delhi, Orient Paperbacks, 1980, p.75.

- diplomacybeyond.com/at-homeaway-from-home-literatures-of-the-new-indian-diaspora/

- en.wikipedia.org/wiki/Anita_Desai

- www.onmanorama.com/news/columns/global-indian/2017/04/01/india-diaspora-literary-expressions-t-p-sreenivasan.html

- www.researchgate.net/topic/Diaspora-Literature/publications

Chapter 21

भारतीय कला, संगीत एवं नृत्य को प्रोत्साहित करने में प्रवासियों की भूमिका

डॉ0 बिनीता पाण्डेय

असिस्टेट प्रोफेसर
हीरा लाल यादव बालिका पी॰जी॰कॉलेज
लखनऊ
ईमेल पता: binitavijay1983@gmail.com

सार

परम पवित्र भारतवर्ष का आधार यहाँ की विविध सांस्कृतिक परंपराएं हैं। हमारी सभ्यता प्राचीन है जिसने विश्व को अठारह विद्या तथा चौसठ कलाओं का प्रकाश प्रदान किया जिसने अपने लोगों को हमेशा यह सिखाया कि –'दुख सहना देवत्व है और दुख देना आसुरी वृत्ति'। इसलिए भारतीय संस्कृति का स्वरूप हमेशा आशावादी रहा है परंतु अफसोस कि इतनी समृद्ध परंपरा के बाद भी भारत में मध्यकाल हो या आधुनिक काल विदेशी आक्रांताओं ने यहाँ अपना प्रवास किया तो उन्हें यह लगता था कि भारतीय अज्ञानी है क्योंकि वह भारतीय संस्कृति की अजरता अमरता को पहचान ना सके। अंग्रेज़ जब भारत आए तो उन्होंने फारसी में राजकाज किया, हिंदी सीखी परंतु निर्णय लेने की भाषा अपनी

अंग्रेजी को ही बनाया। व्यापारिक महत्वाकांक्षाओं की पूर्ति के लिए एशिया के धनी सम्पन्न वैभवशाली एवं गौरवशाली भारत देश को अपना उपनिवेश बनाया तो व्यापार के साथ-साथ भारत से कला-वैभव एवं संपन्नता तथा सस्ते कामगारों को अपने देश व अन्य उपनिवेशों में ले जाने की एक नई परंपरा सी अंग्रेज़ों ने विकसित कर ली, उद्देश्य था मात्र गुलाम भारत को आर्थिक सांस्कृतिक तथा राजनीतिक रूप से हमेशा कमजोर रखना, सस्ते मज़दूरों को प्राप्त करना। इस राष्ट्र ने अपनी कला, संगीत, नृत्य की विविधता अर्थात यूं कहें कि भारत की भौगोलिक संरचना के आधार पर विभिन्न क्षेत्रीय उप क्षेत्रीय, कला, संगीत, नृत्य तथा शास्त्रीय संगीत उप शास्त्रीय संगीत, वादन, लोक कला, चित्रकला आदि को विदेशी आक्रमण भी समाप्त न कर पाए और यह कलाएं सरहद की दीवारों, बंदिशों को तोड़कर औपनिवेशिक काल में विश्व के विभिन्न भागों तक भारतीयों के साथ उनकी संस्कृति के रूप में वहीं पहुंची और आज विश्व का शायद कोई देश ऐसा होगा जहां भारतीय प्रवासी व भारतीय संस्कृति का उनके द्वारा प्रचार प्रसार ना किया जा रहा हो।

मुख्य शब्द: भारतीय संस्कृति, कला, नृत्य, प्रवासियों, लोक कला, चित्र कला, शास्त्रीय संगीत

कलाएं हमेशा जनमानस को जागृत करती हैं भारत विश्व में अपने कला संगीत एवं नृत्य रूपी समृद्ध सांस्कृतिक परंपरा के लिए ही प्रसिद्ध है क्योंकि भारतीय कला संस्कृति हमेशा समृद्ध रही है भले प्राचीन भारत हो मध्यकाल हो या आधुनिक भारत अधिक से अधिक लोगों को इस संस्कृति से जुड़ने का अवसर मिला या यूं कहें कि जो अपनापन भारतीय कला संगीत व नृत्य में है वह कहीं और नहीं है शायद इस बात को प्रवासी भारतीयों से बेहतर कौन समझ सकता है जो विश्व के लगभग सभी देशों में भारतीय कला संस्कृति को फैलाने में महत्त्वपूर्ण योगदान दे रहे हैं। पिछले कई वर्षों में प्रवासी भारतीयों की संख्या में निरंतर वृद्धि हुई है जो या तो स्वतन्त्रता से पूर्व अंग्रेज़ों द्वारा कामगारों के रूप में अपने

उपनिवेशों में ले जाए गए जैसे फिजी, सूरीनाम, गुआना, त्रिनिदाद, अफ्रीका, मॉरीशस आदि देशों में बसे या फिर स्वतंत्रता पश्चात रोज़गार के अवसरों की तलाश में स्वयं विश्व के कई भागों में गए और वहीं बस गए परंतु खून का रिश्ता सबसे बड़ा होता है इस बात को चरितार्थ करते हुए ये प्रवासी भारतीय आज भी अपनी जड़ों से जुड़े हुए हैं और भारत के गौरव को विश्व पटल पर प्रचार-प्रसार कर रहे हैं। भारतीय कला, संगीत एवं नृत्य को प्रोत्साहित करने में प्रवासियों की भूमिका की बात की जाए तो भला आज पश्चिम की कला कितनी ही महामंडित हो जाए, परंतु इन पश्चिमी देशों में रहने वाले प्रवासी भारतीय आज भी जब अंतर्राष्ट्रीय स्तर के मंच से अपनी अभिव्यक्ति प्रस्तुत करते हैं तो नमस्कार या नमस्ते शब्दों का संबोधन करके भारतीय होने का एहसास अवश्य प्रकट करते हैं। अकबर ने भारतीय कला की गौरव गाथा को स्पष्ट करते हुए लिखा था -'कोई कला यदि संपन्न है, चर्चा करने योग्य है, तो वह भारतीय कला है' इस संपन्न कला को अपना स्वाधीनता आंदोलन का अस्त्र बनाते हुए गांधी जी ने कहा था कि यदि अधिक से अधिक लोगों को स्वाधीनता से जोड़ना है तो उनमें भारतीय कला एवं संस्कृति के प्रति प्रेम जगाना आवश्यक है। भारतीय संस्कृति की सम्पन्न परंपरा के अंतर्गत विशिष्ट कला शैली और विकसित पद्धतियाँ, ना सिर्फ भारत में बल्कि प्रवासी भारतीयों द्वारा विश्व में पहचान बना रही है।

भारतीय संगीत में वह सामर्थ्य व क्षमता है जिससे वह संपूर्णविश्व के हृदय में अपनी सरगम एवं भावों को प्रसारित कर सके।यह बात इस ब्रह्मांड की तरह ही सत्य है कि भारतीय संस्कृति व संगीत प्राचीनतम है और समय के साथ-साथ बदलती शैलियों के रूप में इसने गांव, नगर, वैश्विक परिदृश्य को भी भारतीय संगीत कला ने अपनी और आकर्षित किया। संगीत सिर्फ आजीविका का साधन ही नहीं बल्कि खुश रहने का आज एक महत्वपूर्ण स्रोत बन चुका है। न्यूयार्क के डॉक्टर एडवर्ड पोलाबास्की ने अपने अध्ययन में भी स्पष्ट किया कि संगीत से

रक्त संचालन प्रभावित होता है और शिराओं में नवजीवन का संचार होता है। उन्होंने ध्वनि तरंगो का पथरी रोग पर विशेष प्रभाव देखा अर्थात यह कहना गलत ना होगा कि स्वस्थ जीवन शैली के लिए भोजन के साथ-साथ संगीत भी वर्तमान जीवन में आवश्यक अंग बन रहा है। ना केवल भारतियों ने भारत में रहकर कला, संगीत, नृत्य, को अपनाया है बल्कि कला के साथ-साथ भारतीय संगीत, नृत्य, ने अंतर्राष्ट्रीय मंच पर भारतीय सांस्कृतिक मूल्यों एवं विविधता को प्रदर्शित करने का असीम प्रयास किया है। भारतीय प्रवासी नागरिक भारत से बाहर रहकर भी संगीत नृत्य के माध्यम से जहां अपने लिए रोजगार के अवसरों की तलाश कर रहे है वहीं भारतीय गीत संगीत को विश्व में पहचान दे रहे हैं। शुभा बेदुला, फाल्गुनी शाह जिन्होंने अपनी कला से देश का सिर गर्व से ऊंचा किया है, लियोरा इतजाक भारतीय मूल की इजरइली संगीतज्ञ, सनातन कृष्णन पारंपरिक भारतीय गीतों को स्वदेशी भाषा के शब्दों के साथ मिश्रित करने वाले भारतीय मूल के अफ्रीकी गायक, अशोक रामचद्र, वंदना नारन आदि अनेक गायक हैं, जिन्होंने लगभग विश्व के सभी देशो में भारतीय संगीत को वैश्विक बनाने में भूमिका निभाई है। एवं जो भारतीय संगीत की धुनों पर भारतीय भाषाओं में भारतीय फिल्म जगत को अपने प्रेरणा स्रोत मानते हुए अदभुत प्रतिभा के धनी विश्व में भारतीय भाषा एवं भारतीय झंडे को फक्र के साथ थामे हुए भारतीय मूल के होने पर गर्व करते हैं।

पूर्णतः रागों पर आधारित भारतीय शास्त्रीय संगीत हो या शास्त्रीय संगीत के अलग -अलग विधाएँ जैसे हिंदुस्तानी संगीत मूलतः भारत के उत्तर भारतीय क्षेत्र में गाया जाने वाला संगीत हो या कर्नाटक संगीत, द्रविड संगीत, हो या उपशास्त्रीय संगीत जैसे- ठुमरी, कजरी या लोक संगीत हो या फिर फिल्मी संगीत जो अपनी भाव भंगिमा मुद्राएँ आदि के लिए जानी जाती हैं,ने हमेशा समाज, देश व विश्व को जोड़ने का कार्य किया है और भारत के विभिन्न भौगोल्लिक क्षेत्रों से बाहर विश्व में प्रवासन कर चुके

प्रवासी भारतीयों ने इस समृद्ध सांस्कृतिक परम्परा का अनुसरण किया। इसीलिए आज विश्व के लगभग अधिकांश भागों से प्रवासी भारतीय विश्वविद्यालयों में संगीत की शिक्षा लेते हैं। जो भारतीय संस्कृति के प्रति उनके आकर्षण, प्रेम आदि को दर्शाता है।

अंतरराष्ट्रीय स्तर पर अनेक सांस्कृतिक केंद्र जो सांस्कृतिक कार्यक्रमों, सांस्कृतिक संगोष्ठियों एवं सांस्कृतिक कार्यशालाओं के माध्यम से प्रवासी भारतीयों को जोड़ने के अवसर प्रदान कर रहे हैं, स्थापित किए गए हैं। जो भारत सरकार के साथ जुड़कर साहित्य, सांस्कृतिक आदि का संवर्धन एवं मार्गदर्शन कर रहे हैं। मॉरीशस का इंदिरा गांधी भारतीय संस्कृति केंद्र, विभिन्न विश्वविद्यालयों में आयोजित किए जाने वाले सार्वजनिक समारोह में भारतीय प्रवासियों की सहभागिता, भारतीय मूल के प्रवासी भारतीयों का हॉलीवुड का हिस्सा बनना, सिनेमाघर में बॉलीवुड फिल्में दिखाकर भारतीय भाषा तथा संस्कृति से अधिक से अधिक लोगों को जोड़ना, योग दिवस पर अंतर्राष्ट्रीय जगत में प्रवासी भारतीयों द्वारा बढ़ चढ़कर हिस्सा लेने हेतु भारतीय प्रवासियों द्वारा अनेक भारतीय शास्त्रीय नृत्य कार्यशाला केंद्र खोले गये हैं,आदि। आज विश्व में बड़ी संख्या में भारतीय नृत्य संगीत सिखाया जाता है तथा प्रदर्शित किया जाता है एवं नई पीढ़ी द्वारा सीखा भी जाता है। अधिक से अधिक प्रवासी भारतीयों द्वारा उत्साह के साथ प्रतिभाग भी किया जा रहा है, ताकि भारतीय कला, संगीत, नृत्य, रूपी खूबसूरत कला और अतुलनीय भारतीय संस्कृति के प्रोत्साहन में योगदान दिया जा सके।

संदर्भ

* खाडेकर लक्ष्मी नारायण, साहू अजय कुमार, भट्टाचार्य गौरी एण्ड, द इण्डयिन हस्टिोरकिल एण्ड कनटम्पररेी कॉनटेक्सट,रावत पब्लकिेशन्स, पृष्ठ सं० 205

- चौधरी डॉ. विनोद कुमार, *इण्डियन डायसपोरा*, कला एवम् धर्म शोध संस्थान, 2017,पृष्ठ सं० 113

- बन्धोपाध्याय शेखर, *प्लासी से विभाजन तक और उसके बाद,आधुनिक भारत का इतिहास*, द्वितीय संस्करण, ओरियण्टल ब्लैकस्वान प्रा० लि.२०२०पृष्ठ सं० 231.

- लॉ नारमन, *मॉर्डन वर्ड हिस्ट्री*, संस्करण –पाँचवा,पॉलगेन मैकमीलियन पब्लिकेशन. - 2021,पृष्ठ सं० 629

Chapter 22

भारतीय प्रवासी हिंदी साहित्य

सबीहा नूरी

शोध छात्रा
मध्यकालीन एवं आधुनिक इतिहास विभाग
लखनऊ विश्वविद्यालय, उ० प्र०
ईमेल पता: sabeehanoori123@gmail.com

सार

प्रस्तुत शोध पत्र में भारतीय प्रवासी हिंदी साहित्य का अध्ययन किया गया है। पिछले कुछ दशकों के दौरान प्रौद्योगिकी में वृद्धि और वैश्वीकरण के परिणामस्वरूप पिछली शताब्दियों की तुलना में प्रवासन और आव्रजन एक सार्वभौमिक अनुभव बन गया है। भारतीय प्रवासी आम तौर पर जो भारतीय अपनी मातृभूमि से दूर रह रहे हैं उन्हें दुविधा और समायोजन के कई संघर्षों का सामना करना पड़ता है भारतीय आप्रवासी एक ऐसे मानव हैं जो दूसरे मानवीय परिवेश में अपनी पहचान की तलाश में हैं हिंदी अप्रवासी साहित्य उनके अनुभवों और मानसिकताओं को चित्रित करने का एक माध्यम बन गया है।अपने देश से बाहर परदेश में रहने वाले प्रवासियों द्वारा रचित साहित्य प्रवासी साहित्य के अंतर्गत आता है नई साहित्य धारा के रूप में प्रवासी साहित्य का उभराव उत्तर औपनिवेशिक संदर्भ में दृष्टव्य है, प्रवासी लेखक उन प्रवासियों का प्रतिनिधित्व करते हैं जो बेगानी धरती पर कई संघर्षों का सामना

करते हैं प्रवासी हिंदी साहित्य गद्य और पद्य विधाओं में रचा जाता है जिनमें प्रवासी भारतीय जीवन के कई पक्ष का निरूपण होता है। इस अध्ययन का उद्देश्य हिंदी प्रवासी साहित्य में दर्शाए गए भारतीय प्रवासियों के सामाजिक और सांस्कृतिक अनुभवों की पहचान करना और लोगों को समकालीन साहित्य अध्ययन और मानविकी के लिए प्रेरित करना है प्रवासी हिंदी साहित्य ने हिंदी साहित्य संसार में अपनी एक अलग पहचान बनाई है पर राष्ट्रीय प्रवास को प्रवास के ऐसे पैटर्न के रूप में परिभाषित किया जाता है जिसमें हालांकि व्यक्ति अंतर्राष्ट्रीय सीमाओं के पार चले जाते हैं और नए राज्य में बस जाते हैं और सामाजिक संबंध स्थापित कर लेते हैं लेकिन उसे राष्ट्र से सामाजिक संबंध बनाए रखते हैं जिसके भी मूल निवासी होते हैं।

मुख्य शब्दः हिंदी साहित्य, प्रवासी, प्रवासन, विदेश, हिंदी भाषा

प्रस्तावना

वर्तमान समय में जीवन के अन्य क्षेत्रों की भांति लेखन का क्षेत्र विस्तृत हो रहा है और नित्य नए आयाम को छूने लगा है। हिंदी साहित्य आज भारत में ही नहीं रचा जा रहा बल्कि यह विश्व के अन्य कई देशों में भी रचा जा रहा है। प्रवासी भारतीयों द्वारा लिखे जा रहे हिंदी साहित्य को प्रवासी हिंदी साहित्य की संज्ञा दी गई है विश्व में अनेक देश है जहां हिंदी में साहित्य सृजन हो रहा है इनमें जहां एक ओर मॉरिशस, फिजी, सूरीनाम आदि भारतवंशीय बहुल राष्ट्र शामिल है वहीं दूसरी ओर अमेरिका और इंग्लैंड, डेनमार्क, ऑस्ट्रेलिया, कनाडा, नार्वे आदि यूरोपीय देश भी आते हैं वस्तुतः हिंदी साहित्य का अंतरराष्ट्रीय क्षितिज दिन प्रतिदिन व्यापक और विस्तृत होता जा रहा है प्रस्तुत शोध के अंतर्गत भारतीय प्रवासी हिंदी साहित्य के विविध पक्षों को सामने लाने का प्रयास किया गया है।

शोध प्रविधि

शोध पत्र में विश्लेषणात्मक शोध पद्धति का प्रयोग किया गया है। जिसमें आंकड़े द्वितीयक समंक पर आधारित है।

मानव नैसर्गिक रूप से स्वतंत्र जन्म लेता है उसकी यह प्रवृत्ति रही है कि जिस स्थान पर जीवन जटिल होता है वह उस स्थान को छोड़कर ऐसे स्थान की ओर स्थानांतरण करता है जहां जीवन तुलनात्मक रूप से सुगम होता है यह स्थानांतरण ही प्रवास कहलाता है प्राचीन काल से भारतीय विभिन्न कारण से प्रवास कर रहे हैं प्राकृतिक आपदाएं, जलवायु परिवर्तन, महामारियां,गरीबी,सुखा, आकाल, बेरोजगारी, धार्मिक उन्माद और शिक्षा आदि प्रमुख कारण है।

9 जनवरी 2003 को प्रथम प्रवासी भारतीय सम्मेलन का आयोजन किया गया था, तब से 9 जनवरी को हर वर्ष **प्रवासी भारतीय दिवस** के रूप में मनाने का प्रचलन बना हुआ है। 9 जनवरी का दिन भारतीयों के लिए ऐतिहासिक दिन भी है क्योंकि इसी दिन महात्मा गांधी दक्षिण अफ्रीका से भारत लौटे थे। 48 देश में रह रहे प्रवासियों की जनसंख्या करीब 2 करोड़ है इनमें से 11 देश में 5 लाख से ज्यादा प्रवासी भारतीय वहां के औसत जनसंख्या का प्रतिनिधित्व करते हैं और वहां की आर्थिक व राजनितिक दशा व दिशा को तय करने में महत्वपूर्ण भूमिका निभाते हैं आज भारतीय विदेश में इतनी उन्नति कर चुके हैं कि उनका अपना एक प्रवासी समाज निर्मित हो चुका है विदेश गए भारतीयों के लिए प्रवासी भारतीय शब्दावली का प्रयोग सबसे पहले उन भारतीयों के लिए किया जाता है जो 1834 से यूरोपीय उपनिवेशों में गिरमिटिया मजदूर के रूप में भेजे गए थे अभिमन्यु अनंत, रामदेव धुरंधर, जोगिंदर सिंह कंवल, विवेकानंद शर्मा आदि हिंदी के ऐसे प्रवासी उपन्यासकार हैं जिनके पूर्वज वर्षों पूर्व गिरमिटिया मजदूर के रूप में विदेश गए थे अपने पूर्वज के सच को इन उपन्यासकारों ने हिंदी उपन्यास की शक्ल दी है गिरिराज

किशोर पहला गिरमिटिया के अलावा गिरमिटिया प्रवासी भारतीयों को उपन्यास का विषय बनाने वाले अधिकतर हिंदी उपन्यासकार उन्हें गिरमिटिया मजदूरों के वंशज हैं जबकि आजादी के बाद प्रवासी हुए भारतीयों के जीवन को प्रवासी रचनाकारों ने उपन्यास का विषय बनाया।

प्रवासी उन्हें कहा जाता है जो अपने देश को छोड़कर दूसरे देशों में बस जाते हैं भारतीय भी दुनिया के अनेक देशों में रह रहे हैं प्रवासी अपने देश को छोड़कर दूसरे देश में बस जाते हैं तो उनकी स्थिति अनिश्चित होती है, आज भारतीय अर्थव्यवस्था की बदलते स्वरूप और भूमंडलीकरण के कारण प्रवासी लेखन भी महत्वपूर्ण हो गया है] प्रवासी लेखिका उषा राजे सक्सेना के शब्दों में प्रवासी शब्द प्रवास का विश्लेषण है प्रवासी एक मनोविज्ञान है एक अंतर्दृष्टि है जिसे स्वतः तैयार होने में बरसों लगते हैं स्वतंत्रता के पूर्व अंग्रेज भारत से गरीब और सस्ते मजदूर मॉरीशस, त्रिनिदाद, गुयाना, सूरीनाम, कोलंबिया, जावा आदि देशों को ले गए, भारतीय अधिकांशत पंजाब, उत्तर प्रदेश, बिहार, और दक्षिण भारत के तमिल थे, गिरमिटिया प्रथा समाप्त होने के बाद भी ये भारतीय वापस अपने देश नहीं आए और वही जीवन यापन करने लगे ये ही प्रवासी भारतीय कहलाए ये और अब उन्हीं के आगे की पीढ़ी को भारत वंशी कहा जाने लगा है आज हिंदी में प्रवासी साहित्य की चर्चा की जाने लगी है और चर्चा होनी भी चाहिए क्योंकि प्रवासी भारतीयों की संख्या करोड़ों में है और वे देश से बाहर रहकर भी हिंदी भाषा और भारतीय संस्कृति का निर्वाह कर रहे हैं आज प्रवासी साहित्य लेखन बड़ी मात्रा में हो रहा है साहित्य को वैश्विक ऊंचाई पर ले जाने का कार्य भी प्रवासी साहित्य कर रहा है प्रवास के दौरान व्यक्ति जिन समस्याओं से जूझता है अपने देश और समाज से जब दूसरे देश और उसकी परिस्थितियों से समायोजन स्थापित करने करता है और इसमें उसका पूरा जीवन और आने वाली पीढ़ियां जिन समस्याओं का सामना करती हैं और जो मूल्य बोध लेकर वे जाते हैं उनसे अलग

मूल्यों को अपनाने की कश्मकश निरंतर उसमें चलती रहती है प्रवासी साहित्य इन्हीं मूल्यों को उजागर करता है अपने देश से बाहर निकलते ही प्रवासियों को अनेक समस्याओं से जूझना होता है सबसे पहले वीजा की समस्या के साथ ही आवास, नौकरी, भोजन, अजनबीपन, नस्लवाद, भाषा, राजनीतिक तंत्र, भौगोलिक परिस्थितियाँ आदि अनेक समस्याओं से उन्हें गुजरना होता है।

आज मॉरीशस, गुयाना, सूरीनाम, फिजी आदि देशों में आज भी भारतवंशी हिंदुस्तान को हृदय में संजोकर हिंदी साहित्य की शोभा बढ़ा रहे हैं] एक दूसरा प्रवासी वर्ग भी है जो स्वेच्छा से या पारिवारिक मजबूरी से अमेरिका, कनाडा, यू0के0, नॉर्वे, रूस, इटली, डेनमार्क, फ्रांस, स्वीडन, नीदरलैंड, आस्ट्रेलिया आदि अन्य देशों में बसे हैं प्रवासी साहित्य की सबसे विशिष्ट बात यह है कि वहां महिला साहित्यकारों की भागीदारी पुरुष साहित्यकारों से अधिक है, प्रवासी हिंदी साहित्य लेखन में जिन प्रमुख महिला रचनाकारों ने अपनी लेखनी चलाई उनके नाम इस प्रकार हैं अमेरिका से सुषम बेदी, सुदर्शन प्रियदर्शिनी, अनिल प्रभा कुमार, सुधा ओम ढींगरा, रेनू राजवंशी गुप्ता, पुष्पा सक्सेना, प्रतिभा सक्सेना इला प्रसाद, रचना श्रीवास्तव एवं आस्था नवल, अनीता कपूर, मंजू मिश्रा, देवी नागरानी, रेखा मैत्री, अर्चना पांडा, रेखा भाटिया और अंशु जौहरी, ब्रिटेन से-जकिया जुबैदी, दिव्या माथुर, उषा राजे सक्सेना अचला शर्मा, शैल अग्रवाल, नीना पाल, उषा वर्मा, कादंबरी मेहरा, नीरा त्यागी, कनाडा से शैलजा सक्सेना, रीनु पुरोहित, संयुक्त अरब अमीरात से पूर्णिया वर्मन, कुवैत से दीपिका जोशी, जापान से नीलम मलकानिया, डेनमार्क से अर्चना पेन्यूली, शारजाह से पूर्णिमा वर्मन, फ्रांस से सुचिता भट्ट, ऑस्ट्रेलिया से रेखा राजवंशी, नीदरलैंड से पुष्पिता अवस्थी, चीन से अनीता शर्मा, मॉरीशस से राजरानी गैबीन आदि।

मॉरीशस के प्रवासी हिंदी साहित्य पर्यास समृद्ध है, पंडित आत्माराम विश्वनाथ से लेकर कृष्ण लाल बिहारी, अभिमन्यु अनंत, रामदेव धुरंधर आदि के नाम मॉरीशस के हिंदी साहित्य

में प्रचलित है फिजी के प्रवासी हिंदी साहित्य में जैनेंद्र सिंह कंवल, कमला प्रसाद मिश्र, काशीराम कुमुद, महावीर मिश्र बाबू हरनाम सिंह, महेंद्र चंद्र शर्मा, बाबू कुंवर सिंह, राधानंद शर्मा के नाम उल्लेखनीय है, गिरमिटिया मजदूरों के माध्यम से उत्पन्न सूरीनाम के हिंदी साहित्य में भोजपुरी, मगही, मैथिली,ब्रज आदि बोलियां तथा डच, अंग्रेजी आदि की मिश्रित भाषा मिलती है सूरीनाम के हिंदी साहित्य को भारत के हिंदी साहित्य से जोड़ने का श्रेय प्रोफेसर पुष्पिता अवस्थी को मिलता है द्वितीय श्रेणी में अमेरिका का प्रवासी हिंदी साहित्य बहुत प्रचलित है, विगत दशकों में अमेरिका के हिंदी साहित्य में अज्ञेय, सोमवीरा प्रभाकर, उषा प्रियंवदा, कृष्ण बलदेव, सुनीता जैन, श्री गुलाब खंडेलवाल,श्याम नारायण शुक्ल,सुषम बेदी, अंजना संधीर आदि के नाम उल्लेखनीय है, वहां के हिंदी साहित्य में कविता, कहानी, निबंध, संस्मरण, उपन्यास आदि विधाएं बहुत ही विकसित होती जा रही हैं इंग्लैंड में कई संस्थाएं है जो हिंदी साहित्य के प्रति सतत प्रयत्नशील है यू0के0 के हिंदी सीमित 1990, नेहरू केंद्र 1992, कला ज्योति 1995 भारतीय भाषा संगम 1999, हिंदी भाषा समिति 2000, वातायन 2003 आदि उनके अंतर्गत आता है साथ ही पुरवाई, अमरदीप, प्रवासी टुडे, चेतक आदि पत्रिकाएं भी हैं जिनमें हिंदी रचनाएं छापी जाती है, वहां सत्येन्द्र श्रीवास्तव, गौतम सचदेव, उषा राजे सक्सेना, दिव्या माथुर, तेजेंद्र शर्मा, भारतेंदु विमल, नरेश भारतीय महेंद्र भला सूरज प्रकाश, उषा वर्मा, मोहन राणा आदि साहित्यकार प्रसिद्ध है उल्लेखनीय है।

अभिमन्यु अनंत के उपन्यास **लाल पसीना** में मॉरीशस में गए भारतीय मजदूरों के साथ अंग्रेजों द्वारा किए गए क्रूर और अमानवीय व्यवहार का चित्रण किया गया है मजदूरों का जीवन अनेक परेशानियों से गुजरता हुआ आज मॉरीशस में अपना एक मुकाम बना चुका है भारतीय मजदूर के जीवन के इतिहास को यह उपन्यास दर्शाता है इस उपन्यास में पूरी कथा भारतीय मजदूर के इर्द-गिर्द घूमती है,   अभिमन्यु अनंत की कहानी **जहर और**

दवा एक पुत्र और द्वारा पिता को जीवन की सही दिशा की तरफ ले जाने की कहानी है अपनी मां के हक को बनाए रखने के लिए अपने पिता की आंखों पर पड़े पराई स्त्री के मोह का पर्दा हटाकर सच्चाई को सामने लाना है एक व्यक्ति किस प्रकार एक पराई स्त्री केमोह जाल में फंसकर अपने परिवार को नजर अंदाज करता है यह इस कहानी द्वारा कहानी के द्वारा दर्शाया गया है।

सुषम बेदी ने अपने साहित्य में अनेक गंभीर मसलो को उठाया है उन्होंने नस्लीय भेदभाव के शिकार प्रवासी भारतीयों की मानसिकता को भली प्रकार समझा वह अपने साहित्य में प्रकट किया उन्होंने अपने साहित्य में अंतरराष्ट्रीय विवाहों की विडंबना के पीछे कार्यशील नस्लवादी सोच और सांस्कृतिक तनाव को जीवंत रूप में उजागर किया] **अंजोलिया का फूल** कहानी प्रवासी भारतीयों की मानसिक द्वंद्व को प्रकट करती है पश्चिमी समाज में अंतर नस्लीय विवाहों की गिनती बढ़ती जा रही है किंतु उसका अर्थ यह नहीं कि इस कि इससे बेगानापन खत्म हो रहा है प्रवासी भारतीयों के प्रति यह भाव बरकरार ही नहीं बल्कि बढ़ रहा है क्योंकि अंतर नस्लीय विवाह में प्रवासी भारतीय बहू या दामाद को पश्चिमी समाज के लोग स्वीकार नहीं कर पाते इसी कारण वह परिवार में रहते हुए भी अपने आप को बेगाना सा महसूस करते हैं, **तीसरी दुनिया का मसीहा** कहानी प्रवासी भारतीयों के अंधविश्वास को दर्शाती है भारत के किसी भाग का व्यक्ति जब विदेश में जाकर बसता है तब वह अपने साथ अपने संस्कार, संस्थाएं, धार्मिक विश्वास सामाजिक परंपराएं और रूढ़ियों भी ले जाता है वहां उसका अन्य संस्कृतियों के साथ टकराव होता है और ऐसे संघर्ष से अनेक समस्याएं और आंतरिक उलझने जन्म लेती हैं जो ब्रूनो पढ़ा लिखा होने की बावजूद भी धार्मिक अंधविश्वासों में जकड़ा जाता है अपने जीवन की मुश्किलों का हल स्वामी जी के पाखंडों द्वारा ढूंढना चाहता है तनु के साथ अपनी मधुर संबंधों को स्वामी जी के कहने पर तोड़ने के लिए तैयार हो जाता है, **कतरा दर कतरा** में माता-पिता द्वारा अपने बेटे से आवश्यकता

से अधिक अपेक्षाएं रखने के कारण मनोविकारों का उत्पन्न होना दिखाया गया है।

उषा राजे सक्सेना की कहानियों में स्त्री विमर्श पर अधिक बल दिया गया है, बढ़ती हुई वेश्यावृति की ओर भी पाठकों का ध्यान आकर्षित करती हैं उनकी कहानी **वह रात**, विदेश में नारी की असुरक्षा को दर्शाती हुई कहानी है **निशांत,** दिव्या माथुर की प्रवासी भारतीय स्त्री की जीवन में विवाह के उपरांत आए संकट की कहानी है इस कहानी में भारतीय स्त्री शादी करके विदेश आती है किंतु उसका पति उसके प्रति कोई लगाव नहीं रखता है भारतीय नारी की तरह वह पति द्वारा दी जाने वाली हर प्रताड़ना को सहन करती है उसकी भारतीय मानसिकता उसे विरोध करने की इजाजत नहीं देती इसलिए वह चुपचाप इस शोषण का शिकार होती रहती है यही कारण है कि प्रवासी भारतीय समाज में भी स्त्री की दशा दयनीय है।

इस प्रकार प्रवासी हिंदी साहित्य एक भिन्न संवेदना एवं सरोकार का आस्वादन करता है भारत के हिंदी पाठक व शोधकर्ताओं के लिए यह एक नई दिशा है इसमें कथानक और पात्र नए हैं जिसके द्वारा हम स्वदेश विदेश के बीच अपने ही लोगों की समस्याओं को देखते हैं भारतीय हिंदी साहित्य की तुलना में प्रवासी हिंदी साहित्य बहुत छोटा है। प्रवासी जीवन को प्रवासी हिंदी साहित्य के माध्यम से साहित्यकारों ने अलग-अलग ढंग से प्रकट किया है उनकी अभिव्यक्ति की शैली भी एक दूसरे से नितांत भिन्नता लिए हुए हैं कथा साहित्य में हमें प्रवासी भारतीयों के जीवन व उनकी समस्याओं से परिचित कराने का सफल प्रयास है।अंजना अप्पाचना भारतीय डायस्पोरा में हाल की आवाज़ों में से एक है जो संकट में फंसे लोगों के आघात और पुनर्वास से संबंधित है। उनकी लघु कहानी, बहू एक नवविवाहित लड़की के आघात का प्रतीक है जो अपने पति और ससुराल वालों के घर में घुटन का अनुभव करती है। हालाँकि वह एक बैंक में काम करती है और अपने पति की तरह ही एक कमाऊ व्यक्ति के रूप में अपनी भूमिका निभाती

है, फिर भी उसे संकीर्ण नियमों के कारण अपने पति के घर में दबाया जाता है। रूढ़िवादी संकीर्ण परिवार उसे उस स्वतंत्रता से वंचित करता है जो वह चाहती है। परिणामस्वरूप, वह अपने पति का घर छोड़ने का फैसला करती है जहां उसे अपनी स्वतंत्र पहचान से वंचित कर दिया जाता है। अपने माता-पिता के पास वापस लौटे बिना वह अकेले रहना पसंद करती है जहां उसकी अपनी पहचान, अपना स्वयं और अपना घर होगा।

उपसंहार

उक्त तथ्यों पर ध्यान देने से यह निष्कर्ष निकलता है कि प्रवासी हिंदी साहित्य प्रवासी भारतीय जीवन के बाह्य एवं आंतरिक पक्षों का उद्घाटन करते हुए उनका यथार्थ विश्व के समक्ष रखने का सार्थक प्रयास बनता जा रहा है अतः विश्व के प्रवासी साहित्य में प्रवासी हिंदी साहित्य का स्थान भी प्रतिष्ठित होता जा रहा है। प्रवासी हिंदी साहित्य के लिए दिए जाने वाले प्रोत्साहन से इस धारा का व्यापक विकास एवं प्रचलन किया जा सकता है।

संदर्भ

- कुमार,वीरेंद्र, सठोत्तरी हिंदी उपन्यासों में प्रवासी जीवन की समस्याएं,शोध प्रबंध,दिल्ली विश्वविद्यालय)shodhganga. inflibnet.ac.in/bitstream/10603/32070/3/03_preface.pdf

- कुशवाहा, अमित कुमार सिंह, सुषमबेदी के कथा साहित्य में प्रवासी www.researchgate.net/profile/AmitKushawhaha/publication/331638942_susama_bedi_ke_katha_sahitya_mem_pravasi_jivana/links/5c84b077299bf1268d4c860b/susama-bedi-ke-katha-sahitya-mem-pravasi-jivana.pdf

- कौर, गुरप्रीत, सुषम बेदी के कथा साहित्य में प्रवासी भारतीय समाज के विविध पक्ष (पंजाबी विश्वविद्यालय) shodhganga. inflibnet.ac.in/bitstream/06/6/4497/10603_chapter201%.pdf

- कौर, नवनीत, *प्रवासी हिंदी साहित्य वैश्विक परिदृश्य*, हरियाणा ग्रंथ अकादमी, पंचकूला।

- कौर, मनप्रीत, *भारतीय और प्रवासी हिंदी कथा साहित्य वर्तमान परिदृश्य*, अनभै प्रकाशन, सायन माटुंगा रोड,सायन

- बाकोलिया,गगन, प्रवासी जीवन की समस्या के संदर्भ में उषा प्रियंवदा की कथा साहित्य का अध्ययन jmi.ac.in/upload/Research/ab_2014_hindi_gagan.pdf

- बेदी, सुषम, कतरा दर कतरा, लघु उपन्यास archive.org/details/KatraDarKatra-Hindi/mode/2up?view=theater

- राठी,सोनिया, प्रवासी हिंदी साहित्य लेखन की विविध आयाम, इंटरनेशनल जर्नल ऑफ़ हिंदी रिसर्च, अंक 2 जुलाई 2016 oldisrj.lbp.world/ColorArticles/4830.pdf

- hi.wikipedia.org

- Mhalunkar, Shashikant. Breaking the Parochial Cage—Quest for Identity: A Diasporic reading of Anjana Appachana's story, "Bahu" www.academia.edu/11597693/BREAKING_THE_PAROCHIAL_CAGE_QUEST_FOR_IDENTITY_A_DIASPORIC_READING_OF_ANJANA_APPACHANA_S_STORY_BAHU_

- www.abhivyaktihindi.org/kahaniyan/vatan_se_door/2009/teesari_duniyaka_maseh

- www.researchgate.net/publication/351871073_visva_ke_pravasi_sahitya_mem_pravasi_hindi_sahitya_Hindi_Immigrant_Literature_in_universal_Immigrant_Literature

Chapter 23

आर्थिक सशक्तिकरण: वैश्विक व्यापार में भारतीय प्रवासियों का योगदान

डॉ0 विभा पाण्डेय

असिस्टेंट प्रोफेसर, वाणिज्य,
राजकीय महाविद्यालय, ओबरा, सोनभद्र, उ०प्र०
ईमेल पता: vibhaobra@gmail.com

सार

आर्थिक सशक्तिकरण क्या है?

ऐसा माना जाता है कि आर्थिक सशक्तिकरण गरीब लोगों को तत्काल दैनिक अस्तित्व से परे सोचने और अपने संसाधनोंऔर जीवन विकल्पों दोनों पर अधिक नियंत्रण रखने की अनुमति देता है। उदाहरण के लिए, यह परिवारों को स्वास्थ्य और शिक्षा में निवेश करने और अपनी आय बढ़ाने के लिए जोखिम लेने के बारे में अपने निर्णय लेने में सक्षम बनाता है।इस बात के भी कुछ सबूत हैं कि आर्थिक सशक्तिकरण कमजोर समूहों की निर्णय लेने में भागीदारी को मजबूत कर सकताहै। उदाहरण के लिए, माइक्रोफाइनेंस कार्यक्रमों को घर और बाज़ार में महिलाओं के प्रभाव को बढ़ाने के लिए दिखायागया है। सबूत यह भी बताते हैं

कि आर्थिक शक्ति अक्सर आसानी से बढ़ी हुई सामाजिक स्थिति या निर्णय लेने की शक्तिमें परिवर्तितहो जाती है।

मुख्य शब्द: आर्थिक सशक्तिकरण, माइक्रोफाइनेंस कार्यक्रम, संसाधन, निवेश, स्वास्थ्य, शिक्षा

आर्थिक सशक्तिकरण पर साहित्य विशाल है, और इसका एक बड़ा हिस्सा महिलाओं के आर्थिक सशक्तिकरण पर केंद्रितहै - जो लैंगिक असमानता को संबोधित करने में एक महत्वपूर्ण रणनीति है। आम तौर पर, आर्थिक सशक्तीकरण पर चर्चाचार व्यापक क्षेत्रों पर केंद्रित है: क) गरीब लोगों की संपत्ति को बढ़ावा देना; बी) सामाजिक सुरक्षा के परिवर्तनकारीरूप; ग) सूक्ष्म वित्त; और घ) कौशल प्रशिक्षण।

भारतीय अर्थव्यवस्था

भारत की अर्थव्यवस्था को विशाल, जटिल और बढ़ती हुई बताया गया है। यह दुनिया के सबसे रोमांचक और उभरते बाजारों में से एक है। 1951 से भारत एक नियोजित अर्थव्यवस्था के रूप में विकसित हुआ है। पहली कुछ योजनाओं में विनिर्माण क्षेत्र की मजबूती के साथ विकास पर ध्यान केंद्रित किया गया, जिसमें भारी उद्योगों को अर्थव्यवस्था की रीढ़ बनाने पर जोर दिया गया। योजना के अन्य प्रमुख क्षेत्र कृषि और सामाजिक विकास थे। स्वतंत्रता के बाद की अवधि और पंचवर्षीय योजनाओं की अवधि के दौरान, प्रयास अर्थव्यवस्था की जरूरतों की पहचान करने पर केंद्रित थे। इसके अलावा, 90 के दशक की शुरुआत में आर्थिक सुधारों ने भारत के आर्थिक इतिहास में एक नया अध्याय खोला। इसने भारत को अपने अतीत की बेड़ियों को तोड़ने और एक प्रगतिशील राष्ट्र के रूप में विश्व मंच पर उभरने का अवसर दिया।

भारत आर्थिक विकास की ऊंची राह पर है। 2020 के बाद से, COVID-19 महामारी के कारण विश्व अर्थव्यवस्था में गिरावट आई है। संक्रमण की बार-बार लहरें, आपूर्ति-श्रृंखला में व्यवधान और

मुद्रास्फीति ने चुनौतीपूर्ण समय पैदा किया है। इन चुनौतियों का सामना करते हुए भारत सरकार ने तत्काल कार्यवाही की है ताकि भारतीय अर्थव्यवस्था पर इसका कम से कम प्रभाव पड़े।

भारतीय अर्थव्यवस्था 2020-21 की दूसरी छमाही से लगातार सुधार कर रही है। हालाँकि, अप्रैल-जून 2021 में महामारी की दूसरी लहर स्वास्थ्य के दृष्टिकोण से अधिक गंभीर थी। राष्ट्रीय लॉकडाउन ने भारत में छोटे व्यवसायों, आम लोगों और हर किसी को प्रभावित किया है। इससे भारतीय अर्थव्यवस्था नीचे चली गई है. लेकिन अब ये धीरे-धीरे ऊपर उठकर अपना रूप ले रहा है।

कृषि भारतीय अर्थव्यवस्था के सबसे महत्त्वपूर्ण क्षेत्रों में से एक है। यह देश में भोजन एवं कच्चे माल की आपूर्ति करती है।स्वतंत्रता के समय, भारत की 70% से अधिक आबादी आजीविका कमाने के लिए कृषि पर निर्भर थी। तदनुसार, 1950-51 में राष्ट्रीय उत्पाद/ आय में कृषि का हिस्सा 56.6% तक था। हालाँकि, उद्योगों और सेवा क्षेत्र के विकास के साथ, कृषिपर निर्भर जनसंख्या का प्रतिशत, साथ ही राष्ट्रीय उत्पाद में कृषि की हिस्सेदारी में कमी आई है। कृषि खाद्य आपूर्ति कास्रोत है। कृषि निर्यात के माध्यम से विदेशी मुद्रा आय का भी एक प्रमुख स्रोत है। वर्ष 2011-12 में भारत के निर्यात मेंकृषि का हिस्सा 12.3% था। निर्यात की प्रमुख वस्तुओं में चाय, चीनी, तम्बाकू, मसाले, कपास, चावल, फल औरसब्जियाँ आदि शामिल हैं।

उद्योग अर्थव्यवस्था का द्वितीयक क्षेत्र है और आर्थिक गतिविधि का एक अन्य महत्त्वपूर्ण क्षेत्र है। स्वतंत्रता के बाद, भारतसरकार ने लंबे समय में देश के आर्थिक विकास में औद्योगीकरण की भूमिका पर जोर दिया। प्रारंभ में, सार्वजनिक क्षेत्र ने आर्थिक विकास में अधिकतम योगदान दिया। 1990 के दशक की शुरुआत में, यह पाया गया कि सार्वजनिक क्षेत्र के उपक्रम उम्मीद के मुताबिक प्रदर्शन नहीं कर रहे थे। इसलिए, 1991 में, भारत सरकार ने औद्योगिक विकास में निजीक्षेत्र की भूमिका को प्रोत्साहित करने

का निर्णय लिया। यह कदम भारत में औद्योगीकरण की प्रक्रिया को मजबूत करने के लिए उठाया गया था।

1700 से अधिक वर्षों की निरंतर अवधि के लिए, 1 ईस्वी सन् से शुरू होकर, भारत दुनिया की सबसे बड़ी अर्थव्यवस्थाथा, जिसने वैश्विक सकल घरेलू उत्पाद में 35 से 40% का योगदान दिया। ब्रिटिश साम्राज्य के पतन के बाद, भारत पर कुछ समय के लिए शासन करने के लिए संरक्षणवादी, आयात-प्रतिस्थापन, फैबियन समाजवाद और सामाजिक लोकतांत्रिक नीतियों के संयोजन का उपयोग किया गया। अपनी सुस्त वृद्धि, व्यापक विनियमन, संरक्षणवादी नीतियों और सरकारी स्वामित्व के कारण, इस अवधि के दौरान अर्थव्यवस्था को "ड्रिगिज़्म" कहा जाता था। बढ़ते आर्थिक उदारीकरण के कारण 1991 के बाद से देश बाजार आधारित अर्थव्यवस्था के करीब पहुंच गया है। आंकड़े बताते हैं कि2008 तक, भारत की अर्थव्यवस्था दुनिया में सबसे तेजी से बढ़ने वाली अर्थव्यवस्थाओं में से एक थी।

भारत की अर्थव्यवस्था की वर्तमान स्थिति

वित्तीय वर्ष 2022-23 में 7.2% की तीव्र आर्थिक वृद्धि के बाद, 2023 की पहली छमाही में आर्थिक गति मजबूत बनी हुई है। जुलाई के लिए एसएंडपी ग्लोबल इंडिया सर्विसेज पीएमआई बिजनेस एक्टिविटी इंडेक्स ने आउटपुट और नए ऑर्डरमें निरंतर तेजी से विस्तार का संकेत दिया, जबकि जुलाई में विनिर्माण पीएमआई सर्वेक्षण में भी मजबूत विस्तारवादी स्थितियाँ दिखाई दीं।

भारत उद्योगों की एक विस्तृत श्रृंखला में बहुराष्ट्रीय कंपनियों के लिए एक तेजी से आकर्षक स्थान बन गया है, जिसमें प्रत्यक्ष विदेशी निवेश प्रवाह 2021-22 में 85 बिलियन अमरीकी डालर के नए रिकॉर्ड स्तर पर पहुंच गया है। विनिर्माण क्षेत्र में एफडीआई

निवेश प्रवाह 2021-22 में साल-दर-साल 76% बढ़ गया, जो 21 बिलियन अमेरिकी डॉलर से अधिक के स्तर पर पहुंच गया।

2023 की पहली छमाही के दौरान भारत के लिए हालिया आर्थिक संकेतक घरेलू मांग से प्रेरित विस्तारवादी आर्थिक स्थितियों का संकेत दे रहे हैं। अप्रैल-जून तिमाही में स्टील का उत्पादन 11.9% बढ़ा, जबकि स्टील की खपत 10.2% बढ़ी। 2022-23 में वाणिज्यिक वाहनों की बिक्री तेजी से बढ़ी, 34.3% की वृद्धि हुई, जबकि निजी वाहनों की बिक्री 2022-23 में 18.7% बढ़ी।

औद्योगिक उत्पादन सूचकांक, जो आम तौर पर काफी मासिक अस्थिरता दिखाता है, ने अप्रैल-जून तिमाही में 4.5% की वृद्धि दर्ज की, जबकि उसी तिमाही में विनिर्माण उत्पादन में 4.7% की वृद्धि हुई। 2022-23 के लिए अप्रैल से मार्च तक, औद्योगिक उत्पादन 5.2% बढ़ा, इसी अवधि में विनिर्माण उत्पादन 4.7% बढ़ा।

2022-23 के लिए, पूंजीगत वस्तुओं का उत्पादन 12.9% बढ़ गया, जबकि बुनियादी ढांचे और निर्माण वस्तुओं का उत्पादन 12.5% बढ़ गया। हालाँकि, राष्ट्रीय सांख्यिकी कार्यालय के अनुसार, उपभोक्ता टिकाऊ वस्तुओं और गैर-टिकाऊ वस्तुओं का उत्पादन सुस्त था, उपभोक्ता टिकाऊ वस्तुओं का उत्पादन 2022-23 में 0.6 की मामूली गति से बढ़ रहा था, जबकि उपभोक्ता गैर-टिकाऊ वस्तुओं में 0.5% की वृद्धि हुई।

2023 की अप्रैल-जून तिमाही में पूंजीगत वस्तुओं का उत्पादन 4.9% बढ़ा, जबकि बुनियादी ढांचे और निर्माण वस्तुओं का उत्पादन 14% बढ़ा। उपभोक्ता टिकाऊ वस्तुओं का उत्पादन कमजोर रहा, 2.8% की गिरावट आई, हालांकि उपभोक्ता गैर-टिकाऊ वस्तुओं के उत्पादन में मजबूत गति देखी गई, और 6.7% की वृद्धि हुई।

भारत के उपभोक्ता मूल्य सूचकांक (सीपीआई) पर नवीनतम आंकड़ों से पता चला है कि हेडलाइन सीपीआई मुद्रास्फीतिदर जून में 4.8% की गति से बढ़कर जुलाई में 7.4% हो गई।

हेडलाइन सीपीआई मुद्रास्फीति दर में उछाल में योगदान देने वाला एक प्रमुख कारक खाद्य और पेय पदार्थ सीपीआईउप-सूचकांक में और तेज उछाल था। खाद्य और पेय पदार्थ सीपीआई उपसूचकांक जुलाई में 10.6% बढ़ गया, जबकि जूनमें 4.6% बढ़ गया था, जो सब्जियों की कीमतों में वृद्धि के साथ-साथ अनाज और दालों के लिए महत्वपूर्ण मूल्य वृद्धि से प्रेरित था।

सब्जियों के सीपीआई उपसूचकांक में हाल के महीनों में महत्वपूर्ण गिरावट दर्ज की गई है, अप्रैल में 6.5% की गिरावट केबाद मई में 8.2% की गिरावट आई है। हालांकि, जुलाई में सब्जियों की कीमतें 37.3% बढ़ीं। सब्जियों की कीमतों में तेजउछाल का एक महत्वपूर्ण योगदान कारक कुछ क्षेत्रों में फसल की क्षति के कारण टमाटर की कीमतों में तेज वृद्धि थी।दालों की कीमतों में भी जोरदार वृद्धि देखी गई, जुलाई में 13.3% की बढ़ोतरी हुई। भारत सरकार के लिए एक प्रमुख चिंता का विषय चावल की कीमतों में तेजी से बढ़ोतरी है, जिसमें कुल अनाज उप-सूचकांक 13% बढ़ गया है।

उच्च ऊर्जा कीमतें पिछले वर्ष के दौरान भारत के सीपीआई मुद्रास्फीति दबाव में योगदान देने वाला एक महत्वपूर्ण कारक रही हैं, लेकिन हाल के महीनों में इसमें कमी आई है, विश्व तेल की कीमतों में कुछ कमी के साथ-साथ आधार-वर्ष के प्रभाव के कारण वृद्धि में मदद मिली है। विश्व तेल की कीमतें एक साल पहले, 2022 की दूसरी तिमाही में थीं। ईंधन और प्रकाश उप-सूचकांक वृद्धि जुलाई में और कम होकर 3.7% हो गई, जबकि जून में 3.9% थी और मार्च में दर्ज 8.9% कीदर से काफी कम थी।

भारतीय रिज़र्व बैंक (RBI) ने अपने अगस्त के मौद्रिक नीति वक्तव्य में चालू वित्त वर्ष के लिए अपनी अनुमानित सीपीआई

मुद्रास्फीति दर को बढ़ाकर 5.4% कर दिया, जबकि जून के मौद्रिक नीति वक्तव्य में इसका अनुमान 5.1% था।फिर भी यह 2022-23 में सीपीआई मुद्रास्फीति में 6.5% की वृद्धि से एक महत्त्वपूर्ण कमी का प्रतिनिधित्व करता है। आरबीआई के अगस्त मौद्रिक नीति वक्तव्य में सीपीआई मुद्रास्फीति का निकट अवधि प्रक्षेपवक्र जुलाई-सितंबर तिमाही के लिए 6.2%, वित्त वर्ष 2023-24 की अक्टूबर से दिसंबर तिमाही के लिए 5.7%, जनवरी-मार्च में 5.2% तक कम होने का अनुमान लगाया गया है। सामान्य मानसून की धारणा के आधार पर 2024 की तिमाही।

आरबीआई के अगस्त मौद्रिक नीति वक्तव्य में उम्मीद की गई थी कि प्रतिकूल मौसम की स्थिति के कारण खाद्य उत्पादन में व्यवधान के कारण आने वाले महीनों में हेडलाइन सीपीआई मुद्रास्फीति दर में बढ़ोतरी देखी जा सकती है। आरबीआई ने अब तक ख़राब दक्षिण-पश्चिम मानसून के प्रभाव से खाद्य उत्पादन के जोखिमों के साथ-साथ संभावित अल नीनो घटना के साथ-साथ भू-राजनीतिक शत्रुता के कारण खाद्य कीमतों पर बढ़ते दबाव को भी नोट किया है।

प्रत्यक्ष विदेशी निवेश

भारत में शुद्ध नया विदेशी प्रत्यक्ष निवेश हाल के वर्षों में बहुत तेजी से बढ़ा है, पिछले 2020-21 में 82 बिलियन अमेरिकी डॉलर के प्रवाह के बाद, 2021-22 में एफडीआई 85 बिलियन अमेरिकी डॉलर के नए रिकॉर्ड स्तर परपहुंच गया है। इसकी तुलना 2003-04 में मात्र 4 बिलियन अमेरिकी डॉलर के एफडीआई प्रवाह से की जा सकती है।

निरंतर मजबूत एफडीआई प्रवाह ने भारत की बाहरी खाता भेद्यता को कम करने में मदद की है और पिछले दशक मेंभारत के विदेशी मुद्रा भंडार को बढ़ाने में योगदान दिया है।

पिछले दशक में मजबूत एफडीआई प्रवाह में एक प्रमुख योगदानकर्ता प्रौद्योगिकी से संबंधित एफडीआई रहा है, जोनिवेश का एक महत्वपूर्ण स्रोत बन गया है। कंप्यूटर सॉफ्टवेयर और हार्डवेयर क्षेत्र 2021-22 में प्रत्यक्ष विदेशी निवेशइक्विटी प्रवाह का सबसे बड़ा प्राप्तकर्ता था, जो कुल प्रवाह का लगभग 25% था।

अमेरिकी प्रौद्योगिकी कंपनियां भारत में हाल के एफडीआई प्रवाह का प्रमुख स्रोत रही हैं। 2020 में, Google ने "Google for India Digitalization Fund" की स्थापना की, जिसके माध्यम से उसने इक्विटी निवेश, साझेदारी और परिचालन, बुनियादी ढांचे और पारिस्थिति की तंत्र निवेश के मिश्रण के माध्यम से सात वर्षों में भारत में 10 बिलियन अमेरिकी डॉलर का निवेश करने की योजना की घोषणा की। इसके अलावा 2020 में, फेसबुक ने रिलायंसइंडस्ट्रीज लिमिटेड के स्वामित्व वाले Jio प्लेटफ़ॉर्म में 5.7 बिलियन अमेरिकी डॉलर के निवेश की घोषणा की।

बुनियादी ढांचा निवेश भी एफडीआई प्रवाह के लिए एक महत्वपूर्ण क्षेत्र रहा है। 2020 में एक बड़ा एफडीआई सौदाटावर इंफ्रास्ट्रक्चर ट्रस्ट के अधिग्रहण में सिंगापुर के जीआईसी और कनाडा के ब्रुकफील्ड एसेट मैनेजमेंट द्वारा 3.7बिलियन अमेरिकी डॉलर का निवेश था, जो भारतीय दूरसंचार टावरों की संपत्ति का मालिक है।

2020-21 में सऊदी अरब से एफडीआई भी तेजी से बढ़ी और 2.8 बिलियन अमेरिकी डॉलर तक पहुंच गई। सऊदीअरब के सार्वजनिक निवेश कोष ने 2020 में Jio प्लेटफ़ॉर्म में 1.5 बिलियन अमेरिकी डॉलर और रिलायंस रिटेल में1.3 बिलियन अमेरिकी डॉलर की हिस्सेदारी हासिल की।

रिलायंस रिटेल को 2020 में अन्य विदेशी फर्मों से भी निवेश प्राप्त हुआ, जिसमें सिंगापुर की जीआईसी और टीपीजीप्राइवेट कैपिटल ने संयुक्त रूप से 1 बिलियन अमेरिकी डॉलर का निवेश

किया, जबकि अमेरिकी निजी इक्विटी फर्मसिल्वर लेक पार्टनर्स ने भी 1 बिलियन अमेरिकी डॉलर का निवेश किया।

एफडीआई प्रवाह के स्रोत के आधार पर, सिंगापुर, मॉरीशस और संयुक्त अरब अमीरात 2022-23 में संयुक्त राज्यअमेरिका के साथ भारत में एफडीआई प्रवाह के चार शीर्ष स्रोतों में से तीन थे। यह संयुक्त राज्य अमेरिका, जापान,यूरोपीय संघ और ब्रिटेन जैसी उन्नत अर्थव्यवस्थाओं के साथ मजबूत संबंधों के अलावा, उभरते बाजारों में वैश्विकवित्तीय केंद्रों के साथ भारत के द्विपक्षीय आर्थिक और निवेश संबंधों के बढ़ते महत्व को उजागर करता है।

वैश्विक व्यापार में भारत का योगदान

आज के युग में विश्व की अर्थव्यवस्थाओं में अंतर्राष्ट्रीय व्यापार का अत्यधिक महत्व है। यह ब्रिक्स देशों (ब्राजील, रूस,भारत, चीन और दक्षिण अफ्रीका) जैसी तेजी से बढ़ती अर्थव्यवस्थाओं के लिए अधिक महत्व रखता है। अंतर्राष्ट्रीयव्यापार में भारत की वार्षिक वृद्धि दर 8% से ऊपर है।

भारत के पास समृद्ध संसाधन हैं जो अन्य देशों की तुलना में कहीं अधिक हैं। इसीलिए भारत को व्यापार के अवसरतलाशने के लिए सही देश के रूप में देखा जाता है। भारत को व्यवसाय के लिए आकर्षक बनाने वाले कई संसाधनों मेंसे शीर्ष निम्नलिखित हैं:

- उच्च और अर्ध-कुशल जनशक्ति
- देश के भीतर प्रौद्योगिकियाँ
- समृद्ध प्राकृतिक संसाधन
- नवोदित मध्यवर्गीय खंड
- भारत सरकार की विश्व व्यापार में भाग लेने की इच्छा

भारत को दुनिया में चीन के बाद सबसे तेजी से बढ़ती अर्थव्यवस्थाओं में से एक माना जाता है। यह विश्व की 10वीं

सबसेबड़ी अर्थव्यवस्था का स्थान रखता है। यह अनुमान लगाया गया है कि 21वीं सदी की अर्थव्यवस्था पर हावी होने वाले शीर्ष तीन देश हैं; संयुक्त राज्य अमेरिका, चीन और भारत। दुनिया की जीडीपी (सकल घरेलू उत्पाद) का चालीसप्रतिशत हिस्सा इन्हीं देशों से आता है। भारत, जो पहले से ही विश्व बैंक की पीपीपी (क्रय शक्ति समता) विनिमय दर का उपयोग कर रहा है, दुनिया में तीसरी सबसे बड़ी जीडीपी है।

2019-20 में भारत की जीडीपी की वृद्धि 203.39 ट्रिलियन अमेरिकी डॉलर तक पहुंचने का श्रेय दो चैनलों के माध्यम सेघरेलू अर्थव्यवस्था के एकीकरण को जाता है; व्यापार और पूंजी प्रवाह, भारत की प्रति व्यक्ति आय भी इन वर्षों में तीन गुना हो गई है।

भारतीय अर्थव्यवस्था में सेवा क्षेत्र का अत्यधिक महत्व है। भारत की जीडीपी का लगभग 55 प्रतिशत हिस्सा सेवाओं से आता है। पिछले दो दशकों में भारत का सेवा व्यापार उसके निर्यात में एक महत्त्वपूर्ण चालक रहा है। वैश्विक से वाव्यापार में सबसे तेजी से बढ़ते देश के रूप में भारत शीर्ष पर है।

भारत के सेवा क्षेत्र में परिवहन, व्यापार, होटल और रेस्तरां, व्यावसायिक सेवाएँ, वित्तपोषण, बीमा आदि जैसी गतिविधियों की एक विस्तृत श्रृंखला शामिल है। वर्ष 2014-2018 से, भारत के सेवाओं के निर्यात में वृद्धि देखी गई है।

परंपरागत रूप से भारत एक कृषि प्रधान अर्थव्यवस्था है लेकिन 1991 में अर्थव्यवस्था के उदारीकरण के बाद, यह वैश्विक व्यापार के लिए एक खुली बाजार अर्थव्यवस्था बन गया है। 1991 के दशक से, विभिन्न व्यावसायिक मॉड्यूल में निवेश रणनीतियों और बाहरी व्यापार नियमों के रूपों में महत्त्वपूर्ण परिवर्तन हुए हैं। इन बदलावों ने भारत को सबसे तेजी से बढ़ती अर्थव्यवस्था में से एक बना दिया है।

भारत की आर्थिक गतिविधियों में बदलाव देखने को मिल सकता है. अब भारत बुनियादी ढांचे, खुदरा, रक्षा, वित्त औरबीमा, सूचना प्रौद्योगिकी और विनिर्माण सहित विभिन्न क्षेत्रों में पर्याप्त निवेश अवसरों के साथ एक खुली बाजार अर्थव्यवस्था में विकसित हो गया है।

वैश्विक स्तर पर भारत खाद्यान्न के अग्रणी उत्पादकों में से एक है। चावल और गेहूं सबसे अधिक खेती की जाने वाली खाद्य फसलें हैं, जिनमें बाजरा और मक्का का भी काफी उत्पादन होता है। कुल कृषि उत्पादन में दाल और तिलहन का भी योगदान है। नकदी फसलों में, चाय, कपास, जूट और गन्ना चार्ट में सबसे ऊपर हैं। भारत चाय के सबसे बड़े उत्पादकों और निर्यातकों में से एक है।

कपास, लोहा और इस्पात, प्लास्टिक, मछली और क्रस्टेशियंस, विमान, अंतरिक्ष यान, और हिस्से, मांस, और खाद्य मांसके टुकड़े, अन्य निर्मित कपड़ा लेख, सेट, पहने हुए कपड़े और पहने हुए कपड़ा लेख, जहाज, नावें और तैरती संरचनाएं हैंभारत से मुख्य निर्यात भारत में आयात में मुख्य रूप से लोहा और इस्पात, जहाज, नाव और तैरती संरचनाएं, परमाणुरिएक्टर, बॉयलर, मशीनरी और यांत्रिक उपकरण, विद्युत मशीनरी और उपकरण और हिस्से, कार्बनिक रसायन, ऑप्टिकल, फोटोग्राफिक सिनेमैटोग्राफिक माप, सटीकता की जांच करना शामिल है। मेडिकल या सर्जिकल संस्थान, रेलवे या ट्रामवे रोलिंग स्टॉक के अलावा अन्य वाहन, और पार्ट्स और सहायक उपकरण। एफडीआई के लिए भारतीय बाजार खुलने के साथ, यह देश विभिन्न क्षेत्रों में निवेश के अवसरों के लिए विशेषाधिकार प्राप्त स्थलों में से एक बन गया है।

भारतीय निर्यात व्यवसाय की वृद्धि के लिए उत्तरदायी प्रमुख कारक हैं:

एसएमई सेक्टर का विकास

किसी भी देश के विनिर्माण क्षेत्र को स्थापित करने में एसएमई सेक्टर की बहुत बड़ी भूमिका होती है। किसी भी देश की अर्थव्यवस्था बहुत हद तक उसके लघु-मध्यम उद्योगों पर निर्भर करती है। भारत का भी यही हाल है, कौशल सेट और भौगोलिक स्थिति में इतनी विविधता के साथ, एक अलग प्रकार के एसएमई उद्योग विकसित हुए हैं और भारतीय निर्यातकों को दुनिया भर में जाने में सक्षम बनाया है।

ऑनलाइन ट्रेडिंग लेनदेन

ई-कॉमर्स की उपलब्धता के साथ, बी2बी निर्यातकों ने हाल के दिनों में भारतीय व्यापार सांख्यिकी वृद्धि में भारी योगदान दिया है। चूँकि लगभग हर क्षेत्र के लिए बहुत सारे व्यवसाय से व्यवसाय बाज़ार उपलब्ध हैं, भारत के छोटे और मध्यम आकार के उद्यम अपने अद्वितीय उत्पादों और सेवाओं के साथ वैश्विक दर्शकों तक पहुँच गए हैं। वैश्विक दर्शकों तक पहुंचने के लिए कम समय, त्वरित व्यापार लेनदेन, सुपर फास्ट और पूर्ण सुरक्षित भुगतान, और कई अन्य लाभ बी2बी व्यापार लेनदेन और उनकी आश्चर्यजनक वृद्धि से जुड़े हुए हैं।

सरकार का उदारवादी दृष्टिकोण

जैसा कि ब्लॉग की शुरुआत में चर्चा की गई थी, भारत एक बंद अर्थव्यवस्था थी और इतने बड़े निर्यात के अवसर नहीं थे।1991 के तत्कालीन वित्त मंत्री और अपनी उदार नीति के माध्यम से भारतीय अर्थव्यवस्था को खोलने का सबसे बड़ानिर्णय लिया। सबसे बड़े लाभार्थी भारतीय निर्यातक थे, जिन्होंने वैश्विक उपयोगकर्ताओं को अपेक्षाकृत कम कीमत पर उच्च गुणवत्ता वाले उत्पाद और सेवा प्रदान करके अवसर का सर्वोत्तम लाभ उठाया। आज, भारत सरकार निकाय विभिन्न क्षेत्रों में सौ प्रतिशत एफडीआई को मंजूरी, विभिन्न राज्यों में विशेष आर्थिक क्षेत्र और विशेष व्यापार

शिखर सम्मेलन जैसे नए अवसर पैदा कर रही है ताकि भारतीय निर्यात अधिक वैश्विक कंपनियों को आकर्षित कर सके और कुल निर्यातको एक नए स्तर तक बढ़ा सके।

विभिन्न भारतीय निर्यातक संघों का समर्थन

प्रचुर मात्रा में भारतीय निर्यातक संघ हैं जो व्यापार निर्यातकों को सबसे मैत्रीपूर्ण तरीके से व्यापार करने में मदद करते हैं। वे व्यवसाय-अनुकूल नीतियां बनाकर अपने सदस्यों की मदद करते हैं जो अंततः देश को बड़ा मुनाफा दिलाती हैं। बहुत सारे क्षेत्रीय संघ, राज्य-स्तरीय संघ और बहुत सारे उद्योग-विशिष्ट संघ भी हैं जो जरूरत पड़ने पर निर्यातकों को पर्याप्त सहायता और मार्गदर्शन प्रदान करते हैं।

संदर्भ

- indianexpress.com/article/business/economy/vision-document-to-make-india-a-30-trillion-economy-by-2047-in-final-stages-draft-to-be-ready-by-december-9005032/

- m.timesofindia.com/business/30-trillion-economy-document-to-outline-reformspitch/articleshow/104806581.cms

- pib.gov.in/PressReleasePage.aspx?PRID=1894932

- www.businesstoday.in/latest/economy/story/indian-economy-is-in-a-sweet-spot-says-economist-kaushik-basu-403653-2023-10-28

Our Authors

Dr. Shalini obtained her Masters degree and M.Phil degree in English Literature from C.S.J.M University Kanpur. Subsequently she was awarded the doctorate on the topic "British Booker Prize Novelists: A Critical Study of Howard Jacobson, Julian Barnes and Hilary Mantel" from University of Lucknow, Lucknow. Her area of specialization is Modern British Novel, Contemporary British Novel and Indian English Novel. As the programme coordinator, she successfully conducted a national webinar on Ek Bharat Shreshtha Bharat: Dekho Apna Desh (History and Culture of India). As the programme coordinator, she successfully conducted a national e-workshop on (National Education Policy 2020) New Ideas for development of world class digital infrastructure for justified use of online and digital education. As the convenor, she successfully conducted national e-Workshop on Skill Development Programme for Faculty "Adopt, Adapt and Create the OER Based Courses: Moocs and e-content." She has presented research papers in several national as well as international seminars and conferences. Her articles, concerning social issues, women's conditions, yoga and health, environmental studies, English Languages and Literature studies and literary theories have been published in various national and international journals as well as chapters in edited books. She has delivered many lectures in different Universities and colleges. She has authored two text books. After being selected in UPPSC, for Higher Education Service, she is presently appointed as Assistant Professor in English in Govt. Girls' P. G. College, Hamirpur, U.P. from 2015 till now.

Mr. Ajeet Kumar Gupta is a research scholar who is currently pursuing his Ph.D. in English from the University of Lucknow. He is fascinated in exploring the origin and evolution of comics in India. He is a keen observer of the attributes of Indian superheroes and their imprints on young minds. He is also interested in Indian writings in English and contemporary literary theory, especially postcolonial theory.

Prof. Sudheer Chandra Hajela teaches English at the Departmentt of English, Sri JNM P.G. College, Lucknow, associate college of the University of Lucknow. He completed his research work in 1992 on CleanthBrooks under the eminent Indian critic Prof. M.S. Kushwaha. He has written about two dozenresearch articles on Literary Criticism and Indian Writing in English, which have been published in thecountry and abroad. He organised two academic sessions of International Conferences in Japan andThailand in the year 2014 and 2015, respectively, under the aegis of IUAES. His book on CleanthBrooks is enlisted in the suggested readings of Wikipedia. He has also edited one book on Indian Folk Literature. He is the chief editor of a peer reviewed and refereed research journal, 'Dialogue: AJournal Devoted to Literary Appreciation' since 2005.He has attended many national andinternational events of academic and cultural outfits as resource person and guest of honour.

Dr. Mishu Singh is a chemist and a teacher by profession, trying to make students understand how Chemistry is important. She is currently working as an Assistant Professor at Pt. D.D.U. Govt. Girls PG College, Rajajipuram, Lucknow. Having a doctorate in Chemistry, she has many research papers and articles published in various national and international journals of repute. She is also a Diploma holder in Intellectual Property Rights from Indian Institute of Law, New Delhi (2015),Environmental Management & ISO 14000/14001, NILEM, Chennai, and Advance Diploma in Wastewater Treatment and Recycling, Alison Education, Galway, Ireland.

Dr. Madhumita Gupta is a faculty in the Commerce department at Maharaja Bijli Pasi Govt. P.G.College, Lucknow. She holds dual P.G. degrees both in Commerce and Economics. She holds a doctorate in Commerce and her research area is Human Resource. She has more than 17 years of teaching experience of PG and UG students. She has to her credit more than 10 research papers which were published in international and national journals of repute. She has written several chapters in books. Apart from this she has presented numerous papers in international and national seminars. She is an academic counsellor for IGNOU.

She holds membership of All India Commerce Association. Apart from her academic responsibilities, she has worked extensively for promoting awareness towards enrolment of new voters for Central and State elections. Considering her human approach and adaptability to difficult situations, she was chosen to head a Covid Counselling Cell in her college during the peak of pandemic times. Her work has been well appreciated. She is known as a hard task master and her students are testimony to this fact. She is an avid reader and her core competence is team building and leadership development.

Ms. Archika Vishwakarma is a research scholar currently pursuing her Ph.D. in English from the University of Lucknow. In the heart of Prayagraj, she took her first breath, and her educational journey unfolded at the University of Allahabad, where she attained both her undergraduate and postgraduate degrees. By engaging in various creative endeavours, such as composing poems, crafting short stories, and writing essays and articles, she has contributed to several anthologies as a co-author, showcasing the publication of her poems and other literary works. She has also got a chance to compile an anthology named *In Search of Beauty*. She loves to express her emotions through the medium of creativity, and as a determined learner and researcher, she believes in learning new things to create a beautiful chapter of life. Her areas of interest include poetry and science fiction, and her research study focuses on contemporary Indian English poetry.

Mr. Lavkush Kumar, an Assistant Professor,Department of English, is working in Government Girls' Post Graduate College, Hamirpur,U.P. His area of specialization is British poetry, contemporary American poetry and Indian English poetry. He has completed his M.Phil. from C.S.J.M. University Kanpur on the topic "Man and Nature in Robert Frost and William Wordsworth's poetry," in which he has elaborately discussed symbolist and natural elements in the poetry of American writer Robert Frost and British writer William Wordsworth. Many of his research papers have been published in National and International journals of UGC. Many of his papers have been published in edited books on current issues like New Education Policy and prevention of Covid-19, and other relevant literary issues. He is working as the program coordinator of the National Service Scheme in his college. He has worked in different education fields like basic education and secondary education and was selected in Higher Education through UPPSC, where he is currently employed.

Dr. Mohd Faiez is Assistant Professor, Department of English, at Rajendra Prasad (P.G.) College, Meerganj, Uttar Pradesh. He has completed his Ph.D. on the topic "Race, Class and Gender in Hanif Kureishi's Writings." His thrust areas are postcolonial literature, feminist literature and cultural studies.

Mr. Abhishek Kumar Pandey is working as an Assistant Professor-II in the Department of Management, SMS Lucknow. He has submitted his Ph.D. thesis in the area of succession planningand management to the Department of Business Administration(LUMBA), University of Lucknow (NAAC A++) in the year 2023. He has also qualifiedUGC-NET in Management. He has done an MBA in dual specialization HRM (Major)and Marketing (Minor) from

AKTU Lucknow. Prior to MBA, he has completedBachelor of Science in Maths from the University of Gorakhpur (NAAC A++). He has morethan 06 year teaching, 01 year corporate and 05 year research experience. He haspublished 10 research papers. His some papers are indexed in prominent databases like WOS, J-Gate and ABDC. He has presented more than 10 research papersin national and international seminars. He has attended more than 20 seminars andFDPs in RM and Management topics. He has also done two short-term courses fromNPTEL in OB (IIT Madras) and Advance Corporate Strategy (IIM Bangalore). Hisresearch interest caters to area like HRM, OB, Succession Planning, GeneralManagement and Entrepreneurial Orientation. Abhishek is also a life member of the Indian Commerce Association-ICA (Membership ID: UP1089) He has activeParticipation in IIM Bangalore, Center for Corporate Governance and Citizenship PanelDiscussion since 2021. He is also a reviewer in The Organization Studies JournalCollection (Scopus Indexed) since 2021 and the Diversity Journal Collection (ScopusIndexed) since 2021 based on Common Ground Research Networks, University ofIllinois Research Park, USA since 2021.

Dr. Pramod Kumar Upadhyay is working as Assistant Professor in the Department of Commerce, Maharaja Bijli Pasi Govt PG College, Ashiana, Lucknow. He has more than 15 years teaching and 20 years researchexperience. He has interest in teaching subjects like account, financeand management. He has published 20 research papers. He haspresented more than 20 research papers in national and internationalseminars. He has attended more than 30 seminars and FDPs. Hisresearch interest caters to areas like accounting, finance, commerce andgeneral management. Dr Pramod is also a life member of IndianCommerce Association-ICA (Membership ID UP599). He is also alife member of Indian Accounting Association (LC-115). Dr Upadhyay has contributed immensely as the counsellor and question paper setter for several papers related to his subject in IGNOU.

Dr. Nigar Alam is Assistant Professor at Babu Banarasi Das Northern India Institute of Technology, Lucknow. She is also teaching as Guest Faculty (online mode) 'Writing Practice' at Birla Institute of Technology & Science, Pilani for Work Integrated Learning Programme. Her research and publications mostly focus on understanding diasporic identities. She has been exploring the complexities of the immigrants due to their cultural differences with the natives. She enjoys reading biographies and talking politics in her free time.

Dr. Kotra Balayogi was born inVisakhapatnam, Andhra Pradesh, India. He obtained B.Sc., M.Sc. (Mathematics), M.A. (Education), M.A. (Psychology), and M.Ed. from Andhra University, and B.Ed. from Pondicherry University, an M. Phil (Mathematics) from Alagappa University, and an M. Phil. (Education) from Bharathiar University. He was awarded a Ph.D. Degree in Education by Bharathiar University for his work in "Inclusive Education in India and United States of America." Dr Bala has been teaching for the last 20 years, starting his teaching career as a High School Mathematics teacher, lecturer in Mathematics, school Principal and as an Assistant Professor in the Faculty of Education, ICFAI University, Tripura, India and presently working as Assistant Professor (Vice Principal) at Unity College of Teacher Education, Dimapur, Nagaland, India. He is an outstanding classroom practitioner possessing considerable teaching, research, training, administration and management experiences in India, Indonesia and USA. He has to his credit 20 research papers published in reputed national and international Journals, 75 paper presentations in various national and international conferences, workshops and seminars and has contributed 45chapters/papers for national and international edited books. He is a member of various national and international associations and is associated with academic bodies and professional organizations in India and abroad.

Ms. Monika Vishwakarma, a diligent scholar hailing from Lucknow, Uttar Pradesh, is currently immersed in the realm of academia as a Ph.D. candidate at the University of Lucknow. Born to Mr. R. J. Vishwakarma and Mrs. Sheela Vishwakarma, Monika's academic journey began at Nari Shiksha Niketan P. G. College, where she completed her undergraduate studies in 2019. Building on her passion for literature, Monika pursued and excelled in her Masters in English Literature at Maharaja Bijli Pasi Government College, securing the coveted first position. Her academic prowess and passion for English literature have propelled her into the realm of doctoral studies. Monika's research area stands out as a unique and timely contribution to the academic landscape. In an era marked by rapid societal transformations and evolving narratives, her exploration of dystopian themes in Indian English literature reflects a keen awareness of the contemporary socio-cultural milieu.

Monika is a promising scholar contributing to the discourse on the intersection of literature and societal reflection.

Ms. Daksha Kala, MA in Psychology, has to her credit four papers published in international and national books and journals. She has also presented papers in international and national level seminars. Her interest lies in academic research and exploring applications of psychology to help solve social problems and create positive impact.

Presently working as Head, Department of English at NSCB Government Girls' P.G. College Lucknow, Dr. Shalini Srivastava is a dedicated and accomplished English Professor with a passion for fostering intellectual curiosity and critical thinking in students. With an experience of about twenty-five years, she is adept at creating engaging and inclusive learning environments; she brings a wealth of experience in literature and language instruction. Her research interests lie at the intersection of postcolonial literature and contemporary literary theory, with a focus on exploring the impact of globalization on cultural narratives. Committed to contributing valuable insights to academic discourse, she has a proven track record of publication in reputable journals. She is always eager to inspire a new generation of scholars through innovative teaching methods and impactful research. She has handled numerous administrative responsibilities, however, teaching is her first and foremost passion.

Dr. Richa Pandey is CSIR-NET from Central University of Allahabad and has authored several books. She has 20 chapters in various books to her credit, followed by 15 papers in reputed journals. She has bagged many Gold Medals from the Central University of Allahabad and has been awarded by the State Government for her contribution as NSS Programme Officer to Elections 2021-2022. The author continues to seek perfection through her hard work and perseverance.

Dr. Nisha Dubey, currently an Assistant Professor, has cultivated a rich academic profile. Her journey includes completing an HR Management and Analytics course from IIM, Kozhikode, obtaining an M.A. in Economics from Dr R.M.L.A.U., earning an MBA in Banking and Finance from the National Institute of Banking Management, and achieving a Ph.D. in Human Resource Management from Dr R.M.L.A.U. Complementing these, she holds a B.Ed. from IGNOU, a DISM Diploma in IT from APTECH, and a CCC-Computer Course from the National Electronics and Information Technology Institute. Further strengthening her academic prowess, she holds an M.Com. and a B.Com. from Dr R.M. L.A.U. She has 8-10 years of teaching experience of both UG and PG students in B.Com. and M.Com. programs. She seamlessly integrates her extensive qualifications and practical experience to contribute significantly to both academic and industry landscapes.

Dr. Shradha Gupta is an Assistant Professor in the Department of English, RMP PG College, Sitapur (Associated to University of Lucknow). Her research areas are postcolonial studies, gender studies and new literature. Her research articles are published in UGC care listed and peer-reviewed journal. She is a bilingual writer. Shraddha S Sahu is her pen name. Her writings are published in many national and international e-magazines and anthologies, including Muse India, Rhetorica Quarterly and Spillwords.

Dr. Sunita Rawat is currently working as the Head of the Department of Zoology at Government Degree College in Uttar Pradesh. She has published more than 28 research papers/review articles in National and International refereed/peer-reviewed journals and books. She has also received Innovative Faculty Award and Vigyan Bhushan Puraskar.

The state of Birland launched a special edition of a postage stamp for Dr. Brajesh Kumar Gupta "Mewadev". He is a recipient of the Presidency of the International Prize De Finibus Terrae - IV edition in memory of Maria Monteduro (Italy). He has been awarded an honorary doctorate "Doctor of Literature" (Doctor Honoris Causa) from theInstitute of the European Roma Studies and Research into Crime Against Humanity and International Law – Belgrade (The Republic of Serbia).He is the author of 8 books, editor of 20 books, and the principal of S. K.Mahavidyalaya, Jaitpur, Mahoba (U. P.), and resides at Banda (U. P.) India. Visit him as DrBrajesh, facebook. com/brajeshg1, email him at dr.mewadevrain@gmail.com, and www.mewadev.com.

Ms. Varsha Sahebrao Aher is M.A., M.Phil, NET from Savitribai Phule Pune University,Pune, Maharashtra. She has 22 research papers in reputed journals and four chapters in various books, to her credit. She is working as an Assistant Professor at K.J. Somaiya College of Arts, Commerce and Science, Kopargaon, Maharashtra, since September 2016. Since then, she is working as an assistant NCC officer also. The author believes in seeking perfection through honest hard work.

Mrs. Afroz Jahan is an Assistant Professor, Department of English, at Sahu Ram Swaroop Girls P. G. College, Bareilly, Uttar Pradesh. She is working on her Ph.D. on the topic "Concept of Family in the Works of Anita Desai and Jane Austen: A Comparative Study." Her thrust areas are familial concepts and gender studies, Cultural studies, African American Literature, and Indian Diaspora in

Literature. Her research papers have been published in reputed journals. She teaches English literature to undergraduate and postgraduate classes.

डॉ० बिनीता पाण्डेय हीरालाल यादव बालिका पी०जी० कॉलेज लखनऊ में विगत कई वर्षो से सहायक प्रोफ़ेसर के रूप में अध्यापनरत है। वे विभिन्न राष्ट्रीय एवं अंतरराष्ट्रीय संगोष्ठियों में प्रतिभाग करने के साथ ही विभिन्न विषयों पर अपने मौलिक लेखन कला का प्रस्तुतिकरण भी कर चुकी है।

Ms. Sabeeha Noori is a Ph.D. student of History at the Department of Medieval and Modern History, University of Lucknow. She received a Bachelors' degree in Sociology and Medieval & Modern History from Allahabad University and a Masters' degree in

History from IGNOU. Her research interest includes studying the development of education in Medieval & Modern India.

Dr. Vibha Pandey is an Assistant Professor of Commerce in Govt. P. G. College, Obra, Sonbhadra, UP. She is a hardworking and disciplined professional, with a wide-range of experience in, both, academics as well as extra-curricular activities. She has a total of 18 research papers published out of which 3 are included in UGC journals, 2 in edited books with ISBN, and rest in other reputed national and international journals. She is also the Rangers' and NSS incharge in her college.